DECISION-ANALYTIC INTELLIGENT SYSTEMS

Automated Explanation and Knowledge Acquisition

DECISION-ANALYTIC INTELLIGENT SYSTEMS

Automated Explanation and Knowledge Acquisition

David A. Klein
Boston University

Routledge
Taylor & Francis Group

LONDON AND NEW YORK

First published 1994 by Lawrence Erlbaum Associates

Published 2018 by Routledge
2 Park Square, Milton Park, Abingdon, Oxon OX14 4RN
52 Vanderbilt Avenue, New York, NY 10017

First issued in paperback 2018

Routledge is an imprint of the Taylor & Francis Group, an informa business

Library of Congress Cataloging-in-Publication Data

Klein, David A., 1959–
    Decision-analytic intelligent systems: automated explanation and knowledge acquisition / David A. Klein
        p.   cm.
    Includes bibliographical references and index.
    ISBN 0–8058–1105–2
    1. Expert systems (Computer science) 2. Knowledge acquisition (Expert systems) 3. Decision making. I. Title.
QA76.76.E95K535 1994
006.3 '3 – dc20   92–25909
                                                                          CIP

ISBN 13: 978-1-138-87626-2 (pbk)
ISBN 13: 978-0-8058-1105-6 (hbk)

In memory of Dr. Alan C. Geller

Contents

Preface

The prospect of incorporating decision-analytic models in intelligent systems has received significant attention over the past few years. Supported by a rigorously specified foundation and an extensive set of engineering guidelines, these models provide potential advantages for reasoning about value and about uncertainty in intelligent computer programs. However, an obstacle to employing decision-analytic models in intelligent systems is that they do not readily support capabilities that we generally associate with such systems. For example, although experience inidicates that automated explanation of the rationale for computer-based advice is central to acceptance by decision makers, explanation has received little attention in decision-analytic contexts. Similarly, the ability to acquire and integrate new knowledge is central to the ongoing operation of intelligent systems, but this requirement too has not been adequately addressed in the context of computer-based decision-analytic models. By developing computer-based methods for generating qualitative explanations of decision-analytic models and for refining them over time, we potentially can broaden the scope of their employment among nontechnical decision makers and provide a basis for computing choices among alternatives in intelligent systems.

This book presents Interpretive Value Analysis (IVA), a framework for explaining and refining decision-analytic choices automatically. Specifically, IVA increases the transparency of *multiattribute value theory* to provide a framework for modeling choices involving competing considerations that is both formal and transparent. The components of IVA include (a) an *interpretation* of value theory that provides an intuitive yet formally sound vocabulary for talking about choices, (b) a set of *strategies for explaining choices*, and (c) a set of *strategies for refining choices*.

IVA at once addresses problems in artificial intelligence and in decision analysis. From an artificial intelligence perspective, IVA provides a foundation for building formally justifiable, intelligible, modifiable systems for computing decisions involving multiple considerations. Beyond decision models, the methodology underlying IVA's development suggests a more general approach to employing formal mathematical models in transparent intelligent systems. From a decision-analytic perspective, IVA addresses problems of transparency. First, IVA can potentially increase the acceptance of decision-theoretic advice by providing methods for justifying that advice in intuitive terms. Second, IVA provides an approach to managing biases in parameter assessment; the framework provides users with an opportunity to observe the step-by-step effect of a parameter value on the final result, so that users' responses may potentially be influenced less by the fashion in which parameter-assessment questions are posed. Third, IVA can potentially reduce the demands on parameter-assessment methods by providing for the incremental repair of model parameters. Finally, the framework provides an approach to the problem of managing changing preferences over time.

Many of the elements of IVA are implemented in VIRTUS, a shell for building systems that choose among competing alternatives. Three practical systems have been constructed using VIRTUS, in the domains of marketing, process control, and medicine. The book provides details about these applications to supplement the more general description of IVA.

The book is written for readers in both artificial intelligence and decision analysis. Sufficient background material is provided to promote understanding by readers who may be unfamiliar with one field or the other, and such material is labeled to increase the well-versed reader's efficiency in skipping particular sections.

A number of individuals influenced the work reported in this book, which derives from my dissertation research. Ted Shortliffe, my dissertation advisor, contributed guidance and insight, and provided a vibrant environment in which to explore the integration of artificial intelligence and decision analysis—the Medical Computer Science Group at Stanford University. I am indebted to this entire group, particularly to Leslie Perreault and to Curt Langlotz, for their continued challenges, enthusiasm, and support; Harold Lehmann additionally provided the knowledge and effort required to complete the medical application that is described. Martin Weber's decision-analytic expertise and insightful direction were essential to the work. Eric Clemons first pointed me in the right direction, and provided helpful comments on earlier drafts. Tim Finin, my co-advisor, provided many fruitful discussions. Rich Pelavin helped me to resolve a number of issues. David Taub provided valued legal advice.

I am also grateful to the organizations that supported this work: the IBM Corporation, Stanford University (under SUMEX-AIM NIH Grant RR-00785), the IBM Graduate Fellowship Program, the NASA Graduate Student Researcher's Program, and the University of Pennsylvania.

Portions of this book have appeared or will appear in the *Proceedings of the Tenth International Workshop on Expert Systems and Their Applications* (Klein & Shortliffe, 1990), the *Proceedings of the Eighth Biennial Conference of the Canadian Society for Computational Studies of Intelligence* (Klein & Shortliffe, 1990), the *Proceedings of the Fourteenth Annual Symposium on Computer Applications in Medical Care* (Klein, Lehmann, & Shortliffe, 1990), the *Proceedings of the Seventh IEEE Conference on Artificial Intelligence Applications* (Klein & Shortliffe, 1991), and the *Proceedings of the Ninth International Conference on Multiple Criteria Decision Making* (Klein, Weber, & Shortliffe, in press). Adapted portions used with permission.

David A. Klein

Introduction

1.1 CONTEXT

Judgment-intensive choices arise in diverse settings, from the commonplace (e.g., choosing an activity on a Saturday evening) to the technical (e.g., choosing an action to avoid a crisis in a computer complex). Significant research has been devoted to modeling such choices.

Models of choice generally accept as input a set of objective data and subjective judgments that characterize a choice among competing alternatives, and produce as output a recommended alternative. As in other modeling endeavors, computer systems are playing an increasingly important role in building, executing, and interpreting models of choice. Such systems generally vary with the formality of their specification, and with the transparency of their operation.[1] A *formal system* reflects a specific theory of operation that addresses a well-bounded class of applications; a *transparent system* provides an intuitive framework for interpreting its results and for systematically modifying its parameters.

Both formality and transparency contribute to the success of practical systems: Formality guarantees meaningful outputs for a clearly bounded class of inputs, and transparency lends credibility to the system's results in the eyes of users while providing for the system's adaptation to particular problems and user populations. Yet, previous approaches to modeling choices in a systems context generally have emphasized either one property or the other. Computer-based tools for decision analysis (DA), for example, produce meaningful results for any set of inputs that

---

[1]A more detailed description of these properties, and of their pragmatic implications for intelligent systems, is provided in chapter 2.

satisfies a well-defined set of constraints, but they usually lack intuitive facilities for justifying choices and for modifying choice parameters; these limitations render it relatively expensive to construct DA models, and to interpret the results of such models. Heuristic approaches to modeling choices in artificial intelligence (AI) systems, on the other hand, strive for intuitive appeal, but these approaches typically reflect the requirements of only particular domains, and they lack a foundation that permits prediction of their behavior outside the context of particular examples in those domains.

This book is concerned with providing computer-based models of choice that are at once formal *and* transparent.

1.2 APPROACH AND CONTRIBUTIONS

We take the approach of providing a formal and transparent model by embellishing the transparency of a formal model from DA. The result, *Interpretive Value Analysis (IVA)*, is the subject of this book. IVA is a framework for explaining and refining choices in the context of intelligent systems. More specifically, IVA lays the foundation for an array of potential systems that model *multiattribute choices under certainty*,[2] in which multiple competing factors underlie choices (e.g., enjoyment vs. cost of an elegant dinner), and the outcomes of choices are assumed to occur with certainty (e.g., the dinner definitely will be expensive).[3]

IVA increases the transparency of *multiattribute value theory*, a formal model of value, by reformulating the theory and embedding it in a framework for explaining and iteratively refining value-based choices. IVA comprises the following components:

- An *interpretation* that provides an intuitive yet formally sound vocabulary of more than 100 terms for talking about value-based choices. The vocabulary is in part based on analyses of conversations about choices that were collected from both decision analysts and nonanalysts.

- A set of *strategies for explaining value-based choices* that organizes elements of the interpretation to provide insight into how choices are computed.

- A set of *strategies for refining value-based choices* that organizes model parameters for modification. These strategies build on elements of the explanation strategies and of the interpretation.

---

[2]For brevity, we write *value-based choices* to refer to multiattribute choices under certainty, *models of value* to refer to models of value-based choices, and *value-based systems* to refer to intelligent systems that include models of value.

[3]Some authors consider spurious the distinction between certain and uncertain models of choice. Chapter 9 addresses this distinction in more detail.

IVA at once addresses open problems in AI and in DA. From an AI perspective, IVA provides a general foundation for building value-based systems that are formally justifiable, intelligible, and modifiable. Beyond decision models, the methodology underlying IVA's development suggests a more general approach to employing formal mathematical models in transparent intelligent systems. From a DA perspective, IVA addresses problems of transparency. First, IVA can potentially increase the acceptance of decision-theoretic advice by providing methods for justifying that advice in intuitive terms. Second, IVA provides an approach to managing bias in parameter assessment; the framework provides users with an opportunity to observe the step-by-step effect of a parameter value on the final result, so that users' responses may potentially be influenced less by the fashion in which parameter-assessment questions are posed. Third, IVA can potentially reduce the demands on parameter-assessment methods by providing for the incremental repair of model parameters. Finally, the framework provides an approach to the problem of managing changing preferences over time.

Because the book lies at the intersection of theory and practice, it necessarily reports on a number of demonstration systems. Many of the elements of IVA are implemented in VIRTUS,[4] a shell for building value-based systems. VIRTUS implements a view of model construction as an iterative argument with a machine. Aided by a knowledge engineer,[5] the user begins by supplying VIRTUS with an initial model of his preferences. VIRTUS then computes a choice, and justifies that choice with an explanation. If the user finds the explanation convincing, then model construction is complete; if not, the user can request additional explanations, or can initiate the process of refinement to correct a suspicious component of the explanation (i.e., component of the underlying model), and to generate a new explanation that reflects his modification. This process is repeated until convergence is achieved.

VIRTUS is a domain-independent, architecture-independent module that can be used in isolation or in concert with other representations. Three practical value-based systems have been constructed using VIRTUS: JESQ-II (Klein & Shortliffe, 1990b) is a system that chooses among competing alternative actions in managing a large computer complex; RCTE (Klein, Lehmann, & Shortliffe, 1990) is a program for evaluating clinical research in medicine; and ES-SHELL is an application for choosing among competing expert-system shells. These applica-

---

[4]VIRTUS (pronounced *weer-tus*) is Latin for *value* or *virtue*, as in the value or virtue of an alternative in a value-based choice. We thank Mark Steedman (University of Pennsylvania) for these translations.

[5]We employ the terms *knowledge engineer* and *decision analyst* almost interchangeably throughout the book; the distinction between these terms is blurred in the context of intelligent systems that are based on decision theory (Henrion & Cooley, 1987).

tions demonstrate the capabilities of IVA-based systems, and underscore the domain-independence of our approach.[6]

To frame the work more clearly, we mention explicitly objectives that we do *not* attempt to satisfy in the book. First, although IVA is based in part on observations of human discourse, the book makes no contribution to discourse analysis or to natural language processing (in the usual sense of these terms). For example, VIRTUS is not designed to replicate human discourse and employs simple methods for parsing input and for generating text. Second, VIRTUS is not intended as an ideal for any particular system; rather, VIRTUS is a demonstration vehicle for IVA, which represents a general specification for a broad range of potential value-based systems. For example, VIRTUS implements redundant techniques for research-level tasks, and omits the implementation of functions that would be desirable in a production setting, but that are not expected to yield scientific or engineering insights.

1.3 VIRTUS EXAMPLE

VIRTUS can be used in an interactive mode and to generate reports.[7] The interactive mode includes facilities for generating intuitive justifications for choices and for assisting users in modifying model parameters. The reporting mode draws on a number of IVA's explanation strategies to produce intuitive reports about decisions.

The following is an interactive dialog with VIRTUS that demonstrates a sub-

---

[6]Each of these systems is related to other research with which the reader may be familiar. JESQ-II can be viewed as an enhanced component of a larger system for automating computer operations called YES/MVS (Ennis et al., 1984a; Klein, 1988). YES/MVS was constructed by the author and colleagues at IBM's Thomas J. Watson Research Center in Yorktown Heights, New York. The motivating limitations of the original version are described in chapter 2. RCTE is an enhanced version of REFEREE (Haggerty, 1984), which was constructed in EMYCIN at Stanford University's Knowledge Systems Laboratory. The motivating limitations of the original version are described in chapter 8. Concurrent with the development of RCTE, yet another version has been developed at Stanford University, based on belief networks (Chavez & Lehmann, 1988; Lehmann, 1988). We thank Harold Lehmann (Stanford University) for his participation in the development of RCTE. ES-SHELL can be viewed as a component of a larger system called FORECASTER for forecasting revenue in new markets (Klein, 1991). FORECASTER simulates the buying behavior of individual customers to produce a *customer-specific*, *multiproduct* forecast. A preliminary version of FORECASTER was conceived by the author and was implemented by an interdisciplinary team of business analysts and computer scientists under the author's direction at IBM.

[7]A sample report appears in the appendix. Techniques for generating such reports are described in chapter 5.

set of the implemented capabilities.[8] In this example, the user is a computer-operations manager who is verifying and correcting an existing model of value for automatically managing a large computer complex. More specifically, there is a large dataset waiting for a user-requested printer that currently is disabled, and the manager employs VIRTUS to explain and refine its choice among the following actions for removing this dataset from the overloading print queue:

1. COPY: Copy the dataset to tape, and print it later when the requested printer has been repaired
2. EXPENSIVE-PRINTING: Print the dataset on a faster printer that uses forms more expensive than those requested by the user
3. CHEAP-PRINTING: Print the dataset on a slower printer that uses forms of lower quality than those requested by the user
4. DELETE: Delete the dataset from the queue
5. INSTALL: Connect a duplicate of the requested printer for use until the requested printer has been repaired
6. FICHE: Deliver the dataset to the user on microfiche
7. CARDS: Deliver the dataset to the user on punched cards
8. DASD: Transfer the dataset to the user's private disk storage, so that the user can transfer it back to the queue for printing after the printer has been repaired

Which alternative is best?

DASD is the best with regard to overall queue space management effectiveness.

What does DASD involve?

DASD involves transferring the user's dataset to his private disk storage for later printing. This encompasses:
- *.1 minutes of additional operator time*
- *.5 dollars of additional cost*
- *1 minute of problem resolution time*
- *32.1 minutes of additional turnaround time*
- *1 subjective unit of similarity to the user's requested form*

---

[8]We have formatted all the dialogs that appear in this document. **Bold-faced type** is used to display the user's input, including explicit responses to VIRTUS's requests for input (which follow the prompt symbol: >), and VIRTUS's paraphrases of the user's mouse and menu input. Textual responses generated by VIRTUS appear in *italics*. Annotations appear in {normal typeface enclosed in braces}. The names of alternatives are set in CAPITAL letters. Because refined text generation is not a focus of our work, we have made cosmetic corrections in formatting selected VIRTUS examples, such as capitalization and pluralization.

Which alternatives are very similar to DASD with regard to overall queue space management effectiveness?

Close contenders of DASD include EXPENSIVE.PRINTING and CHEAP.PRINTING.

What factors are notably important in the determination of overall queue space management effectiveness?

Overall user satisfaction is notably important in the determination of overall queue space management effectiveness.

Which alternatives are notably good with regard to overall user satisfaction?

EXPENSIVE.PRINTING and CHEAP.PRINTING provide notably good overall user satisfaction.

Give me a summary-level comparison of EXPENSIVE.PRINTING and DASD.

EXPENSIVE.PRINTING provides infinitesimally worse overall queue space management effectiveness than DASD. Compelling reasons to prefer EXPENSIVE.PRINTING, such as overall user satisfaction, are outweighed by considerations of additional cost, along with less compelling reasons that recommend DASD.

Why is additional cost a compelling factor in the choice between EXPENSIVE.PRINTING and DASD?

While additional cost is not notably important in determining overall queue space management effectiveness, DASD provides sufficiently different additional cost from EXPENSIVE.PRINTING relative to other factors to make additional cost a notably compelling factor in this particular decision.

What is the relative quality of EXPENSIVE.PRINTING and DASD with regard to additional cost?

EXPENSIVE.PRINTING provides substantially worse additional cost than DASD.

Which alternatives are better than EXPENSIVE.PRINTING with regard to additional cost?

DASD, CHEAP.PRINTING, COPY, DELETE, FICHE, and CARDS provide qualitatively better additional cost than EXPENSIVE.PRINTING.

Interactively diagnose and repair the choice between DASD and EXPEN-SIVE.PRINTING.

DASD provides infinitesimally better (.05) overall queue space management effectiveness than EXPENSIVE.PRINTING.

If you disagree with this statement, then you must disagree with at least one of the statements that supports it: With which of the following statements are you least comfortable?

1. Additional operator time is an inconsequential (0.0) factor in the choice between DASD and EXPENSIVE.PRINTING.

2. Additional cost is a compelling (.12) factor favoring DASD over EXPEN-SIVE.PRINTING.

3. Problem resolution time is a factor favoring DASD over EXPENSIVE.PRINT-ING, although not a compelling one (.08).

4. Overall user satisfaction is a compelling (−.15) factor favoring EXPEN-SIVE.PRINTING over DASD.

5. The above represents a complete list of factors underlying the determination of overall queue space management effectiveness.

> 2

You selected:

Additional cost is a compelling (.12) factor favoring DASD over EXPEN-SIVE.PRINTING.

If you disagree with this statement, then you must disagree with at least one of the statements that supports it: With which of the following statements are you least comfortable?

1. DASD provides substantially better (.6) additional cost than EXPEN-SIVE.PRINTING.

2. Additional cost accounts for 20.0 percent of the determination of overall queue space management effectiveness when queue space is at an acceptable level.

> 2

You selected:

Additional cost accounts for 20.0 percent of the determination of overall queue space management effectiveness when queue space is at an acceptable level.

This is a primitive statement that you can modify directly. Do you want to change it?

> **YES**

With no other modifications, you must lower the importance of additional cost to less than 12.72 percent in order to prefer EXPENSIVE.PRINTING over DASD.

What is the correct percentage?

> **10**

OK. The statement has been changed to:

Additional cost accounts for 10.0 percent of the determination of overall queue space management effectiveness when queue space is at an acceptable level.

Note that with this change:

1. *Additional operator time accounts for 11.25 percent of the determination of overall queue space management effectiveness when queue space is at an acceptable level.*
2. *Additional cost accounts for 10.0 percent of the determination of overall queue space management effectiveness when queue space is at an acceptable level.*
3. *Problem resolution time accounts for 22.5 percent of the determination of overall queue space management effectiveness when queue space is at an acceptable level.*
4. *Overall user satisfaction accounts for 56.25 percent of the determination of overall queue space management effectiveness when queue space is at an acceptable level.*

Does this seem reasonable?

> **YES**

OK. The choice is now argued for as follows:

Additional cost accounts for 10.0 percent of the determination of overall queue space management effectiveness when queue space is at an acceptable level.

Since it's also true that:

- *DASD provides substantially better (.6) additional cost than EXPEN-SIVE.PRINTING.*

It follows that, in toto:

Additional cost is a factor favoring DASD over EXPENSIVE.PRINTING,
although not a compelling one (.06).

Since it's also true that:

1. *Additional operator time is an inconsequential (0.0) factor in the choice*
    between DASD and EXPENSIVE.PRINTING.
2. *Problem resolution time is a factor favoring DASD over EXPEN-*
    SIVE.PRINTING, although not a compelling one (.09).
3. *Overall user satisfaction is a compelling (−.17) factor favoring EXPEN-*
    SIVE.PRINTING over DASD.

It follows that, in toto:

DASD provides infinitesimally worse (−.02) overall queue space management
effectiveness than EXPENSIVE.PRINTING.

How are alternatives ranked with regard to overall queue space manage-
ment effectiveness?

EXPENSIVE.PRINTING is the best alternative with regard to overall queue
space management effectiveness. DASD is the next best. CHEAP.PRINTING
is the next best. COPY is the next best. FICHE is the next best. DELETE is
the next best. CARDS is the next best. INSTALL is the next best.

1.4 READER'S GUIDE

The book is written for readers in both AI and DA. Because not all potential
readers can be expected to be familiar with both fields, and with the application
domains in which we have applied IVA, the structure of the book reflects the
following approach. Where a referenced concept is essential to understanding
what follows, it is explained in the body of the text, and lengthy expository sections are flagged with footnotes.[9] Where a referenced concept is significant, but
a detailed exposition is not essential to understanding subsequent material, a
glossary-level explanation is provided in a footnote.[10] Terms that are intended

---

[9]Example: Decision theorists will want to skip section 2.5, which introduces multiattribute value
theory, but all readers will need to understand this material to grasp the rest of the work.

[10]Example: Section 3.4.3 defines a *randomized clinical trial* in a footnote. This level of information is probably adequate for the nonmedical reader to grasp the flavor of the RCTE application.

only to clarify a description for readers who are familiar with them are not annotated and can be ignored by other readers.[11]

The book is organized for linear reading from start to finish, but is intended to be sufficiently modular to encourage close examination of particular topics. Chapter 2 examines previous value-based systems, describes the problem addressed in more detail, and summarizes related work. Chapter 3 provides an overview of IVA and VIRTUS and presents additional examples of VIRTUS's application. Chapters 4 through 6 detail the interpretation, explanation strategies, and refinement strategies that constitute IVA; they can be viewed as appendices to chapter 3. Chapter 7 provides an overview of VIRTUS's implementation. Chapter 8 presents an evaluation of IVA and describes general observations derived from developing IVA. Chapter 9 provides a summary of the book, describes its contributions in more detail, and identifies opportunities for future work.

---

[11]Example: Section 4.3.2.2 equates IVA's formulation of the concept *notable* with *z-scores* for clarification, but z-scores are not mentioned again.

Background, Motivation, and Problem Statement

This chapter examines previous value-based systems, describes the hypothesis of this research in more detail, and summarizes related work. Section 2.1 abstractly characterizes *implicit* and *explicit* models of value in intelligent systems. Section 2.2 describes the pragmatic role of explicit models by exposing the limitations of an application that employs an implicit model where an explicit model would have been more appropriate. Having described why explicit models of value are useful, in section 2.3 we describe the advantages of formality and of transparency in such models, and we examine previous value-based systems in light of these properties. This analysis forms the basis for the hypothesis of the work, presented in section 2.4: *We can build on a formal model of value to provide a framework for value-based systems that is both formal and transparent.* Section 2.5 describes *multiattribute value theory*, which provides the starting point for developing IVA in subsequent chapters. Section 2.6 describes the application of value theory in the context of the problematic system described in section 2.2. Section 2.7 reviews challenges in explaining and refining value-theoretic choices. Section 2.8 reviews related work in AI and DA. Section 2.9 provides a summary of this chapter.

2.1 MODELS OF VALUE IN INTELLIGENT SYSTEMS

The reasoning machinery of any intelligent system constructed to perform any task in any domain encompasses one or more paradigms for making choices. A set of like objects in an intelligent system (e.g., rules to fire, subgoals to prove, program statements to execute, recommendations to display for users) can be chosen or ordered by either an *implicit* or an *explicit* model of choice.

An *implicit model of choice*[12] is an ordering (e.g., a table) that captures the *results* of choosing among competing alternative objects; an implicit model contains no representation of the *rationale* for a choice. Under priority-conflict-resolution algorithms (e.g., Cruise et al., 1987), for example, potentially competitive rules are ordered by system developers ahead of time; the rationale underlying the selection of priorities is not encoded in the system. Procedures in traditional programming languages, in which statements are ordered for execution, provide another example. Arbitrary[13] selection schemes in production systems (McDermott & Forgy, 1978) can also be described as implicit models of choice.

In contrast, an *explicit model of choice* computes choices among competing objects, rather than encoding them directly. These models provide an explicit representation of the abstract reasons for choosing one alternative over another. Explicit models of choice include the following elements:

- There exists some natural and clear correspondence between the computational objects of selection (e.g., procedures, symbols) and objects in the domain (e.g., power-plant-recovery strategies, drugs)
- The factors driving choices (e.g., safety, cost) are represented explicitly by identifiable symbols in the system
- The factors driving choices are combined according to some philosophy of choice (e.g., a domain-specific selection scheme) that is represented by a set of identifiable operations in the system

Heuristic evaluation functions in game-playing programs (Berliner & Ackley, 1982; Nilsson, 1980) exemplify explicit models of choice, as do domain-specific therapy-planning models in medical expert systems (Clancey, 1984; Kastner, 1983).

More specifically, we can classify explicit models of choice along two dimensions.[14] The first dimension concerns the number of factors that are relevant to the choice at hand: Some choices are driven by a single factor (e.g., money), whereas others involve multiple, often *mutually competitive* factors (e.g., the classic dilemma of quality vs. quantity). The second dimension concerns the certainty with which the potential outcomes of a choice are known. This view gives rise to four choice types of potential interest:

---

[12]Chapter 4 provides a formal definition of implicit models.

[13]Formally speaking, of course, deterministic computers admit no notion of arbitrariness. In this context, *arbitrary* refers to the absence of any rationale for an ordering even *outside* the system, in the same spirit as software manuals that warn of "unpredictable results" for inputs that deviate from expectations.

[14]This classification has been described elsewhere in a DA context (e.g., Keeney & Raiffa, 1976), and is summarized here in the context of intelligent systems.

- Single-attribute choices under certainty
- Multiattribute choices under certainty
- Single-attribute choices under uncertainty
- Multiattribute choices under uncertainty

Recall from chapter 1 that this book focuses on the multiattribute case under certainty, that is, on models of value. Ignoring uncertainty is, of course, appropriate for modeling decisions in some domains (e.g., managing computer complexes, as we described in chapter 1), where the certainty of outcomes of actions plays a role in decision making, but not a central one, and is less appropriate in other domains (e.g., some instances of therapy planning in medicine), where the uncertainty of outcomes is central to choosing among alternatives. Whether uncertainty can be pragmatically ignored is a choice-specific question; in both instances, preferences or *values* are essential ingredients of decision making, as Keeney noted:

> Values are the basis for any interest in any decision problem. Why is it worth the effort to carefully choose an alternative rather than simply let occur what will? The answer is that some concerned party is interested in the possible consequences that might occur. The desire to avoid unpleasant consequences and to achieve desirable ones, especially when the differences in the relative desirability of the consequences is significant, is the motivation for interest in any decision problem. The relative desirability of the possible consequences in decision problems is based on values. (Keeney, 1986, p. 144)

In computer applications designed principally to assist users in choosing among competing alternatives, an explicit model of value exists in isolation as the central computational machinery of the system. In other applications, an explicit model of value works in cooperation with modules that perform other tasks, such as generating and executing alternatives.

Implicit models of value suffice for points in processing where choices are immaterial, obvious, or inconsistent. No explicit machinery is required when users are unconcerned about a choice, are likely to accept a choice without argument or justification, or cannot be presented with any coherent rationale for a choice. In cases where choices are not subject to change over time, or to user-specific variation, users will generally be unaware of their existence. Many domain tasks, however, encompass choices that are both material and difficult, motivating knowledge engineers to construct explicit models to support such choices. Specifically, explicit models are necessary to support the coherent formulation of choices, to provide a basis for justifying those choices automatically, and to provide for the systematic capture and ongoing modification of the values underlying choices. These requirements are elucidated in the following section, which examines the limitations of a system that employs an implicit model of value where an explicit model would have been more appropriate.

2.2 A MOTIVATING APPLICATION

The initial conception of this work arose in the context of building *intelligent control systems* — that is, systems that aid experts in (or completely automate) the management of complex physical systems, such as nuclear power plants and large computer complexes. Intelligent control systems are distinguished from more traditional control systems (Ray, 1981; Stephanopoulous, 1984) by their employment of heuristic methods that mimic the reasoning of experts to complement (e.g., Astrom, Anton, & Arzen, 1986; DeJong, 1983) or to replace (Chester, 1984; Ennis et al., 1986) rigid algorithms for plant operation. Work in this area is abundant, with applications in manufacturing (Wright, Bourne, Colyer, Schatz, & Isasi, 1982), space systems (Leinweber, 1987; Scarl, 1985), chemical processing (Chester, 1984), nuclear-power generation (Nelson, 1982), computer-operations management (Ennis et al., 1986a), and several other domains.[15]

The need to make careful choices among competing alternatives is ubiquitous in intelligent control. In performing diagnostic tasks, for example, experts must select carefully among potential tests that might be performed to ascertain the state of target-system components. Choices among competing tests involve considerations including the cost of the tests, the value of information yielded by the tests, the disruption to the target system and its environment caused by performing the tests, the degree to which the safety of plant employees and of neighboring residents might be endangered by the tests, and several other factors. In repairing physical systems (usually following a diagnosis), experts must choose among numerous options, ranging from temporary solutions to the replacement of faulty components, guided by similar objectives.

An example of an intelligent control system that encompasses such choices is YES/MVS[16] (Ennis et al., 1986a; Klein, 1988), a forward-chaining rule-based system that is designed to assist computer operators in the management of large industrial computer installations. YES/MVS comprises several domain specialists that perform distinct tasks, such as routine operations (e.g., buffer swaps, startup, shutdown), diagnosis of and recovery from hardware and software failures, and job scheduling.

JESQ (Klein, 1985) is a YES/MVS specialist that continually monitors and actively manages operating-system queue space. JESQ's limitations with regard

---

[15]In fact, there has been sufficient interest in such applications that researchers have constructed special-purpose shells for intelligent control (Cruise et al., 1987; Klein, 1988; Moore, Hawkinson, Knickerbocker, & Churchman, 1984). There has also been significant work on general representations for qualitative reasoning about physical systems (e.g., de Kleer & Brown, 1984; Forbus, 1984), which might prove useful in intelligent control applications. Bobrow (1985) provided a collection of foundational papers.

[16]YES/MVS is an acronym for Yorktown Expert System/Multiple Virtual System Manager.

to choosing among competing operational actions characterize rule-based expert systems in general (Cromarty, 1985; Sauers & Walsh, 1983). In the remainder of this section, we provide a detailed account of these limitations.[17]

The following section provides a detailed description of JESQ's task; this description imparts the background required to understand many examples in the book. Subsequent sections provide a detailed description of JESQ's architecture and of its limitations.[18]

2.2.1 JESQ's Domain

Job Entry Subsystem (JES) queue space is common disk storage in IBM system environments that is used for the staging of computer jobs before, during, and after execution. Jobs normally are deleted from the queue space once output has been processed by an output device such as a printer or a transmission line. The queue space is also used by JES itself. In addition, JES maintains batch job output for online viewing (via IBM's Time Sharing Option [TSO] software) in the queue-space area.

Operations management is concerned with monitoring the amount of available queue space because its allocation is fixed at system-startup time, and its depletion requires restarting the system, potentially inconveniencing all system users for a substantial period.[19] The operator may take several protective and corrective actions when queue space begins to diminish, and these can be described in terms of three general goals:

1. *Protect remaining queue space:* The operator must protect the space that remains when space is at a dangerously low level (e.g., 5%). The operator may, for example, disable the main processor, blocking the initiation of additional jobs that could generate output on the queue.

2. *Free queue space:* The operator can manipulate various devices and operating-system parameters to free queue space. For example, the operator may run *DJ* (Dump Job) to copy large jobs from the queue to tape, and then reinstate

---

[17]The objective of the JESQ and YES/MVS projects was to investigate research issues in real-time, closed-loop control in an expert-systems context; we employed standard techniques (with little or no innovation) for choosing among alternatives, to avoid deviating from the focus of our research. For details regarding this investigation, see (Cruise et al., 1986; Cruise et al., 1987; Ennis et al., 1984a; Ennis et al., 1986b; Klein, 1988; Klein & Milliken, 1984; Milliken, 1984). For a general description of the requirements of closed-loop expert systems that was inspired by the project, see (Klein & Finin, 1987).

[18]Portions of this description are adapted from (Klein, 1985).

[19]Of course, management might solve the problem more easily by allocating more storage than might ever be used, but this brute-force strategy cannot be justified in the absence of identifiable increases in system workload.

them for printing once the queue-space situation has improved. Alternatively, the operator may change parameter settings on printers to allow jobs with special characteristics (e.g., special paper or security requirements) to print. The operator may change the maximum line limits on printers set to favor small jobs in cases where large jobs are waiting and small jobs will soon all be printed. In addition, the operator can reroute large jobs that are destined for slow printers to faster printers that have a relatively light load.

3. *Diagnose and eliminate the cause of queue-space depletion:* In some cases, there exists a direct cause-effect relationship between the actions of an environmental agent (e.g., user, operator, device) and a queue-space problem. For example, a printer might not be operational, or a link to another system might be down. In such cases, the operator must correct the problem, as well as restore the queue to an acceptable state in a reasonable amount of time.

The operator must use significant judgment in choosing among competing actions. For example, the operator can purge output from the queue by using DJ, by requesting action from the user, by printing the job, or even by deleting the job. In general, choices among competing actions are based on a set of underlying decision criteria that includes

- *Anticipated effect* on queue space resulting from the successful execution of the action
- *Operator convenience*, including the amount of time spent by the operator in executing an operational heuristic and the amount of work involved[20]
- *Material cost* of the action in excess of originally scheduled processing
- *User satisfaction*, including considerations of user turnaround time, the additional time expended by the user himself in accomplishing his processing goals,[21] and the difference in the quality of his output from that requested
- *Speed* with which actions can be executed

Because no event in the computer-operations environment is certain, probabilistic factors also come into play. For example, the recent success of particular actions might factor into the decision when some facility is not operating correctly, as in the case of a device that seems to ignore commands that are issued to it. Given that some devices may exhibit this behavior more than once, we might also consider the track record of actions over the history of their execution. Practically speaking, however, we are inclined to ignore such probabilistic concerns

---

[20]Time and work are not equivalent in this context. For example, most operators would rather spend 5 minutes submitting commands through their consoles than spend the same 5 minutes moving heavy boxes of paper.

[21]Resubmitting jobs deleted by operators and talking to operators over the telephone are two examples of actions that consume users' time.

in this domain, because if they become predominant considerations, the devices will be replaced. As any model represents an abstraction of reality, it is appropriate in this domain for choices to reflect the assumption that the outcomes of actions occur with certainty.

2.2.2 Organization of JESQ's Knowledge Base

The essential unit of information in JESQ is the rule. Our goal was to map each operational heuristic recorded in the installation's run book[22] directly into a rule, and to encode a shared set of rules for performing supporting tasks, such as querying the status of the target system. In this way, the benefits of modularity and mutual independence of heuristics often associated with the rule-based paradigm would be realized, allowing the installation to add, modify, and delete operational heuristics with ease as the installation evolved.[23] Rules in JESQ are grouped along two orthogonal dimensions: by function (e.g., query submission, information collection) and by problem severity (as a function of space left on the queue). We address each in turn.

First, JESQ's rules are grouped in functional classes. Each functional class is associated with a priority that determines which rule will be invoked whenever rules from multiple classes are satisfied concurrently in a given iteration of the recognize–act cycle.[24] JESQ's rule groups include:

- *System initialization and control:* This group contains rules that create the internal model of the target system environment, enable and disable groups of rules as a function of the severity of the current queue-space problem, and suppress certain actions when specified by the operator.

- *Periodic query submission and timeout handling:* This group controls the periodic querying of target-system resources. Query intervals are based on estimates of the reliability over time of the information being captured. Rules are also included to resubmit queries that have been lost in transmission.

- *Information collection and data reduction/expansion:* This group includes rules that collect target-system messages and update JESQ's internal model accordingly. Portions of this model appear in the antecedents of the knowl-

---

[22]Definition: A *run book* is a list of procedures supplied to operators that describes the appropriate courses of action for dealing with anticipated problems and routine requirements.

[23]This goal was achieved satisfactorily. As we shall describe, most of JESQ's limitations are due to the system's inability to select the *best* heuristics.

[24]Implementation note: JESQ was implemented in a modified version of OPS5 (Forgy, 1981) and in LISP/VM (1984). We augmented OPS5 conflict resolution with a priority mechanism so that the set of satisfied rules is first reduced to rules of equal priority. The resulting set is resolved on the basis of recency of information and specificity of antecedent conditions (i.e., OPS5 conflict resolution).

edge-based action rules that take space-management actions. Some rules in this group map a single response into a single internal model structure; other rules perform data reduction, manipulating multiple responses to produce a single summary-level structure that is referenced by the knowledge-based action rules; still other rules perform data expansion, supplying attributes with values that are only implied by target-system responses.

- *Miscellaneous cleanup and response collision collection:* This group deletes target-system responses and expert-system-generated goals from working memory. Rules in this group also delete asynchronously arriving responses to duplicate queries that have been delayed by failing or sluggish target-system resources.

- *Knowledge-based action:* The previously described groups exist to support the knowledge-based action rules, which encode queue-space-management policy. Rules are included to protect the remaining queue space, to set up for space-freeing actions, to reset target-system parameters when space returns to an acceptable level, to free queue space when a problem exists, and to alert the operator to potential problems that cannot be diagnosed without additional information. These rules are further decomposed into three subgroups of varying priority: *low-*, *medium-*, and *high-priority knowledge-based actions*.

Thus, priorities are used for two purposes in JESQ: (a) to execute rule groups in a procedural fashion, and (b) to indicate the relative desirability of plans encoded by knowledge-based action rules. In this section, we are concerned with the limitations of priorities as representations of relative desirability.[25]

The second dimension for organizing rules concerns the dynamic enabling and disabling of rules during expert-system execution, according to the severity of the current queue-space problem. For example, a drastic action, such as disabling the main processor, is appropriate when only 3% of the queue space remains, but is not appropriate when 10% remains. This sort of information is implemented by mapping ranges of space left to five symbolic *processing modes* and including processing mode restrictions in the antecedents of knowledge-based action rules.

2.2.3 Critique of JESQ

JESQ surely takes reasonable actions; the system ran successfully at IBM's Thomas J. Watson Research Center for most of 1 year and received a favorable response from operations staff. But we have no justification for believing that

---

[25]The former usage represents an attempt to make declarative code behave procedurally, and reflects limitations in OPS5. This problem (among others) was solved in OPS83 (Forgy, 1984) and in YES/L1 (Cruise et al., 1987; Klein, 1988), an expert-systems shell designed for data-processing applications that was later revised and released by IBM under the name *KnowledgeTool*.

JESQ takes the *best* actions at any time because JESQ contains no explicit model of value. The relative desirability of competing knowledge-based actions is represented by the three priority levels (*low, medium, high*), and the assignment of these priorities to individual heuristics takes place outside the system. Because selecting among competing heuristics is a judgment-intensive task, we have little reason to believe that assigning priorities in this fashion produces optimal results. Because priorities are assigned with some degree of arbitrariness, JESQ's behavior can be described as somewhat arbitrary.

Another limitation of JESQ concerns its lack of transparency. Although JESQ provides explanations regarding how recommended actions achieve the goals of queue-space management, it offers no justification for choosing particular actions over other actions that achieve the same goal. Because the factors underlying priority assignment are not represented in the system, JESQ cannot provide an explanation beyond a display of the priority of the chosen heuristic, or a comparison of priorities. Because JESQ cannot justify its choices, operations managers have no basis for deciding whether JESQ's operation reflects the goals of the installation, or for identifying how JESQ's knowledge base might be enhanced (beyond the introduction of new knowledge-based action rules).

JESQ's principal flaw concerns the difficulty of integrating new heuristics with existing ones, again due to the lack of an explicit model of value. Because the considerations underlying the selection of competing heuristics are not represented in the system, changes to the knowledge base must be addressed as a programming task. To manipulate the priority of a rule in JESQ intelligently, the knowledge engineer must understand the basis for the priorities of all existing rules in the knowledge base, and he must envision all potential conflict sets of interest. Formulating priorities for new heuristics is especially difficult, because the considerations underlying priority selection may be forgotten by the knowledge engineer over time; this problem will almost surely arise when multiple knowledge engineers maintain the system, resulting in priority assignments that fail to reflect any consistent scheme. Thus, although it is easy to augment or to change the rules in JESQ's knowledge base, it is almost impossible to ensure that rules will be invoked at the proper points of execution.

The ability to modify the knowledge base is especially important in JESQ's domain, where the environment—and, hence, the strategy concerning its control—is subject to frequent change. Typical changes in the real world that are reflected in management policies include, for example, changes in the installation's abstract goals (e.g., the introduction of new safety standards); changes in the relationships among those goals (e.g., increased cost consciousness, perhaps at the expense of quality of service); changes to the target-system configuration that create new operational alternatives (e.g., the introduction of a new printer in the machine room); and changes to the target-system configuration that modify the characteristics of existing operational alternatives (e.g., the replacement of parts on existing printers). Given that intelligent control systems such as JESQ will contain hundreds (or, in some cases, thousands) of operational heuristics, the integration of new or modified heuristics cannot be viewed pragmatically as a programming-level task.

From a practical viewpoint, we need to be able to view JESQ as a *storehouse of transparent, evolving heuristics* for managing queue space that reflects the current goals of installation management at any given time. The inclusion of an explicit model of value would have provided a basis for organizing JESQ's numerous operational heuristics and for justifying those heuristics to operations managers. But what sort of explicit model might have best served these purposes? What properties render explicit models of value useful for intelligent systems? We address these questions in the next section.

2.3 FORMALITY AND TRANSPARENCY IN VALUE-BASED SYSTEMS

A *formal* system is supported by a detailed description of the theory that underlies its operation, including a set of constraints on inputs. Langlotz describes formal (or *axiomatic*) systems in terms of "agreements" between those systems and their users:

> How can system users be sure that a system's performance is consistent with their preferences and beliefs? This question can be answered only through an explicit agreement between the decision-making system and its users. An *axiomatic* decision-making framework is the embodiment of that agreement. According to the agreement, the users are obliged to abide by certain desirable properties when structuring communication with the decision-making system; the system is obliged to perform only those manipulations of evidence and goals that are consistent with these properties. If a system could be constructed in accordance with these properties, meeting its assumptions would guarantee consistency between the knowledge that goes into a system and the advice that comes out. In other words, a close correspondence would be achieved among the way knowledge is assessed (knowledge acquisition), the way it is manipulated (reasoning), and the way the results are interpreted (explanation). (Langlotz, 1989, p. 25)

Formality provides a set of related practical advantages in the context of intelligent systems. First, formality provides confidence in a system's results.[26] In the absence of an abstract description of the relationship between a system's inputs and outputs, we have neither a basis for understanding why a system produces seemingly correct results when we intuitively agree with them, nor a basis for

---

[26]Naturally, our confidence in any particular application also varies with the reliability of parameter values for that application. The results produced by carefully defined models can be no more accurate than are the primitive symbols from which they are derived.

understanding presumed failures. Second, formality provides a basis for assessing a system's range of application. In the absence of a well-formed theory of operation, we have no basis for assuming that representations designed to facilitate reasoning in one domain will yield the same benefits in any other; even within the context of a *particular* application, we have no reason to believe that a system will behave appropriately for cases beyond those that have been tested empirically. Third, by imposing constraints on inputs, a formal system limits the space of potential knowledge-acquisition procedures.

In practice, formality often entails generality: The cost of carefully specifying a system or model, and of proving its correctness, is justified usually when there is potential benefit to be derived across several applications, rather than in only one or a few applications.

A *transparent* system reflects an intuitive framework for interpreting its results and for systematically modifying its parameters. Transparent systems generally provide (a) a sufficiently rich and intuitive vocabulary of symbols to permit responses to users' queries, (b) a sufficiently natural set of operations to permit users to understand how symbols are combined in reaching conclusions, and (c) a sufficiently natural and informative set of strategies for relating symbols (to one another) to permit users to understand the system's results and to modify its primitive symbols. Davis described assumptions underlying the development of transparent systems:

> The control structures and representations [must be] comprehensible to the expert (at the conceptual level), so that he can express his knowledge with them. This is required to insure that the expert understands system performance well enough to know what to correct and to assure that he knows how to express the required knowledge. What the expert sees and wants to change is the external behavior of the system. Mapping from the desired (external) behavior to the necessary internal modification is often quite subtle and requires an intimate understanding of the system structure. Part of the "art of debugging" is an understanding of this mapping. . . . [Thus,] the representation of knowledge and the manner in which knowledge is used [must] be sufficiently comprehensible to the expert that he can understand program behavior. (Davis, 1976)

The degree to which a system is transparent is of significant practical importance. First, researchers and knowledge engineers generally acknowledge that automated explanation is a critical determinant of user acceptance in intelligent systems (Teach & Shortliffe, 1981). Second, by providing users with an opportunity to change the system in the context of a step-by-step account of its computation, a transparent system promotes model acquisition, tuning, and ongoing modification.

Thus, both formality and transparency contribute to the success of practical intelligent systems.[27] Yet, previous approaches to representing values have em-

---

[27]Other properties of representations (e.g., complexity) are no less important, but are peripheral to this discussion.

phasized either one property or the other. The formal approach of DA stresses well-formed, general theories, but lacks a framework for justifying the results of formal models to users who are unfamiliar with those models, and for assisting such users with repairing model parameters. Heuristic value-based systems in AI reflect an approach that is more empirically motivated, emphasizing intuitive appeal in the context of particular applications, but often at the expense of concise engineering guidelines and bounds on predictability. The following two sections contrast these approaches in more detail.[28]

2.3.1 Formal Value-Based Systems

Keeney described DA as "a formalization of common sense for decision problems which are too complex for informal use of common sense," and, more technically, as "a philosophy, articulated by a set of logical axioms, and a methodology and collection of systematic procedures, based on those axioms, for responsibly analyzing the complexities inherent in decision problems" (Keeney, 1982, p. 806).

Advocates of DA as a model of choice in intelligent systems stress the benefits of its formality and generality. First, a formal model of choice provides confidence in the integrity of its results with respect to a particular philosophy of choosing among alternatives. Central works on the foundations of DA include those by von Neumann and Morgenstern (1947), Savage (1954), Raiffa (1968), and Keeney and Raiffa (1976). Second, DA provides a basis for distinguishing appropriate applications from inappropriate ones: Decision-analytic assumptions specify required relationships among model inputs that can alert the knowledge engineer to potential failures in an application.[29] Although clear and precise, these assumptions are sufficiently general to characterize problems across diverse domains, from corporate policy (Keeney, 1975) to medicine (Heckerman, 1991) to school busing (Edwards, 1980). Finally, the foundations of formal models suggest guidelines for knowledge acquisition. Authors such as Keeney (1982) and Farquhar (1984) reviewed methodological works in DA. Texts addressing aspects of DA include Holloway (1979), LaValle (1978), Moore and Thomas (1976), Pratt, Raiffa, and Schlaifer (1965), Schlaifer (1969), Tribus (1969), von Winterfeldt and Edwards (1986), and Winkler (1972).

Although decision-analytic models provide these formality-related benefits, authors have criticized these models for their lack of transparency. Several authors noted, for example, that it may be difficult for a nonanalyst to interpret the results of a decision analysis, and, hence, to adopt decision-analytic advice:

---

[28]Chapter 8 describes particular systems and contrasts them with IVA. Here, we provide an informal survey of the relative strengths and weaknesses of formal and heuristic value-based systems.

[29]Section 2.5 addresses this point in detail, providing examples of such failures and of their implications for practice.

> For a formal decision methodology to be useful in solving real problems, its con-
> clusions must ultimately make intuitive sense to the decision maker. It is unreasonable
> to assume that the decision maker will allocate valuable resources merely because
> of a logical argument. Thus, the decision maker must develop an intuitive under-
> standing of the validity of any successful recommendation for action, even if he
> or she does not have detailed knowledge of the underlying formalism that led to
> the recommendation. (Holtzman, 1989)

> An elaborate decision model may obscure the salient features of the problem, trad-
> ing off an ability to explain a choice in intuitive terms in favor of achieving a more
> powerful, generalized characterization of the problem. (Rennels, Shortliffe, & Miller,
> 1985, p. 3)

The difficulty of acquiring models of choice under the decision-analytic framework has also been noted; the task of capturing the parameters of decision-analytic
models generally requires the involvement of a trained decision analyst (Keeney,
1986; Zeleny, 1982). Von Winterfeldt and Edwards noted that

> a set of formal models specifies the relations among responses. This fact is both
> a blessing and a nuisance. It is helpful because it enables the decision analyst who
> is knowledgeable about those logical relations to exploit them in testing the subjec-
> tive numbers the respondent has produced. This gives the decision analyst an ad-
> vantage. . . . It is nuisance because it injects the process of interaction between
> analyst and client into the number elicitation task. (von Winterfeldt & Edwards,
> 1986, pp. 352–353)

Another problem of transparency in DA concerns the reliability of parameter
values that are captured from users. Several authors have noted the effects of
cognitive illusions and biases in parameter assessment (e.g., Hershey, Kunreuther,
& Schoemaker, 1982; Hogarth, 1980; Poulton, 1979; Tversky & Kahneman,
1974, 1981). In particular, normative models admit paradoxical behavior from
the point of view of some users, and user responses may be overly sensitive
to variations in knowledge-acquisition procedures (Fischer, 1979; Fischhoff,
Goitein, & Shapiro, 1982). In part, users have difficulty specifying parameters
because they do not understand how the values they specify affect the final
result.

In summary, the models of DA have been advocated on the basis of their formality and generality; they have been criticized for their lack of transparency.

2.3.2 Heuristic Value-Based Systems

Heuristic approaches to modeling value-based choices focus on models that
capture the spirit of choosing among competing alternatives in particular do-

mains.[30] These approaches have been employed, for example, in domains such as medicine (Clancey, 1984; Haggerty, 1984; Kastner, 1983), spectral analysis (Ferrante, 1985), real estate (Weiner, 1980), and games (Berliner & Ackley, 1982; Nilsson, 1980). Generally speaking, these intuitive frameworks are motivated principally by transparency considerations:

> Because we wanted to formulate judgments that could be provided *by* physicians and would appear familiar *to* them, we decided not to use mathematical methods such as evaluation polynomials or Bayesian analysis. (Clancey, 1984, p. 134)

> The advantage of tailoring a restricted form of a general technique to a particular domain is that such efforts may better capture the character of the domain and allow choice and explanation to be more naturally modelled. . . . Furthermore a general model may not lend itself to terse and concise explanation. (Rennels et al., 1985, p. 2)

Criticisms of heuristic value-based systems focus on their lack of formality. In particular, authors have questioned the integrity of the results of heuristic value-based systems in the absence of a formal foundation and have noted that the range of application of such systems is obscure:

> It can often be quite difficult to separate implementation-dependent weaknesses from failings in a general method. For the QBKG system it is particularly troublesome since we have at present only the outlines of a general method – principles, guidelines, and intuitions – rather than a full-blown knowledge representation language and judgment/reasoning system. Accurate evaluation of the general method will have to await more research into making judgmental systems. . . . (Ackley & Berliner, 1983, p. 47)

> No inference engine builder has yet been successful at defining, in terms understandable to those familiar with tasks, the characteristics a task has to have in order for it to be an appropriate task for his or her inference engine. . . . If we had such a set of concepts, we could develop a wide variety of useful and effective inference engines. Each engine would provide the computational mechanisms required to address a particular class of tasks – i.e., all tasks with a specific set of characteristics. (McDermott, 1989)

> [Heuristic models] cannot be seen as 'general problem solvers' . . . (Rennels et al., 1985, p. 2)

> Relating decisions [produced by the revised MYCIN therapy planning algorithm is] difficult because they require some representation of what the heuristics mean. (Clancey, 1984, p. 144)

---

[30]Models for choosing among alternatives should not be confused with the computational frameworks in which they are implemented. Computational frameworks themselves encode no information about the nature or elements of choices; rather, they are alternative Turing Machines that facilitate the encoding of particular models of choice inspired by particular domains. Thus, it is misguided to debate, for example, whether metarules provide a desirable model of choice; both procedural (Friedman, 1985; Georgeff, 1982) and declarative (Davis, 1976, 1980) frameworks have been employed as metalevel machinery, and the more relevant questions here concern the models that are implemented on top of these frameworks.

In summary, although heuristic value-based systems strive for transparency, they have been criticized for their lack of a formal foundation.

2.4 PROBLEM STATEMENT

DA stresses formal specification and generality, with transparency as a secondary goal; heuristic value-based systems stress transparency, with rigorous specification as a secondary goal. The hypothesis of this book is that **we can build on a formal model of value to provide a framework for value-based systems that is both formal and transparent**. That is, we can develop a framework for value-based systems that is rigorous and general in its definition, and intuitive in its operation. Our approach is to address the explanation and refinement of *multiattribute value theory*, a formal model of value from DA, yielding a general basis for modeling value-based choices in intelligent systems that is both formal *and* transparent.

2.5 MULTIATTRIBUTE VALUE THEORY

Multiattribute value theory is the subfield of DA that addresses the problem of modeling value-based choices. The approach of multiattribute value theory can be stated as follows.[31] We have a set of *alternatives A*, such as a set of actions for purging a dataset. We associate an array of value measurements with each $a \in A$ that reflect our *objectives*, such as the desire to minimize the time it takes to purge a dataset. We describe the degree to which our objectives are satisfied in the context of *attribute values* $x_1, \ldots, x_n$ of alternatives, such as minutes elapsed in purging a dataset. We define a *multiattribute value function* (or simply *value function*) that maps each $a = (x_1, \ldots, x_n)$ into an overall measure of value, and we select alternatives that maximize this function.

The formal justification for a value function's behavior includes a set of assumptions (or *axioms*) concerning the function's parameters, along with proof that these axioms are necessary and sufficient to guarantee desirable behavior. The axioms essentially restrict the relationships among model parameters, and the associated procedures for capturing these parameters are designed with the axioms in mind.

One important variation underlying various axiom systems concerns the type of measurement scale for value. Under the classical utility theory of von Neumann and Morgenstern (1947), for instance, preferences are ordinal: We can

---

[31]This entire section is expository in nature. Portions of this exposition are based on (von Winterfeldt & Edwards, 1986) and on (Keeney & Raiffa, 1976). Figures reprinted by permission. Copyright © 1986 by Cambridge University Press. Readers who are familiar with DA may want to skip to Section 2.6.

represent that "*a* is preferred to *b*" and that "*c* is preferred to *d*," but we cannot represent the strength of preference of *a* over *b* as compared with that of *c* over *d*; similar restrictions characterize conjoint measurement theory (e.g., Green & Srinivasan, 1978; Luce & Tukey, 1964; Tversky, 1967). These models are thus limited to representing statements such as "*a* is better than *b*"; statements such as "*a* is *much* better than *b*" have no formal meaning. The latter sorts of comparisons are valid, however, under axiom systems based on difference measurement (Fishburn, 1970; Krantz, Luce, Suppes, & Tversky, 1971; Suppes & Winet, 1955). Axiom systems based on a ratio scale of measurement (Hauser & Shugan, 1980; Stevens, 1968) lend meaning to proportions of values, supporting statements such as "*a* is *twice as good* as *b*." The relative naturalness of alternative value-measurement systems has been a subject of debate in the literature (Farquhar & Keller, 1988).[32]

IVA is based on a scale of difference measurement. Von Winterfeldt and Edwards (1986) summarized the assumptions that are typically required in formulations of value-difference measurement, as follows. Let *xy* denote "the strength of preference of alternative *x* over alternative *y*" (assuming that *x* is preferred or indifferent to *y*), and let *B* be the set of all such ordered pairs *xy*. Let $wx \overset{\cdot}{\geq}$ *yz* denote "the strength of preference of *w* over *x* is at least that of *y* over *z*." It can be shown that whenever the following axioms are satisfied, there exists a value function *v* such that for all *ab*, *cd* $\in$ *B*, $ab \overset{\cdot}{\geq} cd$ iff $v(a) - v(b) \geq v(c) - v(d)$.

- *Connectivity:* For all *ab*, *cd* $\in$ *B*, either $ab \overset{\cdot}{\geq} cd$ or $cd \overset{\cdot}{\geq} ab$ or both
- *Transitivity:* When $ab \overset{\cdot}{\geq} cd$ and $cd \overset{\cdot}{\geq} ef$, then $ab \overset{\cdot}{\geq} ef$

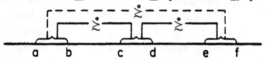

- *Summation:* For all *ab*, *bc* $\in$ *B*, $ac \overset{\cdot}{\geq} ab$ and $ac \overset{\cdot}{\geq} bc$

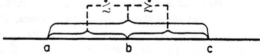

- *Cancellation:* When $ab \overset{\cdot}{\geq} a'b'$ and $bc \overset{\cdot}{\geq} b'c'$ then $ac \overset{\cdot}{\geq} a'c'$

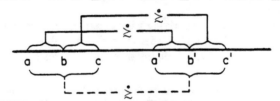

---

[32]We shall return to these debates in chapter 4.

- *Solvability:* Informally, this assumption requires that the value space be "dense," that there be no "holes" in the space
- *Archimedean:* Informally, this assumption requires that we can traverse the value space without running up against a point of infinite positive or negative value

Von Winterfeldt and Edwards (1986) noted that these assumptions can never be verified in practice; rather, they serve to alert the knowledge engineer to potential failures in difference measurement: When the knowledge engineer observes that one of the assumptions is violated systematically in the context of a particular application, he can take specific steps to correct the problem (or, in the worst case, he can decide that the model is inappropriate for a particular user and application). For example, when only a small set of discrete alternatives is available, the solvability assumption may be violated, but this violation may not be considered pragmatically important when certain elicitation techniques are employed.[33] Should the knowledge engineer favor elicitation techniques that rely directly on solvability, he could enrich the space with hypothetical alternatives, if the hypothetical alternatives seem natural to the decision maker. On the other hand, if connectivity is violated (i.e., the decision maker is unable to compare value differences), then difference measurement may not be appropriate for the application. The essential point is that a clearly specified set of general assumptions facilitates the identification of potential pitfalls in particular applications.

In multiattribute theories of value, an additional set of assumptions associates relationships among attributes with forms for the value function. Researchers have developed a variety of functional forms (Farquhar & Fishburn, 1981; Fishburn, 1970; Tamura & Nakamura, 1978), and the relative advantages of different forms also have been debated in the literature. Authors such as Keeney (1981) advocated the approach of investing significant effort in the initial phases of knowledge engineering to select attributes that are related simply; under this approach, we may, in some instances, replace attributes that are related nonlinearly with more *fundamental attributes* that represent the user's preferences more directly. Other authors (e.g., Farquhar & Fishburn, 1981) recommended amortizing the cost of simplifying the value function by retaining complex forms captured from the user initially. The significant majority of practical applications reflect the former approach, employing the *additive multiattribute value function (AMVF)*:[34]

$$v(a) = v(x_1, \ldots , x_n) = \sum_{i=1}^{n} w_i v_i(x_i)$$

---

[33]Solvability violations do not pose a serious problem under *direct-rating techniques*, for instance, because respondents rate alternatives directly and verify alternative differences, without having to match minute increments in value. *Indifference techniques*, on the other hand, require the decision maker to think in terms of matching potentially minute increments in value, so solvability is more important when such techniques are employed.

[34]This notation and terminology is employed by (Keeney & Raiffa, 1976).

where

1. $(x_1, \ldots, x_n)$ is the vector of attribute values for alternative a
2. For each attribute i, v_i is the *component value function*, which maps the least preferable x_i to 0, the best x_i to 1, and other x_i to values in $(0,1)$
3. w_i is the *weight* for attribute i, $0 < w_i < 1$ and $\sum_{i=1}^{n} w_i = 1$

The component value function expresses the preferability of each attribute value of its associated attribute, and the corresponding weight represents the relative importance of the attribute within the range of attribute values in the decision at hand.[35]

IVA is based on the additive form of the *measurable multiattribute value function* (Dyer & Sarin, 1979), which, under difference measurement, requires that the attributes be *difference independent* and *difference consistent*. Informally, these conditions require that strength of preference in a given attribute not depend on the level of other attributes that are held constant. Although the AMVF rests on strong assumptions, its use is standard in practice: According to Weber, for example, approximately 95 percent of all applied analyses employ the additive form.[36]

2.6 EXAMPLE: AN AMVF FOR JESQ

Consider employing the AMVF in the context of JESQ, which suffered a number of problems due to the omission of an explicit model of value (Section 2.2). More specifically, suppose that a user has generated a large dataset that is to be printed on a device that is presently disabled, and that a choice among the following alternative plans for manipulating that dataset must be made to free space on the operating-system queue:[37]

1. COPY: Copy the dataset to tape, and print it later when the requested printer has been repaired
2. EXPENSIVE-PRINTING: Print the dataset on a faster printer that uses forms more expensive than those requested by the user
3. CHEAP-PRINTING: Print the dataset on a slower printer that uses forms of lower quality than those requested by the user

---

[35]Chapter 4 examines the semantics of AMVF parameters in more detail.

[36]The bulk of the remaining applications employ the *multiplicative form*; Keeney maintained that "when the objective functions are complex, meaning they involve more than additive or multiplicative components of single-attribute objective functions, it is often the case that the original objectives were not wisely selected" (Keeney, 1986).

[37]This is the same set of plans that we presented in chapter 1.

4. DELETE: Delete the dataset from the queue

5. INSTALL: Connect a duplicate of the requested printer for use until the requested printer has been repaired

6. FICHE: Deliver the dataset to the user on microfiche

7. CARDS: Deliver the dataset to the user on punched cards

8. DASD: Transfer the dataset to the user's private disk storage, so that the user can transfer it back to the queue for printing after the printer has been repaired

Sections 2.6.1 through 2.6.4 describe an AMVF that can be employed to automate this choice.

2.6.1   The Structure of Objectives

First, we structure management's operational objectives in a *value tree* or *objectives hierarchy*.[38] The essential idea is to capture the hierarchical nature of objectives in a corresponding hierarchical structure, where the satisfaction of a given objective is measured in terms of the satisfaction of its component objectives (i.e., children). Primitive objectives (at the leaves of the tree) are measured in terms of their associated attributes, as described in section 2.5; for example, the primitive objective *minimize cost* might be measured in dollars. An attribute should be both *comprehensive* (i.e., it is indicative of the level to which the associated objective is achieved) and *measurable* (i.e., the decision maker can specify preferences for different possible levels of the attribute) (Keeney & Raiffa, 1976).

Recall that the effectiveness of space-management actions is judged in terms of several objectives (section 2.2), including maximizing the effect on the JES queue space, maximizing the convenience of the operator, maximizing the satisfaction of the user, minimizing costs, and maximizing the speed of actions. These objectives, in turn, were defined in terms of more detailed objectives. We shall simplify this set of objectives for ease of presentation.

Let us assume that a single dataset is to be manipulated, so that the magnitude of the effect of an action on queue space becomes irrelevant; this assumption limits the number of alternative actions to the mentioned eight. We shall thus choose among competing space-freeing alternatives based on four objectives: *minimize additional operator time, maximize user satisfaction, minimize additional cost*, and *minimize problem-resolution time*. In our simplified formulation, *minimize additional operator time* can be considered to correspond directly to "minimize the amount of additional time the operator spends performing an action beyond that originally required" (i.e., before the printer broke down and created the problem), measured in minutes of additional operator time. *Maximize user satisfaction*, on the

---

[38]Both terms are commonly used in the literature, and we shall use them interchangeably.

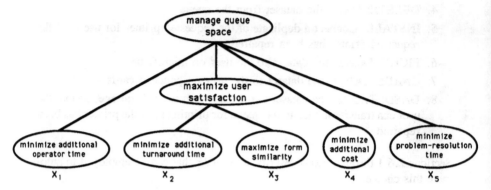

FIG. 2.1.   Objectives hierarchy for simplified queue-space problem.

other hand, might be decomposed into more detailed objectives, such as *minimize additional turnaround time* (measured in minutes of additional turnaround time) and *maximize form similarity* (i.e., maximize similarity between the output medium originally requested and the output medium associated with the chosen action), measured in terms of a subjective index that assigns 0 to forms most inferior to those requested, and assigns 1 to the requested forms, as well as to forms that are better than those requested. Alternatively, we could measure user satisfaction directly in terms of a subjective index, but in this case more detailed objectives are available. *Minimize additional cost* can be measured directly in dollars of additional cost. *Minimize problem-resolution time*, the time that it takes for the dataset to exit the queue (excluding other processing), can be measured directly in minutes of problem-resolution time. Pictorially, we have the objectives hierarchy of Fig. 2.1 for our sample problem.

Our attributes are

- x_1 = additional operator time (minutes)
- x_2 = additional turnaround time (minutes)
- x_3 = form similarity (subjective index)
- x_4 = additional cost (dollars)
- x_5 = problem-resolution time (minutes)

2.6.2 Assessment of Alternative Plans

Next, we represent each alternative as a vector of attribute values. COPY, for example, is represented as (10, 34.2, 1, 1, 15.1) according to the following analysis. It takes the operator approximately 10 minutes to make sure that a tape is mounted, start the copy process, walk the tape to and from the tape library, and

TABLE 2.1
Attribute Vectors for Alternatives

Alternative	x_1	x_2	x_3	x_4	x_5
COPY	10.0	34.2	1.0	1.00	15.1
EXPENSIVE-PRINTING	0.1	0.0	1.0	100.00	25.0
CHEAP-PRINTING	0.1	10.0	0.8	0.00	40.0
DELETE	0.1	inf.	0.0	0.00	0.1
INSTALL	180.0	180.0	1.0	5000.00	210.0
FICHE	0.1	20.0	0.2	70.00	50.0
CARDS	0.1	15.0	0.1	20.00	45.0
DASD	0.1	32.1	1.0	0.50	1.0

so on, so $x_1 = 10$.[39] Repairing the printer, and copying and restoring the user's job takes around 34.2 minutes on average, thereby increasing the user's turn-around time by that amount (so $x_2 = 34.2$). Because COPY encompasses bringing the dataset back onto the queue and printing it (after the printer has been repaired), the user receives his data on the output medium requested (thus $x_3 = 1$). Although tapes and tape drives are reusable, we amortize the cost of copying a job at about \$1 per job, so $x_4 = 1$. We assign $x_5 = 15.1$ because the dataset stays on the queue until the copy operation has been completed (approximately 15.1 minutes). By similar analyses, we obtain the vectors shown in Table 2.1.

We made several assumptions in formulating these vectors, including

1. Our constant dataset size is 1 million lines. In an actual implementation, some attribute values (e.g., the cost of expensive paper) would be computed as a function of the number of lines in the dataset. Here, they are constants.[40]

2. Attribute values that might be recorded as negative (i.e., in cases where the alternative actions are *better* with respect to the associated objectives) are recorded as zero to reflect the wording "additional" in our formulation of objectives. Equivalently, we might have recorded them as negative and treated them as zero in the component value functions described later. We take this approach because the operators will honor the user's request for resources exactly when the printer is not disabled, rather than attempt to *optimize* output processing. They (and hence we) assume that the user will not be made any happier, for example, by expensive paper, if he does not request that paper. Thus, setting these attribute values to zero negates the potential positive value derived from "negative excesses." We would not want these negative excesses to offset true (positive) excesses in choosing the best alternative.

---

[39]In an actual analysis, we might collect historical data to compute these averages.

[40]Appropriate attribute ranges for component value functions thus need to be selected in concert with expectations regarding allowable dataset sizes.

3. Alternatives that involve reestablishment of the dataset on the queue for requested printing (e.g., DASD, COPY) assume approximately a 30-minute waiting time for printer repairs. In an actual implementation, this value would be determined on a situation-by-situation basis, and the affected attribute values would be computed accordingly.

2.6.3 Assessment of Values

Next, we determine the operational preferences of installation management and encode them in the value function. Our conversations with operators suggest that the objectives satisfy the independence assumptions that justify employing the AMVF. Now we need to capture the relative importance of these objectives with respect to choices among competing alternatives. One realistic distribution is depicted in Fig. 2.2.[41]

We thus have the following value function for assessing queue-space-management actions:

$$
\begin{aligned}
v(x_1, x_2, x_3, x_4, x_5) &= .1v_1(x_1) + .5(.5v_2(x_2) + .5v_3(x_3)) \\
&\quad + .2v_4(x_4) + .2v_5(x_5) \\
&= .1v_1(x_1) + .25v_2(x_2) + .25v_3(x_3) \\
&\quad + .2v_4(x_4) + .2v_5(x_5)
\end{aligned}
$$

Note that the hierarchy allows for the isolated assessment of decision problems at different levels of abstraction, with weights summing to 1 at any given level. At the highest level, *maximize user satisfaction* accounts for 50% of the decision, with the remaining objectives accounting for the remaining 50%. As for *maximize user satisfaction* itself, the only decomposed objective, *minimize additional turnaround time* accounts for 50% of the *maximize user satisfaction* assessment, with *maximize form similarity* accounting for the remaining 50%. Multiplying the weights as implied by the hierarchy, we arrive at values of 25% and 25% for these detailed attributes, without requiring the user to specify them directly.

---

[41]In this domain, the relative importance of objectives depends on factors outside the model — primarily on the severity of the current queue-space situation. (See (Langlotz & Shortliffe, 1989) for a general discussion of this problem and of its implications for nonmonotonic reasoning). If, say, 25% of queue space remains free, then the installation is willing to sacrifice more of an operator's time to provide better service (i.e., more user satisfaction). If, on the other hand, only 5% of queue space remains free, there is significant danger that the target system will crash, so an individual's satisfaction is traded off for more judicious use of the operator's time. Chapter 4 introduces the notion of a *decision context* that captures varying weights as a function of exogenous variables. Decision contexts provide an alternative to reformulating the set of chosen objectives (Keeney, 1981) and to employing more elaborate functional forms. For purposes of exposition, we assume here that the situation is still under control — there is sufficient space left to avoid panic.

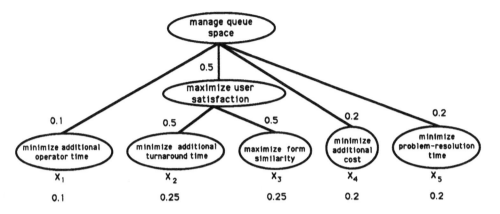

FIG. 2.2. Distribution of weights.

Table 2.2 provides the component value functions for our leaf objectives. Note that, for objectives that are to be maximized (minimized), the value functions assign 0 to the lowest (highest) attribute values and 1 to the highest (lowest) values, with all other values lying in between.[42]

2.6.4 Evaluation of Alternatives

Finally, we evaluate and compare our alternatives as follows, based on the model presented in previous sections.

$v(DASD) = v(.1,32.1,1,.5,1) = .1*v1(.1) + .5(.5*v2(32.1) + .5*v3(1))$
$+ .2*v4(.5) + .2*v5(1) = .85$

$v(EXPENSIVE\text{-}PRINTING) = v(.1,0,1,100,25) = .1*v1(.1) + .5(.5*v2(0)$
$+ .5*v3(1)) + .2*v4(100) + .2*v5(25) = .8$

$v(CHEAP\text{-}PRINTING) = v(.1,10,.8,0,40) = .1*v1(.1) + .5(.5*v2(10)$
$+ .5*v3(.8)) + .2*v4(0) + .2*v5(40) = .78$

$v(COPY) = v(10.0,34.2,1.0,1.00,15.1) = .1*v1(10) + .5(.5*v2(34.2) +$
$.5*v3(1)) + .2*v4(1) + .2*v5(15.1) = .76$

---

[42]The attribute ranges in these definitions reflect the data and the simplifying assumptions of section 2.6.2, with inequalities at the extremes of the ranges representing indifference among extreme cases. v_5 encodes, for example, that all plans requiring more than 1 hour to resolve are "bad," and, more specifically, that 2-hour solutions are not substantively worse than are 1-hour solutions, because solutions exceeding 1 hour are so "bad" in the context of queue-space management. In subsequent chapters, we shall simply employ discrete points for attribute values and for component value functions in this domain, and assume that extreme values for attributes are fixed.

TABLE 2.2
Component Value Functions for the Queue-Space Problem

Additional operator time (minutes)		Additional turnaround time (minutes)	
x_1	$v_1(x_1)$	x_2	$v_2(x_2)$
$x_1 \leq 5$	1.0	$x_2 \leq 5$	1.0
$5 < x_1 \leq 20$	0.5	$5 < x_2 \leq 10$	0.8
$20 < x_1 \leq 60$	0.3	$10 < x_2 \leq 20$	0.6
$x_1 > 60$	0.0	$20 < x_2 \leq 40$	0.4
		$40 < x_2 \leq 60$	0.2
		$x_2 > 60$	0.0

Form similarity (subjective index): $v_3(x_3) = x_3$

Additional cost (dollars)		Problem-resolution time (minutes)	
x_4	$v_4(x_4)$	x_5	$v_5(x_5)$
$x_4 \leq 10$	1.0	$x_5 \leq 10$	1.0
$10 < x_4 \leq 40$	0.8	$10 < x_5 \leq 20$	0.8
$40 < x_4 \leq 80$	0.6	$20 < x_5 \leq 30$	0.6
$80 < x_4 \leq 100$	0.4	$30 < x_5 \leq 40$	0.4
$100 < x_4 \leq 150$	0.2	$40 < x_5 \leq 60$	0.2
$x_4 > 150$	0.0	$x_5 > 60$	0.0

$v(\text{DELETE}) = v(.1, \infty, 0, 0, .1) = .1 * v1(.1) + .5(.5 * v2(\infty) + .5 * v3(0))$
$+ .2 * v4(0) + .2 * v5(.1) = .5$

$v(\text{CARDS}) = v(.1, 15, .1, 20, 45) = .1 * v1(.1) + .5(.5 * v2(15) + .5 * v3(.1))$
$+ .2 * v4(20) + .2 * v5(45) = .475$

$v(\text{FICHE}) = v(.1, 20, .2, 70, 50) = .1 * v1(.1) + .5(.5 * v2(20) + .5 * v3(.2))$
$+ .2 * v4(70) + .2 * v5(50) = .46$

$v(\text{INSTALL}) = v(180, 180, 1, 5000, 210) = .1 * v1(180) + .5(.5 * v2(180) +$
$.5 * v3(1)) + .2 * v4(5000) + .2 * v5(210) = .25$

This formulation of the problem imposes the following ordering on the desirability of alternatives: DASD > EXPENSIVE-PRINTING > CHEAP-PRINTING > COPY > DELETE > CARDS > FICHE > INSTALL.

2.7 CHALLENGES IN EXPLAINING AND REFINING THE AMVF

Although including the AMVF of section 2.6 would increase the competence of JESQ's choices, this model would fail, by itself, to address JESQ's transparency problems, as section 2.3 described in general terms. The following sections elucidate some of the challenges of explaining and refining AMVF-based choices.

2.7.1 Justification of AMVF-Based Choices

What is a "convincing" justification for a choice? Clearly, we need to do better than to display the value function and its arguments. Referring again to JESQ's domain, imagine an explanation of the form

> *Your best option is DASD because your value function is* $v(x_1, x_2, x_3, x_4, x_5) =$ *.1$v_1(x_1)$ + .25$v_2(x_2)$ + .25$v_3(x_3)$ + .2$v_4(x_4)$ + .2$v_5(x_5)$ where x_1 = additional operator time in minutes, x_2 = additional turnaround time in minutes, x_3 = form similarity (subjective index), x_4 = additional cost in dollars, and x_5 = problem-resolution time in minutes, and DASD maximizes v over all available alternatives.*

There are several obvious problems with this justification. First, the explanation does not appeal to intuition; it does not associate components of the value function with notions such as "desirability" and "importance," for example.

Second, the explanation does not compare alternatives explicitly. Although the explanation communicates the *results* of such a comparison by mentioning the highest-rated alternative, it provides little insight into how that alternative compares with its closest contenders.

Third, the explanation refers to only the most detailed attributes on which the decision is based. For example, the concepts of *additional turnaround time* and *form similarity* are both associated with the higher-level concept *user satisfaction*, but this information is omitted from the explanation. It might even be appropriate to talk solely in terms of *user satisfaction* in some situations, omitting references to this objective's more detailed supporting measures.

Fourth, the explanation reflects the brute-force approach of elucidating *all* the attributes that underlie the decision, whereas it is most likely that only one, or perhaps a few, distinguish the chosen alternative from its closest contenders. For example, EXPENSIVE.PRINTING, like DASD, involves little additional operator time. Thus, the attribute *additional operator time* plays a relatively minor role in distinguishing these two alternatives in terms of their overall relative desirability.

Fifth, the explanation makes no reference to the presumed conditions under which the value function is applicable. Is *maximize user satisfaction* always the most important objective? Or are there circumstances under which it would be weighted differently?

We might also enhance the explanation in other ways, such as reassuring the user that value functions built by several operations managers reflect the same preferences, or by providing a higher level description of the basic goals of the installation, or by substituting qualitative descriptions for quantitative values.

The essential point is that justifications for choices should be more than displays of the models and of the parameters that compute those choices. How can we provide such explanations? What information beyond the value function is required? How should this information be represented? IVA addresses these and related questions.

2.7.2 Refinement of the AMVF

Suppose the user is unconvinced by the system's justification for a choice. Should he be forced to rebuild the underlying model from scratch? Should he call on decision analysts and programmers to help change the model? As in explanation, we need to do better than to display candidate parameters for modification. To demonstrate this point, we can imagine an extremely poor system that produces help of the following form:

> *OK, so you disagree with the choice. Select the parameter that you would like to modify, or add additional objectives:*
> - w_1,
> - w_2,
> - w_3,
> - w_4,
> - w_5,
> - x_1 *for COPY,*
> - x_2 *for COPY,*
> - x_3 *for COPY,*
> - x_4 *for COPY,*
> - x_5 *for COPY,*
> - x_1 *for EXPENSIVE.PRINTING,*
> - x_2 *for EXPENSIVE.PRINTING,*
> - x_3 *for EXPENSIVE.PRINTING,*
> - x_4 *for EXPENSIVE.PRINTING,*
> - x_5 *for EXPENSIVE.PRINTING,*
> - x_1 *for CHEAP.PRINTING,*
> - x_2 *for CHEAP.PRINTING,*
> - x_3 *for CHEAP.PRINTING,*
> - x_4 *for CHEAP.PRINTING,*
> - x_5 *for CHEAP.PRINTING,*
> - x_1 *for DELETE,*
> - x_2 *for DELETE,*
> - x_3 *for DELETE,*
> - x_4 *for DELETE,*
> - x_5 *for DELETE,*
> - x_1 *for INSTALL,*
> - x_2 *for INSTALL,*
> - x_3 *for INSTALL,*
> - x_4 *for INSTALL,*
> - x_5 *for INSTALL,*
> - x_1 *for FICHE,*
> - x_2 *for FICHE,*

- x_3 *for FICHE,*
- x_4 *for FICHE,*
- x_5 *for FICHE,*
- x_1 *for CARDS,*
- x_2 *for CARDS,*
- x_3 *for CARDS,*
- x_4 *for CARDS,*
- x_5 *for CARDS,*
- x_1 *for DASD,*
- x_2 *for DASD,*
- x_3 *for DASD,*
- x_4 *for DASD,*
- x_5 *for DASD,*
- $v_1(x_1)$ *for COPY,*
- $v_2(x_2)$ *for COPY,*
- $v_3(x_3)$ *for COPY,*
- $v_4(x_4)$ *for COPY,*
- $v_5(x_5)$ *for COPY,*
- $v_1(x_1)$ *for EXPENSIVE.PRINTING,*
- $v_2(x_2)$ *for EXPENSIVE.PRINTING,*
- $v_3(x_3)$ *for EXPENSIVE.PRINTING,*
- $v_4(x_4)$ *for EXPENSIVE.PRINTING,*
- $v_5(x_5)$ *for EXPENSIVE.PRINTING,*
- $v_1(x_1)$ *for CHEAP.PRINTING,*
- $v_2(x_2)$ *for CHEAP.PRINTING,*
- $v_3(x_3)$ *for CHEAP.PRINTING,*
- $v_4(x_4)$ *for CHEAP.PRINTING,*
- $v_5(x_5)$ *for CHEAP.PRINTING,*
- $v_1(x_1)$ *for DELETE,*
- $v_2(x_2)$ *for DELETE,*
- $v_3(x_3)$ *for DELETE,*
- $v_4(x_4)$ *for DELETE,*
- $v_5(x_5)$ *for DELETE,*
- $v_1(x_1)$ *for INSTALL,*
- $v_2(x_2)$ *for INSTALL,*
- $v_3(x_3)$ *for INSTALL,*
- $v_4(x_4)$ *for INSTALL,*
- $v_5(x_5)$ *for INSTALL,*
- $v_1(x_1)$ *for FICHE,*
- $v_2(x_2)$ *for FICHE,*
- $v_3(x_3)$ *for FICHE,*
- $v_4(x_4)$ *for FICHE,*
- $v_5(x_5)$ *for FICHE,*

- $v_1(x_1)$ *for CARDS,*
- $v_2(x_2)$ *for CARDS,*
- $v_3(x_3)$ *for CARDS,*
- $v_4(x_4)$ *for CARDS,*
- $v_5(x_5)$ *for CARDS,*
- $v_1(x_1)$ *for DASD,*
- $v_2(x_2)$ *for DASD,*
- $v_3(x_3)$ *for DASD,*
- $v_4(x_4)$ *for DASD,*
- $v_5(x_5)$ *for DASD.*

Obviously, such methods are inadequate even in this case, where a relatively small model is employed. In particular, this hypothetical refinement facility fails to organize the parameters in a coherent fashion, and offers no help in understanding how particular parameters participate in producing the final result. The facility fails to distinguish sensitive parameters from less sensitive ones, and the user receives no indication of whether a particular change will affect the final result at all. In general, there can be as many as $n(2|A| + 1)$ candidate parameters for modification, where n is the number of (leaf) objectives appearing in the AMVF, and A is the set of alternatives under consideration.[43] For larger value trees, such as the RCTE and ES-SHELL trees described in chapter 3, there are *hundreds* of candidates for modification, rendering refinement difficult.

A more sophisticated approach is required to maximize the reliability of model repairs while minimizing user effort. How should we accomplish this goal? What additional information is required? How should it be represented? IVA addresses these and related questions.

2.8 RELATED WORK

We can describe related work in terms of three broad research areas: intelligent systems based on decision theory, automated explanation, and automated knowledge acquisition.

2.8.1 Decision Theory in Intelligent Systems

We are hardly the first to advocate the use of decision theory in intelligent systems; in part, our motivation for developing frameworks to explain and refine

---

[43]There are $n|A|$ attribute values x across all alternatives, as many as $n|A|$ component value function evaluations $v(x)$ when all x are unique for each attribute, and n instances of w across objectives, so $n|A| + n|A| + n = 2n|A| + n = n(2|A| + 1)$. Alternatively, we can view entire component value functions as primitive objects, yielding the number of potential modifications $n|A| + n + n$ $= n|A| + 2n = n(|A| + 2)$. In applications that do not employ a mapping from a natural scale to a value scale, there are $n|A|$ component value function evaluations and n instances of w across objectives, so there are $n|A| + n = n(|A| + 1)$ candidate parameters for modification.

decision-theoretic models derives from the increasing popularity of such models as inference machinery for intelligent systems.

For example, a number of researchers have explored the use of decision theory as a general knowledge representation for intelligent systems, and its integration with representations that are more commonly employed in such systems. Langlotz (1989), Wellman (1987), and Sycara (1988) described planners that are based on decision-theoretic principles. Horvitz (1988) describes a decision-theoretic approach to inference under varying resource limitations. White and Sykes (1986) used multiattribute utility theory for conflict resolution in a rule-based system. Holtzman (1989) described the employment of influence diagrams in an intelligent-system context. Heckerman (1991) described extensions to this formalism with applications in large medical domains. Pearl (1986) described foundational work on inference using belief networks. Cooper (1988a) provided efficient algorithms for calculating probabilistic propositions in belief networks, and Suermondt and Cooper (1988) described methods for updating probabilities in multiply connected belief networks. Cooper (1988c) provided an overview of belief networks and of their employment in intelligent systems.

Many of these representations have been applied in the context of intelligent-system applications. Coles, Robb, Sinclair, Smith, and Sobek (1973) and Jacobs and Keifer (1973) used utility theory to evaluate robot plans as a means for coping with uncertainty. Feldman and Sproull (1975) employed decision theory to direct the application of planning operators in an implementation of the monkey and bananas problem. Horvitz, Heckerman, Nathwani, and Fagan (1984) described the use of decision theory for medical diagnosis. Langlotz, Fagan, Williams, and Sikic (1985) described a cancer-therapy-planning system that generates a small set of plausible plans, simulates them to predict their possible consequences, and uses decision theory to rank them. Langlotz, Shortliffe, and Fagan (1986) also used decision theory to justify heuristics in MYCIN. Sykes and White (1986) described the employment of multiobjective decision theory in the context of intelligent computer-aided design. Slagle and Hamburger (1985) described an interactive planning system that uses decision-theoretic models to rank competing plans for allocating military resources. O'Leary (1986) discussed the use of multiattribute decision theory in expert systems for financial-accounting decisions. Klein and Finin (1989) described the use of decision theory in the context of intelligent safety systems. Cooper (1988b) described the application of belief networks in medical diagnosis. Beinlich, Suermondt, Chavez, and Cooper (1989) reported on an alarm-monitoring system based on belief networks. Klein (1991) described the application of multiattribute value theory to the problem of forecasting new markets.

A general perspective on the benefits of integrating techniques from AI and from operations research is provided by Simon (1987). Keeney (1986) provided a general discussion of the explicit representation of values in expert systems. Horvitz, Breese, and Henrion (1988) and Farquhar (1986) reviewed additional applications of decision theory in AI contexts. The apparent utility of decision-theoretic models as inference machinery in intelligent systems motivates our research on techniques for explaining and refining such models.

2.8.2 Automated Explanation

Explanation is a fundamental supporting capability for intelligent systems. A well-known study by Teach and Shortliffe, for example, revealed that high-quality explanation capabilities were the most important requirement for user acceptance of a clinical consultation system, concluding that a "system should be able to justify its advice in terms that are understandable and persuasive. . . . A system that gives dogmatic advice is likely to be rejected" (Teach & Shortliffe, 1981, p. 651). Explanation has become a central topic of research, with experiments in diverse domains, such as the blocks world (Winograd, 1972), medicine (Aikens, 1980; Clancey, 1981; Davis, 1976; Swartout, 1981), complex physical machinery (de Kleer & Brown, 1984; Forbus & Stevens, 1981; Stevens, 1981; Weld, 1984), and financial planning (Kosey & Wise, 1984). We do not provide an exhaustive overview of explanation research here; rather, we cite only those approaches that are particularly pertinent to the research reported in this book.

A number of research programs focus on presenting the results of uncertain inferences. Authors such as Suermondt (1992), Druzdzel and Henrion (1990), and Elsaesser (1990) described techniques for explaining Bayesian inferences. Langlotz, Shortliffe, and Fagan (1988) described a system that generates justifications for choices based on decision trees. Wiecha and Henrion (1988) described the Demos and Demaps systems, which improve the understandability and modifiability of computer-based tools for DA by integrating documentation with model statements and by graphically displaying model structures. Strat (1987) described techniques for generating explanations in the context of systems for evidential reasoning. Jimison (1988) described a system for explaining Bayesian decision networks. Barsalou, Chavez, and Wiederhold (1989) described a hypertext interface for systems based on belief networks. Ben-Bassat et al. (1980), Speigelhalter and Knill-Jones (1984), and Reggia and Perricone (1985) described more quantitative approaches to automated explanation in the context of probabilistic models.

Decision theory has also been employed as machinery for *controlling* explanation. McLaughlin (1987) and Horvitz (1987) described systems that employ multiattribute utility functions as metalevel machinery for balancing the costs and benefits of various levels of completeness in explanations.

As we described in section 2.3, researchers have developed heuristic value-based systems to explain choices in the context of particular domains. Clancey (1984), for example, addressed the explanation of therapy plans in medicine, as did Kastner (1983). Weiner (1980) described a question-answering system in the financial domain. Berliner and Ackley (1982) described an explanation system for choosing among alternatives in the backgammon domain. Schulman and

Hayes-Roth (1987) described a system for choosing and explaining actions in the context of modeling protein structure. Haggerty (1984) described the original EMYCIN implementation of the RCTE system (called REFEREE) for evaluating medical research. IVA extends the range of application, the formal correctness, and the transparency of these approaches. These systems contribute basic ideas that underlie the development of any transparent value-based system, such as pruning irrelevant information from explanations, and separating factors that support a choice from factors that do not. But these systems provide neither a general, well-formed vocabulary for talking about choices (such as the interpretation of chapter 4), nor a basis for systematic refinement (chapter 6), and most of the systems provide explanation strategies that reflect implicit domain-specific expectations about the volume of and relationships among values (unlike the strategies we shall present in chapter 5).

Also relevant is work on explaining quantitative models outside the realm of decision theory. The ROME system (Kosey & Wise, 1984), for example, answers queries about financial spreadsheets. In formulating explanations, ROME employs strategies such as distinguishing relevant parts of the underlying model from irrelevant parts, identifying significant variables in particular situations, and translating quantitative values to qualitative ones for presentation. Such strategies are useful in virtually any system for explaining quantitative models (Langlotz et al., 1988).

2.8.3 Automated Knowledge Acquisition

Automated knowledge acquisition is another fundamental supporting capability for intelligent systems. Because the acquisition of knowledge often represents a significant cost in intelligent-system development (Waterman, 1986), there has been significant research on its automation. Various approaches to automating the construction and improvement of intelligent systems have been proposed over the past several years, ranging from the interactive transfer of expertise (Davis, 1976) to machine learning (Michalski, Carbonell, & Mitchell, 1983, 1986). As in the case of explanation, we do not review the field of knowledge acquisition here; rather, we cite those approaches that are particularly pertinent to the work reported in this book.

In describing knowledge acquisition for decision-theoretic models, it is convenient to distinguish between two phases of model development: acquisition and refinement.[44] Initial *acquisition* involves such activities as problem structuring, model selection, and parameter assessment. Starting with an initial problem structure, iterative *refinement* involves incremental problem restructuring and parameter tuning.

---

[44]Chapter 3 describes in detail the relationships among acquisition, explanation, and refinement.

There exists a well-developed literature regarding the initial acquisition of decision-theoretic models. First, researchers have produced a number of tools to aid in problem structuring, including value trees, inference trees, event trees, fault trees, and decision trees (see, e.g., von Winterfeldt & Edwards, 1986, for a review). More recently introduced structuring aids include influence diagrams (Howard & Matheson, 1980) and analytic hierarchies (Saaty, 1980). In addition, computer programs have been developed for problem structuring (Humphreys & Wishuda, 1980, 1987); although such works represent important advances, problem structuring generally still requires significant involvement with a trained decision analyst. Second, investigators have worked on the automated selection of appropriate functional forms for a decision analysis; Wellman (1985) described an automated system for reasoning about assumptions to select appropriate forms for particular applications. Third, the systematic assessment of utility functions is a relatively mature topic of research (see, e.g., Farquhar, 1984, for a review). Many methods have been implemented in interactive computer programs (Keeney & Sicherman, 1976; Nair & Sicherman, 1979; Novick et al., 1980; Schlaifer, 1971; Seo, Sakawa, Takanashi, Nakagami, & Horiyama, 1978; Klein, Moskowitz, & Ravindran, 1982; Weber, 1985; von Nitzsch & Weber, 1988). More recently, researchers have explored the use of sophisticated graphical environments for assessing values in probabilistic expert systems: Lehmann (1988), for example, described recent work on knowledge acquisition in probabilistic expert systems, and Chavez and Cooper (1988) described an expert-systems-style shell for building such systems. Finally, researchers such as Heckerman (1991) addressed the problem of reducing the number of parameters in decision-theoretic models that need to be captured.

Refinement involves the incremental modification of the value function over time to correct errors and to reflect new preferences as the system evolves. A fundamental decision-analytic tool for refinement is *sensitivity analysis* (see, e.g., Howard, 1968; Keeney & Raiffa, 1976), which involves varying parameters over the range of their possible values, and analyzing the results to reveal the sensitivity of results to parameter modifications. Although powerful, decision-analytic training is required to use sensitivity-analysis techniques effectively. Edwards and Newman (1982), for example, found that nonanalysts had considerable difficulty interpreting even simple tables of quantities derived from sensitivity analysis. We do not mean to suggest that IVA in any way replaces sensitivity analysis; rather, IVA complements traditional methods for sensitivity analysis by providing an intuitive framework for performing what-if-style sensitivity analyses that allow the user to observe how parameter modifications affect the final result in the context of an intuitive supporting argument.

Another approach to refinement, analogous to machine learning in expert systems, involves learning the parameters of a function from examples: Madni, Samet, and Purcell (1985) described a system for learning weights in an additive utility function; a related approach, adaptive utility theory (Cohen, 1984; Cyert &

DeGroot, 1975), encompasses methods for converging on a precise utility function by inferring parameters based on experience. IVA is essentially unrelated to this research; rather, we are concerned with approaches involving the *interactive* refinement of preferences.

IVA's refinement strategies are influenced strongly by Teiresias (Davis, 1976), a system constructed to explore applications of metalevel knowledge in the context of rule-based systems (Davis & Buchanan, 1977). IVA shares some of the general themes of Teiresias, such as capturing and verifying new information in the context of specific situations, and employing explanation facilities as a window into system behavior that facilitates modification. In addition, just as Teiresias assumes an initial problem structure, IVA assumes an initial problem structure (constructed using the tools described previously). Loosely speaking, VIRTUS can be viewed as a "Teiresias for value-theoretic models."

2.9 SUMMARY

In this chapter, we examined previous value-based systems, described the problem addressed in this book, and summarized related work. We began by distinguishing explicit models of value in intelligent systems from implicit models. We demonstrated the pragmatic role of explicit models of value in intelligent systems by exposing the limitations of JESQ, an application that employs an implicit model where an explicit model would have been more appropriate. Having described why explicit models of value are useful in intelligent systems, we addressed the advantages of formality and of transparency in such systems, and we examined previous value-based systems in light of these properties. This analysis provided the basis for the hypothesis of our research, that we can build on a formal model of value to provide a framework for value-based systems that is both formal and transparent. Next, we reviewed multiattribute value theory, which provides the starting point for developing IVA, and we demonstrated the application of value theory in the context of JESQ. We concluded by reviewing the challenges in explaining and refining value-theoretic choices, and we reviewed related work in AI and DA.

IVA and VIRTUS:
Overview and Applications

IVA is a framework for explaining and refining the AMVF. VIRTUS is an IVA-based shell for implementing value-based systems. This chapter provides an overview of IVA and VIRTUS, and demonstrates their breadth of application. The chapter is an introduction to chapters 4 through 6, which present the details of IVA.

Section 3.1 details the general assumptions on which IVA is based, making explicit the perspective that underlies IVA's construction. Section 3.2 provides an overview of IVA. Section 3.3 introduces VIRTUS and describes VIRTUS's potential operational contexts and user populations. Section 3.4 describes implemented applications of VIRTUS in the domains of marketing (ES-SHELL), process control (JESQ-II), and medicine (RCTE). Section 3.5 provides a summary of this chapter.

3.1 PERSPECTIVE AND APPROACH

IVA is based on a particular view of justifying and modifying value-based choices. The following sections impart our perspective on related issues that underlie the development of IVA.

3.1.1 Intelligent Systems as Modular Media

We do *not* seek to develop a cognitive model of human choice or a descriptive model of how any particular population of users goes about making choices. Rather, we seek to develop a *medium* for decision making that is coherent and intuitive.

IVA is consistent with a divide-and-conquer, eclectic approach to system construction that involves decomposing a system into logical components that work in concert to perform a subsuming task. Under this approach, IVA is intended as a framework for representing choices in the context of multiple, distinct representations, as well as for addressing isolated decisions. IVA might be employed, for example, to support conflict resolution in a rule-based system, to support subgoal selection in a theorem prover, or to support the test phase in a generate-and-test paradigm.

In short, the goal of IVA is to provide a formal and transparent medium for modeling choice-related values in the context of single-representation and multirepresentation practical intelligent systems.

3.1.2 Formal Theories of Value: Inherently Opaque?

Chapter 2 described problems of transparency that represent obstacles to employing decision theory in intelligent systems. Some researchers might argue that these problems cannot be overcome, that decision theory is *inherently* opaque. IVA is based on the opposing view: It seems unlikely that a counterintuitive theory would have a history of application to pragmatic and consequential decisions; moreover, professional decision analysts are effective at explaining decision-theoretic models to clients who are not familiar with such models, and at guiding clients through the refinement of the models.

Some authors regard decision theory as inherently counterintuitive. Keen and Scott Morton, for example, wrote, "The rational tradition is completely unrealistic. . . . there is virtually no descriptive support whatsoever for its conception of decision-making. . . . MIS and management science has almost entirely ignored descriptive models of the decision process. . . . they are emotionally and philosophically biased toward rational conception" (1978, p. 65). But such statements are strong, and some authors consider them to be dated. According to von Winterfeldt and Edwards, for example,

> Descriptive considerations have changed the context of normative models of decision making over the years. The earliest normative models of decision making in effect attempted to prescribe not only how one should go about implementing one's value system, but also to some extent what that value system should be. Such prescriptions turned out to be so different from the actual behavior of reasonable people that the content of the normative model was reexamined and much of the prescription of values was removed. Contemporary normative models for decision making are little more than sets of rules designed to ensure that acts will be competent or internally consistent with one another in the pursuit of whatever goals the decision maker may have. (1986)

In addition, several empirical studies suggest a correspondence between the results of normative models and the results derived from intuition in the context of *simple* decisions (Fischer, 1972; Fischer, 1976; Fischer, 1977; Gardiner, 1974; Goodman, Saltzman, Edwards, & Krantz, 1979; Hoepfl & Huber, 1970; Pollack, 1964; Yntema & Klem, 1965). Although one can also cite studies that report systematic deviations from normative principles (Einhorn & Hogarth, 1981; Pitz & Sachs, 1984), some authors argued that, for complex decision problems, unaided human decision making should be *expected* to deviate from principles of consistent thinking (Keeney, 1982); such deviations provide the essential motivation for building artifacts to support better choices. Empirical evidence is subject to interpretation, but decision theory clearly cannot be dismissed as inherently counterintuitive. Perhaps *any* particular philosophy of choosing among alternatives—formal or heuristic—would encourage *some* debate regarding its intuitive appeal.

Another popular argument is that mathematical models generally require too much precision for use in practical intelligent systems; indeed, a number of intelligent-system representations are developed expressly to accommodate the sort of imprecision that inconveniently characterizes many application domains. This argument, however, misses the point that mathematics provides only the *machinery* for computing choices; the information captured in a mathematical model for any particular (domain-specific) choice can be as vague or as detailed as an application requires. Moreover, decision theory provides a basis for calculating the value of additional information (LaValle, 1968; Merkhofer, 1977), and more recent research in decision theory provides methods that explicitly account for incomplete information in a systematic fashion (Weber, 1985, 1987).

If we consider these objections to decision theory to be misunderstandings, how do we account for them? There are at least two explanations. First, transparency has been a secondary goal in the formal development of DA, which is hardly surprising; DA has evolved in the context of manual applications, not automated ones, with trained decision analysts playing a central role in both the interpretation of outputs and the formulation of inputs. That the field lacks a formal body of research on intuitive explanation and refinement does not imply that one cannot be developed. In part, IVA represents an endeavor to address this void.

The second potential source of misunderstanding concerns the packaging of formal theories. As a matter of clarity and convention, a formal model is described in terms of only those axioms and proofs that are perceived as necessary and sufficient to provide a complete and convincing presentation. As the intuition that underlies such a theory may fail to appear in the paper that presents the theory, some readers may regard *the theory itself* as opaque. The development of IVA involves *recovering* this intuition and expressing the theory in a fashion that makes this intuition more accessible.

3.1.3 A Unified View of Acquisition, Explanation, and Refinement

IVA is based on a view of model construction as an iterative argument with a machine. Aided by a knowledge engineer, the user supplies the machine with an initial problem structure. This *acquisition* phase includes activities such as problem structuring, model selection, and parameter assessment. The machine then computes a choice and justifies that choice with an *explanation*. If the user finds the explanation convincing, then model construction is complete. If not, the user can request more detailed explanations or can initiate the process of *refinement* to correct a suspicious component of the explanation (i.e., component of the underlying model). The explanation is then regenerated, and the process is repeated until convergence is achieved.

This view assumes that convergence will in fact *be* achieved eventually; there is empirical evidence to support this assumption. Experiments by John (1984) and by Kimbrough and Weber (1989), for example, revealed that clients chose to adjust model parameters rather than to reject decision models in the face of inconsistencies between their intuitive judgments and the results of those models. If convergence is not achieved for a particular application, we need to look again for potential systematic violations of the assumptions of chapter 2. Ultimately, we may conclude that the decision maker does not have any consistent set of values, so an implicit model of value is probably more appropriate (chapter 2).

IVA thus rests on a view of acquisition, explanation, and refinement as distinct but tightly coupled processes. The computer provides a medium for interactive, intuitive sensitivity analysis; the user can perform what-if analyses in the spirit of a spreadsheet program until the system's explanation meshes with the sort of justification he might present to a colleague.

Underlying this view of explanation, acquisition, and refinement is the notion that the "meaning" of a parameter is essentially "how the parameter affects the final result": Irrespective of the intuitive concepts that parameter *names* connote, it is variations in the final result due to corresponding parameter-value variations that give parameters their semantics. IVA's explanation and refinement strategies are intended to clarify the meanings of parameters by allowing the user to observe directly the effects of parameter-value variations in the context of intuitive justifications for choices.

3.1.4 A Modular Approach to the Task of Representation

According to Barr and Feigenbaum, "the most important consideration in examining and comparing knowledge representation schemes is the eventual *use* of the knowledge" (Barr & Feigenbaum, 1981, p. 145). Heuristic models of value reflect this perspective, providing representations that are designed to support two uses of knowledge: reasoning about choices *and* justifying choices. In contrast, IVA reflects the approach of addressing considerations of reasoning and of transparency separately: Decision theory reflects an emphasis on formal reasoning (chapter 2), and IVA — as a separate research endeavor — embellishes the theory with transparency. Devising a representation that at once supports multiple uses obviously is more difficult than is devising a representation to support a single use. By focusing on formal specification and transparency separately, we reduce our burden in attempting to support multiple uses of knowledge.

3.1.5 Formal and Heuristic Components in Intelligent Systems

One of our objectives in developing IVA is to achieve a separation of formal and heuristic components in value-based systems. As we describe in chapters 4 and 5, for example, the functions employed in strategies for pruning objectives from explanations have a formal interpretation in IVA, but the choice of functions for pruning in VIRTUS is a heuristic one.

This clean separation of formal and heuristic components has practical implications. If explanations are deemed unconvincing by a particular user population, for example, the task of enhancing the explanation facility can be focused on choosing more appropriate functions, because the meanings of the functions themselves are not subject to interpretation. In a system that did not achieve a clean separation between formal and heuristic components, the task of enhancing the explanation facility would necessarily involve addressing issues of semantics and of intuitive appeal simultaneously.

3.2 ELEMENTS OF IVA

IVA comprises the following components, as depicted in Fig. 3.1. The design of IVA reflects empirical observations; interviews with both decision analysts and nonanalysts suggest an intuitive framework for talking about value and value-based choices. The intuitive framework provides a basis for developing an alternative *interpretation* for the AMVF that retains its rigor but is more intuitive. The interpretation is developed in two stages: reformulation and analysis. *Reformulation* involves the development of a *difference function* that is proved to be consistent with value theory. Difference functions are embedded in a *value superstructure* that is also consistent with value theory. *Analysis* takes the reformulated model into a set of packaged insights about the model's operation. Collectively, the objects of the interpretation (called *interpretation concepts*) provide a formal vocabulary for talking about value-based choices. Chapter 4 describes the interpretation in detail.

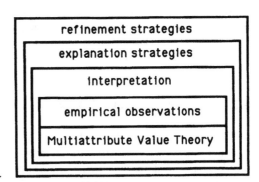

FIG. 3.1.   Elements of IVA.

A set of *explanation strategies* is defined based on the vocabulary of interpretation concepts. The purpose of explanation is to provide the user with sufficient insight into a model's operation either (a) to become convinced that the chosen alternative is indeed preferred, or (b) to identify for correction a model parameter that deviates from his preferences. Interpretation concepts are employed as the primitive elements of explanations and as evaluation functions that guide the organization and content of explanations.

IVA includes four classes of explanation strategies. *Interpretation-concept invocation* involves providing the user with simple interfaces for arbitrarily invoking interpretation concepts in exploring a decision. *Value-tree pruning and presentation* involves summarizing a choice between two particular alternatives in a population, guided by the structure of the value tree. *Difference-function traversal* exposes the details of a choice between two particular alternatives in a population. *Model traversal* provides an abstract description of how choices are computed. Together, the explanation strategies provide a space of options that can be implemented in isolation or in combination by knowledge engineers. IVA thus provides a general specification for a variety of explanation systems. Chapter 5 describes these explanation strategies in detail and demonstrates how designers can combine explanation strategies to implement common intelligent-system commands such as WHY and HOW, and to produce intuitive reports that describe decisions.

A set of *refinement strategies* is defined based on the explanation strategies and on the interpretation. *Interactive diagnosis and repair* guides the user through the computation of a choice, and provides the user with an opportunity to identify, modify, and verify the correction of a faulty parameter value. This strategy is potentially useful for resolving perceived inconsistencies with reality in an existing model of value. *Direct parameter modification* allows the user to initiate repair directly; under this strategy, the user decides on his own to modify a parameter, without performing interactive diagnosis. This facility is potentially useful when a change in an environment (e.g., a corporate directive to reduce costs) necessitates a corresponding change to an existing model of value, but the appropriate degree of change is unclear. Finally, *parameter suggestion* is a set of heuristic strategies for presenting candidate parameters for modification. The user might initiate parameter suggestion to identify logical parameters to investigate. Chapter 6 describes these refinement strategies in detail.

3.3 VIRTUS: A SHELL FOR VALUE-BASED SYSTEMS

VIRTUS is an IVA-based shell for building value-based systems. The shell includes a number of alternative strategies for explaining and refining AMVFs. In value-based systems that employ the AMVF as the sole knowledge base, VIRTUS provides an intuitive medium for explaining and refining an application. Where the AMVF is one component of a larger, multirepresentation system, VIRTUS can be integrated with other explanation and refinement facilities.

3.3.1 Operational Contexts

VIRTUS is intended as a domain-independent module that might be used in a variety of intelligent-system settings.

A Tool for Brainstorming about Values. The construction of every VIRTUS application involves the capture of a particular decision maker's preferences. Thus, VIRTUS is fundamentally a brainstorming tool for organizing values to produce a choice and a supporting justification. In some applications, there is no distinction between user and expert, and VIRTUS's use is limited to brainstorming. In the context of the ES-SHELL system described in section 3.4, for example, a software-development manager might use VIRTUS to converge iteratively on a set of preferences regarding the purchase of an expert-system shell.

A Tool for Explaining Expert Advice. In applications designed to provide a particular user population with access to a particular expert's values (i.e., where there *is* a distinction between user and expert), VIRTUS serves as an isolated explanation facility. In the context of JESQ-II (section 3.4), for example, an operations manager's preferences can be encoded in VIRTUS in a brainstorming mode, and VIRTUS's explanation facility can be employed to justify JESQ-II's choices to staff computer operators who execute its advice, and to higher level managers who review the computer installation's operations and policies.

A Tool for Managing Changing Preferences over Time. In applications involving values that are subject to change over time, VIRTUS can be employed to manage those values on a continuing basis. In the context of JESQ-II, for example, an operations manager might use VIRTUS to reflect the continuing evolution of management policies.

A Tool for Reducing the Cost of a Decision Analysis. VIRTUS might be used by professional decision analysts (in conjunction with traditional DA tools) to reduce the cost of a decision analysis, in three respects. First, VIRTUS permits the client to perform a portion of the analysis without the assistance of the analyst. The analyst would perform problem-structuring tasks, such as helping the client to identify objectives and alternatives, and to capture initial parameter values. The client might then use VIRTUS on his own to tune the AMVF. The analyst could then return to perform additional consistency tests and analyses.

Second, VIRTUS allows the analyst to employ relatively inexpensive acquisition procedures, because VIRTUS provides a vehicle for incremental model repair. Of particular interest are acquisition methods that do not require the user to think hard initially about trade-offs among objectives; holistic methods (Green & Srinivasan, 1978), for example, which require only that the user make judgments over small sets of representative alternatives, are appropriate in this context, as are methods that accommodate incomplete information in a structured fashion (Weber, 1985, 1987). Alternatively, an analyst may omit entirely the acquisition of parameters, supplying defaults for initial parameter values.[45] Whatever acquisition methods are chosen, the existence of a refinement facility permits the capture of only rough approximations of parameters in acquisition because the user is provided with an opportunity to effect subsequent refinements in the context of model operation, when he is already thinking hard about particular choices.

Third, VIRTUS might be used by the analyst to provide clients with intuitive summaries of decision-analytic results. In this respect, VIRTUS may reduce the cost of a decision analysis by reducing the cost to the analyst of interpreting model results for the client.

A Tool for User Modeling. In applications involving a number of similarly structured knowledge bases, VIRTUS can be used as a tool for tailoring a generic knowledge base to a particular user's preferences. The generic knowledge base would contain default values for AMVF parameters (e.g., those of an experienced manager), and these values could be modified by the user via VIRTUS's refinement facilities, until he judged the explanations to be consistent with his own values. This strategy might be used, for example, by a new operations manager to reflect his own preferences in JESQ-II.

3.3.2 Potential Users

VIRTUS might be employed by three classes of users that differ in their knowledge of DA and of VIRTUS. For the trained decision analyst, VIRTUS provides a supplement to traditional DA tools, as described in section 3.3.1. For the user

---

[45]One reasonable set of default values is $w_i = 1/n$, and $v_i(x_i) = 0.5$ (except for the best and worst attribute values).

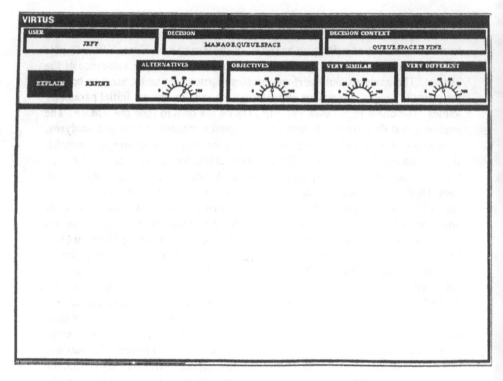

FIG. 3.2.   VIRTUS interface.

who is unfamiliar with DA but is trained in VIRTUS concepts, VIRTUS is intended to serve as a tool for performing intuitive analyses. Of course, this class of user would require decision-analytic assistance with establishing an initial problem structure (i.e., objectives hierarchy, independence verification, alternative generation) before using VIRTUS. The user who is not trained in either DA or VIRTUS should be able to comprehend VIRTUS's explanations, but he may not understand VIRTUS terms beyond their usual conversational meanings.

3.3.3 VIRTUS Interface

VIRTUS's interface is shown in Fig. 3.2.[46] The user selects the USER, DECISION, and DECISION CONTEXT[47] windows with the mouse, and types the appropriate names to load a knowledge base that represents a particular choice. Selecting EXPLAIN or REFINE icons initiates pop-up menus of explanation

---

[46]This section provides a brief summary of the operation of the interface. Chapter 7 provides more detail, in the context of a description of VIRTUS's implementation.

[47]Chapter 4 describes these terms in detail.

or refinement commands (chapters 5 and 6). The dials to the right of these icons are set by the user (using the mouse) to control VIRTUS parameters. The OB-JECTIVES dial, for example, controls the terseness of explanations with regard to the volume of objectives that is mentioned: The higher the setting, the fewer objectives appear in explanations.[48] Dialogs with VIRTUS are conducted in the large blank window. In some cases where VIRTUS requires user input, the user types to a prompt in this window; in other cases, VIRTUS displays pop-up menus of objectives and alternatives for selection with the mouse.

3.4   APPLICATIONS

We describe three practical applications that were constructed using VIRTUS. JESQ-II is a system that chooses among competing alternative actions in managing a large computer complex. ES-SHELL is an application for choosing among competing expert-system shells. RCTE is a program for evaluating clinical research in medicine. The following sections provide a glimpse of VIRTUS in the context of these domains.[49]

3.4.1   Evaluation of Process-Control Actions

Chapter 2 described the JESQ system for automating computer operations. JESQ-II (Klein & Shortliffe, 1990b) is a system for choosing among competing actions in JESQ's domain using the AMVF of chapter 2. Chapter 1 included a JESQ-II dialog, in which an operations manager explored a choice with JESQ-II and interactively diagnosed and repaired a portion of the underlying AMVF.

JESQ-II might serve as a realtime advisor to operators who physically execute its advice. Alternatively JESQ-II might be used in a background mode to compute priorities in JESQ: Operations managers would recompute priorities with each change to the underlying AMVF, and JESQ would select among and execute operational alternatives directly, in realtime.

3.4.2   Evaluation of Expert-System Shells

ES-SHELL is a VIRTUS application for evaluating expert-system shells that run on IBM mainframe computers. ES-SHELL might be used by a data-processing

---

[48]Objective pruning is *not* accomplished only by simple thresholding: The dials do not directly set the *number* of objectives that are included in explanations. Chapters 4 and 5 describe why such straightforward pruning schemes can produce counterintuitive results.

[49]Chapters 5 and 6 detail a number of VIRTUS capabilities that are not demonstrated in this section. The objective of this section is to demonstrate the domain-independence of IVA.

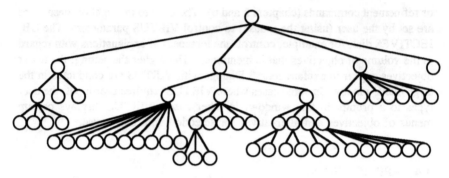

FIG. 3.3.   ES-SHELL value tree.

manager who is making a purchase decision, or by a vendor who is analyzing the expert-system market. As an example of the latter usage, ES-SHELL was used in a project at IBM to formulate forecast assumptions regarding expert-system revenues. The resulting ES-SHELL knowledge base was employed in a larger system for revenue forecasting in new markets, called FORECASTER (Klein, 1991), which simulates the buying behavior of individual customers to produce a customer-specific, multiproduct forecast. Once FORECASTER determines that a particular customer is likely to purchase an expert-system shell, the ES-SHELL knowledge base simulates the customer's selection of a particular product.

The structure of the value tree for choosing among competing expert-system shells is shown in Fig. 3.3. The root of the tree corresponds to the overall value of an expert-system shell. At the next level of the tree are instances of Kotler's (1980) four Ps of marketing management: price, product, promotion, and place. For expert-system shells, *product* refers to the quality of a vendor's shell, *promotion* refers to confidence in the vendor's product, and *place* corresponds to the support provided by the vendor. Except for *price*, objectives are further decomposed into subobjectives. *Product*, for example, is decomposed into *quality of delivery environment*, *quality of development environment*, and *functionality*. The weights associated with objectives represent the decision maker's (e.g., manager's or customer's) preferences: The weight of *price*, for example, is a representation of the decision maker's price sensitivity in the market for expert-system shells. The flavor of ES-SHELL's output[50] is demonstrated in the following VIRTUS dialog fragment.[51]

---

[50]Recall from chapter 1 that **bold-faced type** is used to display the user's input, and that textual responses generated by VIRTUS appear in *italics*.

[51]In this demonstration, we have changed the names of all shells, the weights on objectives, and the values for attributes.

What is the set of alternatives under consideration?

Alternatives under consideration include SHELL.C, SHELL.A, and SHELL.B.

Which alternative is best with regard to overall value?

SHELL.B is the best with regard to overall value.

What is the relative quality of SHELL.B and SHELL.C with regard to overall value?

SHELL.B provides substantially better overall value than SHELL.C.

What are notably compelling reasons in the choice between SHELL.B and SHELL.C with regard to overall value?

Price provides the most compelling reason for the choice.

Why is price a compelling factor in the choice between SHELL.C and SHELL.B with regard to overall value?

While price is not notably important in determining overall value, SHELL.C provides sufficiently different price from SHELL.B relative to other factors to make price a notably compelling factor in this particular decision.

What are relatively uncompelling reasons in the choice between SHELL.B and SHELL.C with regard to overall value?

Overall product support, confidence in the vendor, and overall product quality are relatively uncompelling factors.

What is the relative quality of SHELL.B and SHELL.C with regard to overall product quality?

SHELL.B provides only marginally better overall product quality than SHELL.C.

What are notably compelling reasons in the choice between SHELL.C and SHELL.B with regard to overall product quality?

Development environment support provides the most compelling reason.

Why is development environment support a compelling factor in the choice between SHELL.C and SHELL.B with regard to overall product quality?

Development environment support is notably important in determining overall product quality, and SHELL.C provides notably different development environ-

*ment support from SHELL.B relative to other factors, so development environ-
ment support is a notably compelling factor in this particular decision.*

**What is the relative quality of SHELL.C and SHELL.B with regard to
development environment support?**

*SHELL.C provides somewhat worse development environment support than
SHELL.B.*

**How are alternatives evaluated with regard to development environment
support?**

*Evaluating the development environment support of an alternative involves con-
siderations of quality of documentation, syntactic familiarity to data processing programmers, quality of front end, reliability, and interactive development
facilities. Quality of documentation accounts for 30.0 percent of the determination of development environment support when a novice FORTUNE 500 customer is making the choice. Syntactic familiarity to data processing
programmers accounts for 20.0 percent. Quality of front end accounts for 20.0
percent. Reliability accounts for 20.0 percent. Interactive development facilities accounts for 10.0 percent.*

*Evaluating the syntactic familiarity to data processing programmers of an al-
ternative involves considerations of similarity to C, similarity to COBOL, and
similarity to PLI. Similarity to C accounts for 33.33 percent of the determination of syntactic familiarity to data processing programmers when a novice
FORTUNE 500 customer is making the choice. Similarity to COBOL accounts
for 33.33 percent. Similarity to PLI accounts for 33.33 percent.*

**What are notably compelling reasons in the choice between SHELL.C and
SHELL.B with regard to development environment support?**

Quality of documentation provides the most compelling reason.

**Why is quality of documentation a compelling factor in the choice between
SHELL.C and SHELL.B with regard to development environment
support?**

*Quality of documentation is notably important in determining development en-
vironment support, and SHELL.C provides notably different quality of documentation from SHELL.B relative to other factors, so quality of documentation
is a notably compelling factor in this particular decision.*

**What is the relative quality of SHELL.C and SHELL.B with regard to
quality of documentation?**

SHELL.C provides far, far worse quality of documentation than SHELL.B.

What factors are notably important in the determination of development environment support?

Quality of documentation is notably important in the determination of development environment support.

How are alternatives ranked with regard to quality of documentation?

SHELL.B is the best alternative with regard to quality of documentation. SHELL.C is the next best. SHELL.A is the next best.

What are the reasons for and against SHELL.C vs. SHELL.B with regard to development environment support?

Reliability, interactive development facilities, and syntactic familiarity to data processing programmers are reasons to prefer SHELL.C over SHELL.B with regard to development environment support. Quality of documentation and quality of front end are reasons not to prefer SHELL.C over SHELL.B with regard to development environment support.

What is the relative quality of SHELL.C and SHELL.B with regard to interactive development facilities?

SHELL.C provides somewhat better interactive development facilities than SHELL.B.

How are reasons pertinent to development environment support ranked by compellingness in the choice between SHELL.C and SHELL.B?

Quality of documentation is the most compelling reason underlying the choice with regard to development environment support. Quality of front end is the next most compelling. Reliability is the next most compelling. Interactive development facilities is the next most compelling. Syntactic familiarity to data processing programmers is the next most compelling.

Why isn't syntactic familiarity to data processing programmers a compelling factor in the choice between SHELL.C and SHELL.B with regard to development environment support?

Syntactic familiarity to data processing programmers is not notably compelling in this particular choice because syntactic familiarity to data processing programmers is not notably important in determining development environment support and SHELL.C does not provide notably different syntactic familiarity to data processing programmers from SHELL.B relative to other factors.

What is the relative quality of SHELL.C and SHELL.B with regard to syntactic familiarity to data processing programmers?

SHELL. C provides infinitesimally better syntactic familiarity to data processing programmers than SHELL. B.

{And so on}

3.4.3 Evaluation of Medical Research

RCTE (Klein et al., 1990) is a VIRTUS application designed to assist the journal referee or reader of the medical literature in evaluating the overall merit of a reported randomized clinical trial.[52] The system might be used by practicing physicians or by journal referees who are evaluating the credibility of studies concerning related treatments.

Unlike JESQ-II and ES-SHELL, RCTE is viewed most naturally as a mechanism for evaluating an isolated alternative in the context of a population of similar alternatives, rather than as a mechanism for choosing among them.[53] The population of similar alternatives is assumed to be somewhat familiar to the user. In the case of a journal referee, for example, the population of alternatives is a set of papers previously deemed acceptable for publication, and RCTE is a system for evaluating a new paper in the context of this population.

The alternatives in RCTE are papers that report randomized clinical trials; the value tree for evaluating them appears in Fig. 3.4. The root of the tree corresponds to the overall credibility of a paper. The next level in the tree contains four objectives. *Equivalence of group composition* concerns the uniformity of the experimental and control groups with regard to factors that are relevant to the study. *Equivalence of execution* concerns the degree to which experimental and control groups are exposed to the same clinical environment. *Endpoint assessment* concerns the sufficiency of the data that support the reported results of a study. *Statistical analysis* concerns the degree to which the statistical techniques employed support the study's conclusion, as well as the potential level of bias introduced into the analysis.

The following dialog fragment demonstrates the exploration of a new study, RCT7. The relative merit of this study is examined by the journal referee in the context of RCT2, an older study he knows quite well.

---

[52]Definition: A *randomized clinical trial* is an experimental study that compares the relative effectiveness of treatments by randomly assigning treatments to subjects and observing the resulting effects.

[53]As we describe in chapter 4, however, the former view is actually a specialization of the latter, and overlooking this relationship in designing explanations can impede their effectiveness, as we describe in chapter 8.

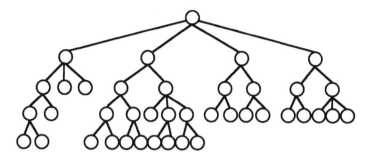

FIG. 3.4.   RCTE value tree.

What is the relative quality of RCT7 and RCT2 with regard to credibility?

RCT7 provides infinitesimally better credibility than RCT2.

What are the reasons for and against RCT7 vs. RCT2 with regard to credibility?

Equivalence of group composition and equivalence of care are reasons to prefer RCT7 over RCT2 with regard to credibility. Endpoint assessment and statistical analysis are reasons not to prefer RCT7 over RCT2 with regard to credibility.

What are notably compelling reasons in the choice between RCT7 and RCT2 with regard to credibility?

While endpoint assessment provides a compelling reason to prefer RCT2, this is outweighed by considerations of equivalence of group composition, along with other less compelling reasons, which provide motivation for choosing RCT7.

Why is endpoint assessment a compelling factor in the choice between RCT7 and RCT2 with regard to credibility?

While endpoint assessment is not notably important in determining credibility, RCT7 provides sufficiently different endpoint assessment from RCT2 relative to other factors to make endpoint assessment a notably compelling factor in this particular decision.

Why is equivalence of group composition a compelling factor in the choice between RCT7 and RCT2 with regard to credibility?

While RCT7 does not provide notably different equivalence of group composition from RCT2 relative to other factors, equivalence of group composition is sufficiently important in determining credibility to make equivalence of group composition a notably compelling factor in this particular decision.

What are the reasons for and against RCT7 vs. RCT2 with regard to equivalence of group composition?

RCT7 is as least as good as RCT2 regarding all objectives that underlie the choice with respect to equivalence of group composition.

How are alternatives evaluated with regard to equivalence of group composition?

Evaluating the equivalence of group composition of an alternative involves considerations of equivalence of treatment assignment and equivalence at study outset. Equivalence of treatment assignment accounts for 66.66 percent of the determination of equivalence of group composition when referee standards for a typical journal are in effect. Equivalence at study outset accounts for 33.33 percent.

What are notably compelling reasons in the choice between RCT7 and RCT2 with regard to equivalence of group composition?

Equivalence of treatment assignment provides the most compelling reason for the choice.

Why is equivalence of treatment assignment a compelling factor in the choice between RCT7 and RCT2 with regard to equivalence of group composition?

While RCT7 does not provide notably different equivalence of treatment assignment from RCT2 relative to other factors, equivalence of treatment assignment is sufficiently important in determining equivalence of group composition to make equivalence of treatment assignment a notably compelling factor in this particular decision.

What is the relative quality of RCT7 and RCT2 with regard to equivalence of treatment assignment?

RCT7 provides infinitesimally better equivalence of treatment assignment than RCT2.

What is the relative quality of RCT7 and RCT2 with regard to statistical analysis?

RCT7 provides infinitesimally worse statistical analysis than RCT2.

What are the reasons for and against RCT7 vs. RCT2 with regard to statistical analysis?

Attention to P-value alpha threshold is the only reason to prefer RCT7 over RCT2 with regard to statistical analysis. Statistical techniques is the only reason not to prefer RCT7 over RCT2 with regard to statistical analysis.

{And so on}

3.5 SUMMARY

IVA is a framework for explaining and refining the AMVF. VIRTUS is an IVA-based shell for implementing value-based systems. In this chapter, we provided an overview of IVA and VIRTUS and demonstrated their breadth of application.

We began by describing the general assumptions that underlie the development of IVA. In particular, we described a view of intelligent systems as modular media, rather than as cognitive models, and we addressed arguments that formal models of value may not provide a sufficiently intuitive decision-making medium for intelligent systems; we described a unified view of acquisition, explanation, and refinement in the context of intelligent systems; next, we addressed the decomposition of the *task* of representation itself and argued for a clean separation between the formal and heuristic components of value-based systems.

Having made explicit the perspective that underlies IVA's construction, we provided an overview of IVA's components: an interpretation of the AMVF, a set of strategies for explaining AMVF-based choices, and a set of strategies for refining the AMVF. The following three chapters, respectively, detail the designs of these components.

Next, we introduced VIRTUS and described VIRTUS's potential operational contexts and user populations. Finally, we presented three implemented applications of VIRTUS, in the domains of marketing (ES-SHELL), process control (JESQ-II), and medicine (RCTE).

CHAPTER 4

Interpretation

This chapter provides an interpretation of the AMVF that will be shown (in chapters 5 and 6) to facilitate explanation and refinement in value-based systems. The interpretation is based in part on conversations with both decision analysts and nonanalysts. We develop the interpretation in two steps: *Reformulation* takes the AMVF into a provably equivalent model that corresponds more closely to intuition; *analysis* takes the reformulated model into a set of packaged insights about its operation. Together, reformulation and analysis yield a vocabulary of more than 100 terms for talking about values and value-based choices.

The terms of this vocabulary, the *interpretation concepts*, serve as the primitives of explanation and refinement (chapters 5 and 6), in three respects. First, interpretation concepts define a space of queries that can be invoked directly by users to explore a value-based choice.[54] Second, interpretation concepts are the primitives that are combined by strategies for explanation and refinement to produce more sophisticated interactions. Third, interpretation concepts serve as evaluation functions in the explanation and refinement strategies themselves.

This chapter consists mostly of interpretation-concept definitions. The essential point of the chapter lies in its presentation *as* a separate chapter: Our central objective in developing the interpretation is to *isolate* the meanings of vocabulary terms (interpretation concepts) that are employed in explanation and refinement strategies from the strategies themselves. In this light, readers may find it useful

---

[54]More specifically, interpretation concepts are the operands of *interpretation-concept interfaces*, which might produce text, graphics, or speech; interpretation-concept interfaces are simply interfaces for presenting interpretation-concept results. Chapters 5 and 7 describe interpretation-concept interfaces and the implementation thereof in more detail.

to, at first, only skim this chapter (gaining an understanding of the nature of the interpretation and of its structure), and then to refer back to the chapter from chapters 5 and 6, where we shall demonstrate how elements of the interpretation are employed.

This chapter is organized as follows. Section 4.1 describes empirical observations on conversations about choices. Section 4.2 describes the reformulation. Section 4.3 describes the analysis. Section 4.4 provides a summary of this chapter.

4.1 EMPIRICAL OBSERVATIONS

IVA is based in part on analyses of conversations about choices. We collected conversations in a series of interviews with decision analysts and nonanalysts. Both groups were presented with a choice among alternative actions in the JESQ domain (chapter 2). The decision analysts were in addition presented with a decision problem involving choices among competing plans for an evening in New York City. Analyses of these conversations provide empirical guidelines for interpreting the AMVF in a fashion that is likely to be intelligible to most users.

4.1.1 Nonanalysts

The following observations are derived from a series of interviews with 12 computer operators at IBM's Thomas J. Watson Research Center in Yorktown Heights, New York. The operators had no familiarity with DA. Each operator was presented with the following description of a choice situation concerning the management of JES queue space:

> *Queue space is low. We have a large dataset destined for a 3800 printer, to be printed on 1part forms, but the 3800 is down, awaiting repairs. The following alternatives are available:*
> - *DJ to tape (DJ)*[55]
> - *Print on a 3211 (3211)*[56]
> - *Call the user and negotiate the fate of the dataset (CALL)*
> - *Do nothing; wait until the 3800 has been fixed (WAIT)*
> - *Install a new printer (INSTALL)*

The operator was asked to rank the actions. Next, the operator was asked to compare various alternatives according to the ranking. Two sorts of comparisons were requested. First, we asked why the chosen alternative was the best

---

[55]*DJ* is operator jargon for alternative COPY.
[56]*3211* is alternative CHEAP-PRINTING.

one; for example, if an operator produced the ranking DJ > CALL > 3211 > WAIT > INSTALL, we asked, "Why is DJ the best?" Second, we asked the operator to compare particular pairs of alternatives, by asking, for example, "Why is DJ better than CALL?" and "Why is CALL better than 3211?" Our observations of the operators' justifications are described in the following sections.[57]

Objectives and Abstraction. When asked to compare alternatives, operators referred to objectives, the associated attributes, the levels of attainment for particular alternatives, and other value-related concepts.

The operators mentioned both abstract and detailed objectives in justifying their choices. Justifications sometimes included a statement of general mission, as shown in the following quotations:

> As operations, our responsibility is to have the system up and as much as possible operational at all times.

> We need the *best and quickest solution* we can find to recover the error. *That's what operations is all about.*

> We're *serving the people*, you know.

The operators sometimes were more specific about which objectives are best satisfied by alternatives, as indicated by these comments:

> [CALL] saves the operator a lot of *work*.

> Well, [CALL is] the *quickest* way and the *easiest* way.

Focus on Alternative Differences. When asked to evaluate a single alternative, the operators often compared that alternative with others. In response to "Why is CALL the best?" for example, operators replied

> Take one of the other ones; by the time you get the tape or whatever, by the time it prints out or whatever, that's a slower process.

> Because the user may not necessarily need the dataset, and to just purge it if he doesn't need it rather than dump it to tape or print it would be easier.

Comparing alternative differences is a fundamental operation in justifying value-based choices.

Compellingness. In justifying a choice, the operators focused on those objectives that particularly distinguish the alternatives under consideration; their

---

[57]Rambling, thinking out loud, and pause words such as "ugh" and "hmm" have been deleted from transcripts of the interviews. The essential structure and content of the interviews, however, have been preserved.

responses reflected a concept of some objectives "counting more than" others in selecting between two particular alternatives. When a particular set of objectives significantly influenced the choice, objectives not in that set were omitted from the justification.

For example, when asked why WAIT was preferred to INSTALL, one operator laughed and proclaimed, "Cost!"; that same operator, in justifying why DJ was better than WAIT, explained that "going out to tape is quick." Although both cost and speed clearly influenced his decisions, he focused on the more compelling objective in each justification.

When asked why DJ was preferred to WAIT, the operator said, "Dumping it out to tape could save a lot of hassle." When asked why DJ was preferred to 3211, the operator answered, "He might just throw it away and that's a waste of paper." Here, both work and cost were considered meaningful factors, but the less compelling factor was omitted from each explanation.

Importance. The operators' responses also reflected the concept of the importance of objectives in the context of a decision problem, as indicated by these comments:

An operator's time is important.

You look at the easiest way and go from there.

We also noted comparisons of importance:

Some people here might think that their waiting time is a lot more valuable than the cost of the new printer, but that's their opinion.

Importance seems to be an abstraction of compellingness in the context of a particular choice. The operators described the importance of objectives in the context of a particular population of alternatives, but outside the context of any particular pair of alternatives within that population.

Relative Quality. The operators' responses also reflected the concept of the relative quality of two alternatives with respect to an objective. Some of the operators' statements reflected ordinal preferences:

Calling saves time [in comparison with DJ].

Printing is better because. . . .

Other statements encompassed a strength of preference interpretation:

Dumping it out to tape could save *a lot* of hassle [as opposed to WAIT].

It saves the operator *a lot* of work [to choose CALL over DJ].

We also noted iterations of relative quality over all alternatives:

The *slowest* way would be printing it.

Absolute Quality. The operators' responses also included implicit comparisons of a given alternative with others in a population, as in the following quotations:

[DJ is] a *simple* fix.

[INSTALL involves] an *enormous* expense.

These responses reflect a concept of absolute quality that seems to capture the relative quality of a particular alternative and a special alternative (such as the worst or best) in the population.

Qualitative and Quantitative Values. In general, the operators employed qualitative values to refer to quantities:

That's an *enormous* expense.

I'm assuming that the queue space is *real full* here.

It saves the operator *a lot* of work.

In the context of more detailed explanations, particularly those involving particular plans, we also noted mention of quantitative values:

You can contact the user in say *10 seconds*. You say he's got this dataset and he's got to look at it. You can solve your problem or make your decision in like *a minute*.

Explicit Identification of the Decision-Making Context. Operators identified not only the elements of decision making (the objectives, their relative importance, etc.), but also the *context* in which the relationships among those elements were assumed to hold. For example,

If the system's going down or something, you go with the quickest.

If queue space is at an intermediate point where there's not going to be much problem, I'd just let it sit there.

I'm not too crazy about destroying the person's dataset, but *it all depends on how critical the situation is*.

I'm assuming that the queue space is real full here.

These utterances imply that different alternatives would be chosen under different circumstances. In the queue-space domain, these circumstances correspond to the severity of the current situation, measured by the amount of space left on the JES queue.

Reference to Other Decisions and Decision Makers.   In justifying a choice, the operators sometimes referred to the decisions of other decision makers. For example, consider

> That's fine as long as we have authorization from high above. Then we handle it differently.

> We can do it without asking about the decision we have to make.

> Based on our own experience or the title you have, you may make your own decision.

> *On my own*, chances are that I would not delete the dataset.

4.1.2   Decision Analysts

The dialogs we collected from two decision analysts contained many of the same elements as those we collected from the operators. The interviews addressed choices in two domains: (a) managing queue space, as in the interviews with operators, and (b) choosing among competing activities for an evening in New York City. Regarding the second domain, the alternatives included a MOVIE, a RESTAURANT, and a PLAY. The objectives included *minimize cost, maximize entertainment value*, and *maximize travel convenience. Maximize travel convenience* was decomposed into *maximize travel comfort* and *minimize travel time*. The decision analysts were given complete value models, including weighted value trees, alternative vectors, and component value functions.

We asked the same sort of questions of the decision analysts that we posed to operators. The analysts were asked to imagine that they were explaining choices to a client, rather than to a colleague. The following sections describe the analysts' responses.

Objectives and Abstraction.   As we would expect, the analysts mentioned objectives and abstract relationships among objectives in justifications for choices. In fact, one of the analysts *added* a layer of abstraction in his explanations:

> So, DELETE wins pretty well on the attributes not affecting the user directly. Again, it's basically a tradeoff of the satisfaction of this particular user and of the rest of the users.

Focus on Alternative Differences. Like the operators, the analysts justified the choice of an alternative by comparing explicitly that alternative with others. For example, in response to "Why is DASD the best?" an analyst answered:

> Let's compare DASD with its closest contenders. Comparing DASD with EXPENSIVE.PRINTING,
> - They're the same on additional operator time
> - EXPENSIVE.PRINTING has 0.0 additional turnaround time, so it's better than DASD there
> - They're the same on form similarity
> - EXPENSIVE.PRINTING costs a good deal more, at $100
> - EXPENSIVE.PRINTING takes 25 minutes (as opposed to 1 minute for DASD) to clear
>
> So, EXPENSIVE.PRINTING falls down on the last two attributes. So it turns out that these attributes bring EXPENSIVE.PRINTING down below DASD, which is worse only on the second attribute.

When asked "Why is MOVIE the best?", the analyst answered:

> MOVIE is the cheapest, has the highest travel convenience, and is still moderate in entertainment value. RESTAURANT is more expensive, but has the same entertainment value and travel convenience.

Compellingness. The decision analysts were explicit about the concept of compellingness:

> RESTAURANT is not as cheap as MOVIE, so cost and travel convenience *together* get torn down a little bit. Comparing PLAY and RESTAURANT, then, entertainment value *takes over in your mind.*

> Cost and entertainment value sort of *cancel each other out*, more or less.

> Well, the *main* difference is cost, as one might expect.

> Additional cost of course is going to *weigh substantially* in favor of CHEAP.PRINTING.

As in the previous interviews with the operators, the concept of one factor or objective in the choice "counting more than" another was a prominent component in the decision analysts' justifications.

Importance. Both the analysts interpreted the weights on objectives as measures of relative importance.[58] In particular, the analysts compared weights on both an ordinal and a ratio scale:

---

[58]This interpretation is a point of debate in DA; we return to this issue in section 4.2.3.2.

You say entertainment value is most important. . . .

Entertainment value is 1.8 times as important as travel convenience, and cost is 2.0 times as important as travel convenience.

Relative Quality. The analysts described value differences with a strength of preference interpretation:

But MOVIE is *much better* on cost than PLAY. . . .

Between the PLAY and MOVIE was a *close call*.

The difference between 1.0 and 0.2 is a *pretty substantial* difference right there.

Absolute Quality. Like the operators, the analysts' explanations encompassed a concept of absolute quality, an implicit comparison of an alternative with an anchoring alternative:

On turnaround time, INSTALL is also *disastrous*, at 180 minutes.

The PLAY is *very good* on entertainment value.

Relating the Component Concepts. The analysts alluded to relationships among concepts such as compellingness and relative quality. For example, in the analysts' explanations, the compellingness of various factors arguing for and against the choice of one alternative over another collectively determined the relative quality of the two alternatives in question:

Because EXPENSIVE.PRINTING is so much better on turnaround time, 0.6 there, and an extra 0.2 on form quality, and is better on clearing time, with a difference of 0.2, all together, those things are enough to outweigh the increased cost of EXPENSIVE.PRINTING. They're [CHEAP.PRINTING and EXPENSIVE.PRINTING] almost the same in the overall evaluation.

Now you put a slightly higher value on cost and travel convenience *together* than on entertainment value alone. So MOVIE does a little better than PLAY overall.

In determining the compellingness of objectives in the decision, the analysts combined the relative quality of two alternatives in the context of particular objectives with the relative importance of those objectives:

Given the *weights* are roughly equal, the *difference* of 0.8 on additional cost of course is going to weigh substantially in favor of CHEAP.PRINTING.

COPY is *slightly worse* on operator time, which has a *low weight* anyway.

Qualitative and Quantitative Values. Like the operators, the analysts spoke in terms of both quantitative and qualitative values:

Entertainment value is *1.8 times as important* as travel convenience.

That's about *a 0.6 difference* on that value function.

MOVIE does *a little better* than the PLAY overall.

Because EXPENSIVE.PRINTING is *so much better* on turnaround time. . . .

4.1.3 An Intuitive Framework for Talking About Value

Our interviews with the analysts and with the operators share important similarities. Both populations focused on *differences* among alternatives and qualitatively assessed the magnitudes of these differences. Both populations alluded to a set of trade-offs of varying strength that determined a final decision, and to related component concepts. Both summarized the quality of a specific alternative by gross comparison with the population of alternatives. These similarities suggest an intuitive framework for talking about value and about value-based choices.[59] More specifically, both sets of explanations encompass the following value-related concepts:[60]

- COMPELLINGNESS: The strength of a reason—either for or against—the choice of one alternative over another, as in,[61] "Additional cost is a compelling reason to prefer CHEAP.PRINTING over EXPENSIVE.PRINTING."

- IMPORTANCE: The general strength of a factor in choosing among a particular population of alternatives, as in, "Additional cost is an important factor in managing queue space."

- RELATIVE-QUALITY: The strength of preference for one alternative over another with regard to a particular factor in the decision,[62] as in, "DASD provides much better problem-resolution time than COPY."

---

[59]We stress again that we are seeking neither a cognitive model of decision making, nor a system that replicates the choice-related discourse of any particular user population. Rather, we are developing a *medium* for talking about choices that captures the central elements of choices as people describe them.

[60]To promote naturalness of prose, we use the terms *reason* and *factor* in these informal definitions of IVA concepts. The formal definitions of these concepts (section 4.2) employ more carefully defined terminology.

[61]As we shall describe in section 4.2, the informal examples provided here actually refer to *abstractions* of the concepts.

[62]Section 4.2.1 describes a view of the decision itself as the all-encompassing factor or objective. The RELATIVE-QUALITY concept applies naturally to this factor as well.

- ABSOLUTE-QUALITY: The strength of desire for a particular alternative with regard to a particular factor in the decision, as in, "DASD provides good problem-resolution time."

The relationship among these concepts is as follows. We start with the assumption that it makes sense to speak of preferences for one alternative over another, or of the RELATIVE-QUALITY of two alternatives. The RELATIVE-QUALITY of two alternatives is determined by supporting reasons of various strength (or COMPELLINGNESS) that recommend or condemn a choice between these alternatives. The greater the COMPELLINGNESS of a reason, the greater that reason's role in the choice.

The COMPELLINGNESS of a reason or factor depends, in part, on that factor's general IMPORTANCE in the context of the choice. The higher the IMPORTANCE of a factor in the general context of the choice, the greater its COMPELLINGNESS for any two particular alternatives. The COMPELLINGNESS of a reason or factor also depends on the RELATIVE-QUALITY of the two alternatives under consideration with respect to that factor.[63] The higher the RELATIVE-QUALITY of two alternatives with respect to a factor, the greater that factors' COMPELLINGNESS in the choice between them.

It also makes sense to speak of the ABSOLUTE-QUALITY of an alternative, both in the context of a particular factor and at the general level of the choice at large. To speak of the ABSOLUTE-QUALITY of an alternative is to compare implicitly that alternative with others. To say that an alternative is good, for example, is to say that it is significantly better than the worst alternative (or not much worse than the best alternative). Thus, ABSOLUTE-QUALITY can be viewed as a special case of RELATIVE-QUALITY.

4.2 REFORMULATION

Our empirical observations provide a basis for developing a version of the AMVF that conforms more closely to intuition. This *reformulation* involves the development of a *hierarchical-value-difference function* that is proved to be consistent with value theory. This function provides a decompositional representation of the difference between two alternatives and captures the hierarchical nature of objectives. A set of subexpressions of the difference function called *reformulation concepts* is defined, and a value-theoretic interpretation is provided for each concept. A set of *reformulation algebras* is defined based on the reformulation concepts. These algebras provide a conceptual framework for abstraction in explanation and refinement. Hierarchical-value-difference functions for particular

---

[63]Thus, the framework is recursive: RELATIVE-QUALITY is defined in terms of COMPELLINGNESS, which is defined in terms of the RELATIVE-QUALITY of a more detailed factor.

choices are embedded in a *value superstructure* to organize choices for interuser, interdecision, and intercontext comparison.[64]

4.2.1 Terminology, Notation, and Special Objects

Alternatives and Objectives.   Where a single alternative is relevant to a description, it is denoted by $\mathbf{a}^{65} = (a_1, \ldots, a_n)$. Multiple alternatives are denoted by $\mathbf{a1} = (a1_1, \ldots, a1_n)$, $\mathbf{a2} = (a2_1, \ldots, a2_n)$, and so on. The universe of available alternatives is denoted by A.

A single objective is denoted by $\mathbf{o}$,[66] and multiple objectives are denoted $\mathbf{o1}$, $\mathbf{o2}$, and so on. The subscript i is used in descriptions that are limited to leaf objectives. Where a description applies more generally to any objective $\mathbf{o}$ in the value tree, the subscript o is employed instead. For example, $v_i(a_i)$ refers to the component-value-function evaluation of alternative $\mathbf{a}$ with respect to the ith leaf in the value tree, and $v_o(a)$ refers to the value-function evaluation of alternative $\mathbf{a}$ with respect to objective $\mathbf{o}$.

Recall from chapter 2 that every nonleaf objective in the value tree can be viewed as the root of a more specific subtree of value. Many interpretation-concept definitions encompass this notion, defining an objective $\mathbf{o}$'s role in computation in terms of such subtrees. We shall refer to the root of the relevant subtree as the *reference objective*, abbreviated **refo**.[67]

Special Alternatives.   The *all-dominating alternative*, abbreviated BEST, is the best imaginable alternative in a particular value-based choice. Its dual, the *all-dominated alternative*, or WORST, is the worst imaginable alternative. More specifically,

Definition: BEST is that alternative such that $(\forall i)v_i(\text{BEST}_i) = 1$. ■

Definition: WORST is that alternative such that $(\forall i)v_i(\text{WORST}_i) = 0$. ■

BEST and WORST are not to be confused with the highest- and lowest-rated alternatives in a particular decision problem. Rather, they are hypothetical alternatives that *uniformly* perform the best and worst, respectively, across all objectives. From the point of view of a decision analysis performed at a given point in time,

---

[64]None of these comparisons involve comparing interfunction values directly; such comparisons are problematic (Fishburn, 1969; Fleming, 1952; Keeney & Raiffa, 1976).

[65]Where **a** appears in the parameter list of a function, we display it in ordinary typeface rather than in bold typeface.

[66]Where **o** appears in the parameter list of a function, we display it in ordinary typeface rather than in bold typeface.

[67]Where **refo** appears in the parameter list of a function, we display it in ordinary typeface rather than in bold typeface.

these alternatives are fictitious: WORST would be excluded from the analysis right from the start, and the existence of BEST eliminates the need for a decision analysis entirely.

Contextual Weights on Objectives. We need to distinguish between the weight associated with an objective o when **refo** = PARENT(o), and the (lower) weight associated with that same o when **refo** is an ancestor of PARENT(o).

Definition: The *primitive weight* of objective o, denoted w_o, is its assigned weight in the value tree. ■

Definition: The *composite weight* of objective o, denoted w(o refo), is defined recursively as follows:

IF o = **refo**, then return 1
ELSE IF PARENT(o) = **refo**, then return w_o
ELSE return w_ow(PARENT(o) refo) ■

The All-Encompassing Objective. The special objective VALUE is the root of the value tree. It is distinguished as having no context. VALUE serves as a proxy for all component objectives in a choice. By convention, $w_{value} = 1$, and v_{value} is abbreviated v.

Objective Populations. An objective population is a set of objectives that is rational for mutual comparison. More specifically,

Definition: An *objective population*, denoted **opop**,[68] is a set of objectives such that o∈**opop** → x∉**opop** for every x ∈ANCESTOR(o). ■

Examples of objective populations that we employ in explanation and refinement include CHILDREN(VALUE) and LEAVES(VALUE).

4.2.2 The Hierarchical-Value-Difference Function

The *hierarchical-value-difference function* captures alternative differences and hierarchical objectives.[69] We develop the hierarchical-value-difference function in two steps: The *flat-value-difference function* captures component differences

---

[68]Where opop appears in the parameter list of a function, we display it in ordinary typeface rather than in bold typeface.

[69]In chapter 5, we introduce an explanation strategy called *difference-function traversal*, which involves stepping through the calculation of the hierarchical-value-difference function in a computation-by-computation fashion. In chapter 6, we employ this strategy for refinement, by permitting the user to "change an explanation" in the course of difference-function traversal.

between two alternatives; the hierarchical version of this function captures the hierarchical nature of objectives.

The Flat-Value-Difference Function. The flat-value-difference function captures intermediate steps in a value-difference calculation with respect to the leaves of a value tree.

Definition: Let $a1 = (a1_1, \ldots, a1_n)$ and $a2 = (a2_1, \ldots, a2_n)$ be two alternatives. The *flat-value-difference function* is defined as

$$f(a1,a2) = \sum_{i=1}^{n} w_i(v_i(a1_i) - v_i(a2_i)) \quad \blacksquare$$

Measurable multiattribute value functions (Dyer & Sarin, 1979) allow the comparison of differences of value-function evaluations $v(a1) - v(a2)$ and $v(a3) - v(a4)$ whenever a set of attributes meets the conditions described in chapter 2. It is easy to show[70] that the flat-value-difference function yields the same results as the difference between value functions:

$$\sum_{i=1}^{n} w_i(v_i(a1_i) - v_i(a2_i)) = w_1(v_1(a1_1) - v_1(a2_1)) + \cdots + w_n(v_n(a1_n) - v_n(a2_n))$$
$$= (w_1v_1(a1_1) - w_1v_1(a2_1)) + \cdots + (w_nv_n(a1_n) - w_nv_n(a2_n))$$
$$= w_1v_1(a1_1) + \cdots + w_nv_n(a1_n)) - (w_1v_1(a2_1) + \cdots + w_nv_n(a2_n))$$
$$= \sum_{i=1}^{n} w_iv_i(a1_i) - \sum_{i=1}^{n} w_iv_i(a2_i)$$
$$= v(a1) - v(a2)$$

As an example, consider the simple value tree of Fig. 4.1 with leaves c, d, and e. The flat-value-difference function for this tree is[71]

$$f(a1,a2) =$$
$$[\ w(c \ \text{VALUE}) \ (v_c(a1_c) - v_c(a2_c))]$$
$$+ \ [\ w(d \ \text{VALUE}) \ (v_d(a1_d) - v_d(a2_d))]$$
$$+ \ [w_e(v_e(a1_e) - v_e(a2_e))]$$

Hierarchical Objectives. Recall from chapter 2 that the value tree is a tool for hierarchically organizing preferences in problem structuring. This struc-

---

[70]Technical note: This proof implies the existence of negative difference structures as well as of positive difference structures. Although axiom systems exist for negative difference structures (Scott & Suppes, 1958), measurable value theory is based on the axioms of Krantz, Luce, Suppes, and Tversky (1971), which define only positive difference structures.

[71]Here, $w(c \ \text{VALUE}) = w_cw_b$ and $w(d \ \text{VALUE}) = w_dw_b$, by the definition of section 4.2.1.

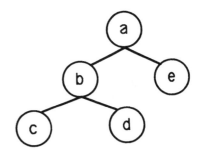

FIG. 4.1. Simple value tree.

ture is useful in explanation and refinement as well, as is demonstrated in chapters 5 and 6. We can embellish the flat-value-difference function to reflect the hierarchical nature of objectives as follows.

> **Definition:**[72] A *hierarchical-value-difference function* (or simply *difference function*) $h(a1,a2)$ is a flat-value-difference function such that each composite weight is rewritten as a product of primitive weights.[73] ∎

For example, consider again the value tree of Fig. 4.1. We can reflect the structure of the value tree in the flat-value-difference function by representing explicitly the calculation of w(o VALUE) for an objective o, yielding the following hierarchical-value-difference function:

$$h(a1,a2) = w_b[w_c(v_c(a1_c) - v_c(a2_c)) + w_d(v_d(a1_d) - v_d(a2_d))]$$
$$+ [w_e(v_e(a1_e) - v_e(a2_e))]$$

The equivalence of the flat-value-difference function and the hierarchical-value-difference function follows immediately from the distributive property of multiplication.

4.2.3 Reformulation Concepts

Reformulation concepts delineate and provide interpretations of subexpressions of the difference function. Reformulation concepts are the primitives of analysis, which in turn provides additional primitives for explanation and refinement. Each reformulation concept is associated with an intuitive interpretation and with a value-theoretic interpretation.

---

[72]This somewhat informal definition is provided to avoid the introduction of richly descriptive structures such as *tree domains* (Gorn, 1965), the power of which is not required here. The example immediately following should dispel any ambiguity.

[73]*Primitive weight* and *composite weight* were defined in section 4.2.1.

4.2.3.1 Compellingness

COMPELLINGNESS is an indication of how much a particular objective "counts" in a choice between two alternatives. More specifically,

Definition:
COMPELLINGNESS(o a1 a2 refo) $= w(o\ refo)(v_o(a1_o) - v_o(a2_o))$. ∎

COMPELLINGNESS(o a1 a2 refo) returns a real number $\in (-1, +1)$.

The term COMPELLINGNESS(o a1 a2 refo) has not been defined formally in value theory,[74] but we can supply a value-theoretic interpretation without requiring any additional assumptions. We can interpret the COMPELLINGNESS of **o** as a measure of **o**'s strength in determining the overall value difference of **a1** and **a2**, other things being equal. More formally, when we consider the COMPELLINGNESS of a leaf objective **o** in the context of the root, we imagine two alternatives α and β that differ only with respect to their **o**th attribute, with $\alpha_o = a1_o$, $\beta_o = a2_o$, and $\alpha_k = \beta_k$ for $k \neq o$. Thus,

$$v(\alpha) - v(\beta) = w(o\ root)[v_o(\alpha_o) - v_o(\beta_o)]$$
$$= \text{COMPELLINGNESS}(o\ \textbf{a1 a2}\ root).$$

We interpret the COMPELLINGNESS of nonleaf objectives analogously, with the nonidentical attributes of α and β corresponding to the leaves of the value subtree with root **o** and with v_o as recursive multiattribute evaluation. When $refo \neq root$, we consider only the leaves of the value subtree with root $refo$ in defining α and β.

4.2.3.2 Derived Concepts

Three specializations of COMPELLINGNESS are of interest:

- IMPORTANCE
- RELATIVE-QUALITY
- ABSOLUTE-QUALITY

Each concept corresponds to an object in value theory. The intuitive interpretations of these objects are subjects of debate in the DA community. Because the specificity of value theory bounds the set of potential interpretations, however, the debates are much more focused than would be possible in the context of a heuristic model.[75] In part, IVA represents a set of commitments to particular arguments in these debates.

---

[74]Its closest analog is the notion of a *part worth* in conjoint analysis. See, for example, (Green & Srinivasan, 1978).

[75]Chapter 8 addresses this point in detail in the context of a broader discussion of formality and transparency.

Importance.   IMPORTANCE is essentially an *alternative-independent* concept of COMPELLINGNESS; it measures how much an objective counts outside the context of any two particular alternatives, *but within the bounds of* BEST *and* WORST.[76] IMPORTANCE answers the question, "Concentrating on only refo, how important is o relative to other objectives?" More specifically,

Definition:
IMPORTANCE(o refo) = COMPELLINGNESS(o BEST WORST refo). ■

IMPORTANCE(o refo) returns a real number $\in (0,1)$. Under IVA, we assume that IMPORTANCE(o refo) is measured on a ratio or absolute scale.

Note that IMPORTANCE(o refo) corresponds to the expression w(o refo), since

IMPORTANCE(o refo)
= COMPELLINGNESS(o BEST WORST refo)
= w(o refo) $(v_o(\text{BEST}) - v_o(\text{WORST}))$
= w(o refo)$(1 - 0)$
= w(o refo)

The interpretation of w(o refo) as a measure of the importance of an objective has been debated in the DA literature: Many standard techniques for capturing weights (e.g., ratio estimation, rank exponent)[77] treat weights explicitly as measures of importance, and the design of IVA reflects this view; on the other hand, authors such as Keeney and Raiffa (1976) described this use of weights as misleading. The discussion centers on the *context* of the use of the term "importance." Critics point out that the meaning of the term is problem-specific; for example, in choosing among competing apartments of approximately the same cost, the objective *minimize cost* would be associated with a low weight, but we could not say that this objective was unimportant to the apartment hunter in general. A counterargument is that, in assessing weights, users think in terms of the choice at hand, so that "importance" is most naturally interpreted as "importance in this particular choice," as is required. Chapter 5 demonstrates that this problem is more manageable in an intelligent-system environment, because explanations can describe explicitly the context in which IMPORTANCE is employed in the difference function.

Relative-Quality.   RELATIVE-QUALITY is essentially a *context-independent* concept of COMPELLINGNESS; it captures the COMPELLINGNESS of an objective outside any particular value subtree (i.e., the objective of interest and the refer-

---

[76]In chapter 5, we exploit this relationship between IMPORTANCE and COMPELLINGNESS to explain the result of multiplication in the difference function.

[77]Techniques for capturing and refining IMPORTANCE are described in chapter 6.

ence objective are the same).[78] RELATIVE-QUALITY(a1 a2 o) answers the question, "How much better (worse) is **a1** than **a2** with regard to **o**?" When **o** = VALUE, this question reduces to the simpler one, "How much better (worse) is **a1** than **a2**?" More specifically,

Definition:
RELATIVE-QUALITY(a1 a2 o) = COMPELLINGNESS(o a1 a2 o). ■

RELATIVE-QUALITY(a1 a2 o) returns a real number $\in [-1, +1]$.

Note that RELATIVE-QUALITY(a1 a2 o) corresponds to the expression $v_o(a1) - v_o(a2)$, since,

RELATIVE-QUALITY(a1 a2 o)
= COMPELLINGNESS(o a1 a2 o)
= $w(o\ o)(v_o(a1) - v_o(a2))$
= $1(v_o(a1) - v_o(a2))$
= $v_o(a1) - v_o(a2)$

$v_o(a1) - v_o(a2)$ has a strength of preference interpretation (Dyer & Sarin, 1979), so it is meaningful to say, for example, that **a1** is *much better* or *slightly better* than **a2** (as long as we agree that *much better* is "more better" than *slightly better* is). The relative naturalness of strength of preference is also a point of debate in the DA community: Some researchers are of the mind that strength-of-preference interpretations lack intuitive appeal and are unreliable; other researchers argue that measurement of strength of preference "greatly enriches the vocabulary of responses available to us in discovering utilities and consequently makes the measurement of utility much easier" (von Winterfeldt & Edwards, 1986), concluding that "judgments based on strength of preference are not inferior in either reliability or validity to judgments based on preference itself; if anything, it is the other way around." The design of IVA reflects this view.

RELATIVE-QUALITY bears another important relationship to COMPELLINGNESS that has already been presented indirectly in the definition of the difference function (section 4.2.2):[79]

RELATIVE-QUALITY(a1 a2 o)
= $v_o(a1) - v_o(a2)$
= $\displaystyle\sum_{i\ \in\ CHILDREN(o)} w(i\ o)(v_i(a1_i) - v_i(a2_i))$
= $\displaystyle\sum_{i\ \in\ CHILDREN(o)}$ COMPELLINGNESS(i a1 a2 o)

---

[78]In chapter 5, we exploit this relationship between RELATIVE-QUALITY and COMPELLINGNESS to explain the result of multiplication in the difference function.

[79]In chapter 5, we exploit this relationship between RELATIVE-QUALITY and COMPELLINGNESS to explain the result of addition in the difference function.

That is, the difference function yields RELATIVE-QUALITY as a sum of COMPEL-LINGNESS measures across siblings in a value subtree.

Absolute-Quality.   The term ABSOLUTE QUALITY(a o) essentially serves as shorthand for RELATIVE-QUALITY(a WORST o).[80] ABSOLUTE-QUALITY answers the question, "How good (bad) is a with respect to o?" More specifically,

Definition:
ABSOLUTE-QUALITY(a o) = RELATIVE-QUALITY(a WORST o). ∎

Note that ABSOLUTE-QUALITY(a o) corresponds to the expression $v_o(a)$, since

ABSOLUTE-QUALITY(a o)
= RELATIVE-QUALITY(a WORST o)
= $v_o(a) - v_o(\text{WORST})$
= $v_o(a) - 0$
= $v_o(a)$

This relationship formalizes the idea that, strictly speaking, there *are* no absolute notions of quality—there are only relative ones. A car is inexpensive, for example, only relative to more expensive cars; a car cannot be inexpensive in any absolute sense.[81] To say that "a is *good*" or that "a rates 7 on a 0-to-10 scale" is to compare a with other alternatives implicitly.

4.2.3.3 Data Selectors

We define two data selectors.

Absolute-Quantity.   In IVA-based applications that employ a mapping from a natural scale to a value scale, ABSOLUTE-QUANTITY is a selector of primitive data over alternatives and leaf objectives. ABSOLUTE-QUANTITY answers the question, "What quantity of i do I get (incur) for selecting a?"

Definition: ABSOLUTE-QUANTITY(a i) returns a_i for alternative a and attribute i. ∎

For convenience, we sometimes write ABSOLUTE-QUANTITY(a o) to denote ABSOLUTE-QUANTITY(a i), where i is the attribute associated with leaf objective o.

---

[80]In chapter 5, we exploit this relationship between ABSOLUTE-QUALITY and RELATIVE-QUALITY to explain the result of subtraction in the difference function.

[81]Chapter 8 describes how overlooking this subtlety caused problems in the rule-based implementation of the REFEREE application for evaluating medical research.

Abstract-Quality.   ABSTRACT-QUALITY is a selector of ABSOLUTE-QUALITY values over alternatives for a given objective. ABSTRACT-QUALITY answers the question, "How good (bad) are various levels of o?"

Definition: ABSTRACT-QUALITY(o) returns ABSOLUTE-QUALITY(a o) for every possible **a** as a function of **a**. ∎

4.2.4 Reformulation Algebras

With the reformulation concepts in place, there are three heterogeneous algebras,[82] called *reformulation algebras*, that describe the reformulation. These algebras differ with respect to the reformulation concepts that are applied *outside* a system, versus the concepts that are applied *inside*. The multiple versions provide a conceptual framework for considering abstractions of the difference function in explanation and refinement.[83] The most detailed algebra is[84]

R_1 = [ABSOLUTE-QUALITY, RELATIVE-QUALITY, IMPORTANCE, COMPEL-
LINGNESS ; +, *, −]

The operations on carriers is as follows:

−:   ABSOLUTE-QUALITY × ABSOLUTE-QUALITY →
RELATIVE-QUALITY
*:   IMPORTANCE × RELATIVE-QUALITY → COMPELLINGNESS
+:   COMPELLINGNESS × · · · × COMPELLINGNESS →
RELATIVE-QUALITY

In R_1, ABSOLUTE-QUALITY and IMPORTANCE are primitive objects that are captured or computed outside the system.

---

[82]Definition (Lipson, 1981): A *heterogeneous algebra* [$\{A_i\}_{i \in I}$; Ω] consists of a family of different types or *carriers* A_i of elements, and a collection Ω of *operations* defined on these carriers. Associated with each *n*-ary operation $\omega \in \Omega$ is an $(n+1)$-tuple $(i1, \ldots, in, i(n+1)) \in I^{n+1}$; ω is then a map $\omega : A_{i1} \times \cdots \times A_{in} \to A_{i(n+1)}$. See Birkhoff and Lipson (1970) for a more detailed description of heterogeneous algebras. There are several related formulations of this structure in the literature, such as Σ-*algebras* (Higgens, 1962) and *many-sorted algebras* (Gallier, 1986).

[83]The set of reformulation algebras provides an analytical tool; a designer can implement combinations of algebras in particular systems according to taste.

[84]Theoretically, we could define an even more detailed algebra that includes function application as an operation on carriers ABSTRACT-QUALITY and ABSOLUTE-QUANTITY. However, this algebra would be awkward in the context of the difference function: Function application in this context is simply a data-selection operation over the entire population of alternatives, whereas the difference function captures a choice between two particular alternatives in that population. Under IVA, we accommodate natural scales by embellishing the explanation and refinement of ABSOLUTE-QUALITY with references to ABSOLUTE-QUANTITY, as we shall describe in chapters 5 and 6.

A knowledge engineer may want to omit some of the details of the computation of the difference function. To make such omissions in a systematic fashion, we progressively eliminate operations and their carriers from R_1 as dictated by the algebraic precedence of operators in the difference function. The first candidate operation and set of carriers for elimination is subtraction and ABSOLUTE-QUALITY, yielding R_2:

$$R_2 = [\text{RELATIVE-QUALITY, IMPORTANCE, COMPELLINGNESS} ; +, *]$$

In R_2, RELATIVE-QUALITY and IMPORTANCE are primitive objects that are captured or computed outside the system.

Next, we can omit multiplication, IMPORTANCE, and primitive measures of RELATIVE-QUALITY, leaving

$$R_3 = [\text{RELATIVE-QUALITY, COMPELLINGNESS} ; +]$$

In R_3, COMPELLINGNESS is a primitive object that is captured or computed outside the system, and RELATIVE-QUALITY is a singleton set that contains the final result (i.e., difference between two alternatives). Note that R_3 eliminates recursion in the difference function, because there is no way to combine RELATIVE-QUALITY and IMPORTANCE measures.

Discarding COMPELLINGNESS and $+$ yields $R*$:[85]

$$R* = [\text{RELATIVE-QUALITY} ; \text{NIL}]$$

In $R*$, RELATIVE-QUALITY is a primitive object that is captured or computed outside the system. Thus, $R*$ is the formal definition for the implicit models of value discussed in chapter 2, and R_1 through R_3 are explicit models that vary in their explicitness. In R_2, for example, RELATIVE-QUALITY(a1 a2 o) can be viewed as an implicit model of $-$(ABSOLUTE-QUALITY(a1 o),ABSOLUTE-QUALITY(a2 o)).

4.2.5   A Superstructure for Value Models

Difference functions for particular choices are embedded in a *value superstructure* (or simply *superstructure*) to organize choices for interuser, interdecision, and intercontext comparison, as depicted in Fig. 4.2. Each difference function is assumed to be applicable under a particular decision context. A *decision context* is a list of variables that are exogenous to the difference function, along with the values under which the difference function is applicable. In JESQ's domain (chapter 2), for example, decision contexts are defined in terms of a single variable—the amount of space left on the operating-system queue—and different

---

[85]We define $R*$ only for completeness.

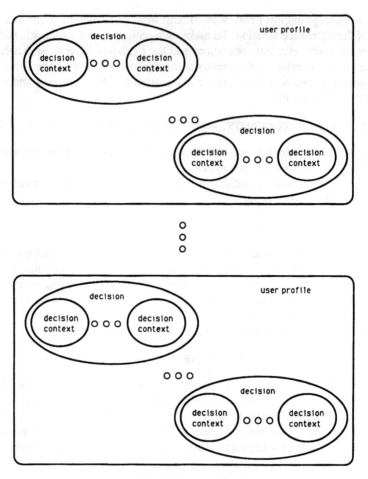

FIG. 4.2.   Value superstructure.

sets of IMPORTANCE measures are assumed to apply under different levels of space left. Decision contexts represent an alternative to nonlinear value functions and to reselecting attributes to meet the independence constraints of linear value functions (Keeney, 1981). A collection of difference function/decision-context pairs forms a *decision*. A decision addresses a particular choice for a particular user, possibly under multiple sets of assumptions about exogenous variable values. A set of decisions for a given user forms a *user profile*. In an implementation of IVA, such as VIRTUS, a user profile exists for every user in an organization. Unless otherwise specified, all difference-function references throughout the book pertain to a fixed user, a fixed decision, and a fixed decision context.

4.3 ANALYSIS

Analysis involves the development of relations over reformulation-concept results called *analysis concepts*. Analysis concepts are choice-independent, packaged insights into the operation of a difference function. We define the following classes of analysis concepts:

- *Ordinal-relation concepts* (section 4.3.1) are Boolean relations on alternatives and objectives. These concepts answer questions such as, "Is **a1** at least as good as **a2** with regard to **o**?"

- *Abstraction concepts* (section 4.3.2) take continuous-valued reformulation-concept results into a discrete quantity space of qualitative values such as {*good, mediocre, poor*}. *Absolute abstraction concepts* take numbers to symbols in a *context-insensitive* fashion, independent of the particular set of related numbers under consideration. *Contextual abstraction concepts* take numbers to symbols in a *context-sensitive* fashion, strictly depending on the particular set of related numbers under consideration.

- *Iteration over alternatives* (section 4.3.3) involves using the abstraction and ordinal-relation concepts as predicates for sorting and selecting alternatives. These concepts answer questions such as, "Which alternatives are at least as good as **a**?"

- *Iteration over objectives* (section 4.3.4) involves using the abstraction and ordinal-relation concepts as predicates for sorting and selecting objectives. *Pattern-classification concepts* answer questions such as, "Is **a1** much better than **a2** with regard to *all* objectives?" *Sorting and selection concepts* answer questions such as, "What factors support the choice of **a1** over **a2**?"

- *Intermodel relations* (section 4.3.5) compare decision models and decision-model results, answering questions such as, "Do users **u1** and **u2** agree on this decision?"

The following sections describe the concepts in detail.

4.3.1 Ordinal-Relation Concepts

Ordinal-relation concepts are Boolean relations on alternatives and objectives. These relations are ordinal abstractions of reformulation concepts that take results into {*T, NIL*}. A set of primitive ordinal-relation concepts is defined with the predicate $\geq$, and concepts defined with predicates $>$, $=$, $<$, $\leq$ are trivially derived from these concepts.

4.3.1.1 Primitive Ordinal-Relation Concepts

Primitive ordinal-relation concepts comprise primitive relations on alternatives and primitive relations on objectives.

Primitive Relations on Alternatives. MORE-OR-SAME?(a1 a2 o) answers the question, "Does **a1** provide at least as much **o** as **a2** does?" More specifically,

> **Definition:** MORE-OR-SAME?(a1 a2 o) returns
> - T if ABSOLUTE-QUANTITY(a1 o) $\geq$ ABSOLUTE-QUANTITY(a2 o)
> - NIL otherwise ■

MORE-OR-SAME? is meaningful only when a natural scale is employed, and **o** must be a value-tree leaf, since ABSOLUTE-QUANTITY is defined only over attributes.

PREFERRED-OR-INDIFFERENT-TO?(a1 a2 o) answers the question, "Is **a1** at least as good as **a2** with regard to **o**?" More specifically,

> **Definition:** PREFERRED-OR-INDIFFERENT-TO?(a1 a2 o) returns
> - T if ABSOLUTE-QUALITY(a1 o) $\geq$ ABSOLUTE-QUALITY(a2 o)
> - NIL otherwise ■

Primitive Relations on Objectives. MORE-OR-EQUALLY-COMPELLING?(o1 o2 a1 a2 refo) answers the question, "Focusing on **refo**, is **o1** at least as compelling as **o2** in the choice between **a1** and **a2**?" More specifically,

> **Definition:**[86] MORE-OR-EQUALLY COMPELLING?(o1 o2 a1 a2 refo) returns
> - T if ABS(COMPELLINGNESS(o1 a1 a2 refo)) $\geq$ ABS(COMPELLINGNESS(o2 a1 a2 refo))
> - NIL otherwise ■

We need to provide a value-theoretic interpretation for MORE-OR-EQUALLY COMPELLING?. Consider two alternatives α and β that differ with respect to only their ith attribute, with

$$\alpha_i = a1_i \text{ and } \beta_i = a2_i \text{ if } v_i(a1_i) \geq v_i(a2_i)$$
$$\alpha_i = a2_i \text{ and } \beta_i = a1_i \text{ otherwise}$$

---

[86]ABS denotes absolute value.

Similarly, consider two other alternatives γ and δ that differ with respect to only their jth attribute, $i \neq j$, with

$\gamma_j = a1_j$ and $\delta_j = a2_j$ if $v_j(a1_j) \geq v_j(a2_j)$
$\gamma_j = a2_j$ and $\delta_j = a1_j$ otherwise

Then, we have

$\alpha = (\ldots, \alpha_i, \ldots)$
$\beta = (\ldots, \beta_i, \ldots)$
$\gamma = (\ldots, \gamma_j, \ldots)$
$\delta = (\ldots, \delta_j, \ldots)$

Thus,

$v(\alpha) - v(\beta) = w(i\ refo)(v_i(\alpha_i) - v_i(\beta_i))$

and

$v(\gamma) - v(\delta) = w(j\ refo)(v_j(\gamma_j) - v_j(\delta_j))$

Then, MORE-OR-EQUALLY-COMPELLING?(o1 o2 a1 a2 refo) iff

$v(\alpha) - v(\beta) \geq v(\gamma) - v(\delta)$ ∎

MORE-OR-EQUALLY DIFFERENT?(o1 o2 a1 a2) answers the question, "Are **a1** and **a2** at least as different with regard to **o1** as they are with regard to **o2**?" More specifically,

Definition: MORE-OR-EQUALLY DIFFERENT?(o1 o2 a1 a2) returns
- T if ABS(RELATIVE-QUALITY(a1 a2 o1)) $\geq$ ABS(RELATIVE-QUALITY(a1 a2 o2))
- NIL otherwise ∎

We need to provide a value-theoretic interpretation for MORE-OR-EQUALLY-DIFFERENT?. Consider two alternatives α and β that differ with respect to only their ith attribute, with

$\alpha_i = a1_i$ and $\beta_i = a2_i$ if $v_i(a1_i) \geq v_i(a2_i)$
$\alpha_i = a2_i$ and $\beta_i = a1_i$ otherwise

Similarly, consider two other alternatives γ and δ that differ with respect to only their jth attribute, $i \neq j$, with

$\gamma_j = a1_j$ and $\delta_j = a2_j$ if $v_j(a1_j) \geq v_j(a2_j)$
$\gamma_j = a2_j$ and $\delta_j = a1_j$ otherwise

Then, we have

$$\alpha = (. \ . \ . \ , \alpha_i, \ . \ . \ .)$$
$$\beta = (. \ . \ . \ , \beta_i, \ . \ . \ .)$$
$$\gamma = (. \ . \ . \ , \gamma_j, \ . \ . \ .)$$
$$\delta = (. \ . \ . \ , \delta_j, \ . \ . \ .)$$

Thus,

$$v(\alpha) - v(\beta) = w(i \text{ refo})(v_i(\alpha_i) - v_i(\beta_i))$$

and

$$v(\gamma) - v(\delta) = w(j \text{ refo})(v_j(\gamma_j) - v_j(\delta_j))$$

Now, assume that

$$w(i \text{ refo}) = w(j \text{ refo})$$

Then, MORE-OR-EQUALLY DIFFERENT?(o1 o2 a1 a2) iff

$$v(\alpha) - v(\beta) \geq v(\gamma) - v(\delta) \ \blacksquare$$

MORE-OR-EQUALLY IMPORTANT?(o1 o2 refo) answers the question, "Focusing on **refo**, is **o1** at least as important as **o2** in the context of this choice?" More specifically,

> **Definition:** MORE-OR-EQUALLY IMPORTANT?(o1 o2 refo) returns
> - T if IMPORTANCE(o1 refo) $\geq$ IMPORTANCE(o2 refo)
> - NIL otherwise $\blacksquare$

We need to provide a value-theoretic interpretation for MORE-OR-EQUALLY-IMPORTANT?. Consider two alternatives α and β that differ with respect to only their ith attribute, with

$$\alpha_i = a1_i \text{ and } \beta_i = a2_i \text{ if } v_i(a1_i) \geq v_i(a2_i)$$
$$\alpha_i = a2_i \text{ and } \beta_i = a1_i \text{ otherwise}$$

Similarly, consider two other alternatives γ and δ that differ with respect to only their jth attribute, $i \neq j$, with

$$\gamma_j = a1_j \text{ and } \delta_j = a2_j \text{ if } v_j(a1_j) \geq v_j(a2_j)$$
$$\gamma_j = a2_j \text{ and } \delta_j = a1_j \text{ otherwise}$$

Then, we have

$$\alpha = (. \ . \ . \ , \alpha_i, \ . \ . \ .)$$
$$\beta = (. \ . \ . \ , \beta_i, \ . \ . \ .)$$
$$\gamma = (. \ . \ . \ , \gamma_j, \ . \ . \ .)$$
$$\delta = (. \ . \ . \ , \delta_j, \ . \ . \ .)$$

Thus,

$$v(\alpha) - v(\beta) = w(i \text{ refo})(v_i(\alpha_i) - v_i(\beta_i))$$

and

$$v(\gamma) - v(\delta) = w(j \text{ refo})(v_j(\gamma_j) - v_j(\delta_j))$$

Now, assume that

$$v_i(\alpha_i) - v_i(\beta_i) = v_j(\gamma_j) - v_j(\delta_j) \neq 0$$

Then, MORE-OR-EQUALLY IMPORTANT?(o1 o2 refo) iff

$$v(\alpha) - v(\beta) \geq v(\gamma) - v(\delta) \; \blacksquare$$

4.3.1.2 Derived Ordinal-Relation Concepts

The predicates $>$, $=$, $<$, and $\leq$ are trivially derived from $\geq$. The following is one possible derivation:

$$\text{NOT}(b \geq a) \rightarrow a > b$$
$$\text{AND}(a \geq b, b \geq a) \rightarrow a = b$$
$$\text{NOT}(a \geq b) \rightarrow a < b$$
$$\text{OR}(a < b, a = b) \rightarrow a \leq b$$

The concepts in the following sections are derived in this fashion from the primitive ordinal-relation concepts. Because their semantics are obvious, we simply list them.

Derived Relations on Alternatives.

MORE-OR-SAME?(a1 a2 o)
- MORE?(a1 a2 o)
- SAME?(a1 a2 o)
- LESS?(a1 a2 o)
- SAME-OR-LESS?(a1 a2 o)

PREFERRED-OR-INDIFFERENT-TO?(a1 a2 o)
- PREFERRED?(a1 a2 o)
- INDIFFERENT?(a1 a2 o)
- DISPREFERRED?(a1 a2 o)
- INDIFFERENT-OR-DISPREFERRED?(a1 a2 o)

Derived Relations on Objectives.

MORE-OR-EQUALLY-COMPELLING?(o1 o2 a1 a2 refo)
- MORE-COMPELLING?(o1 o2 a1 a2 refo)

- EQUALLY-COMPELLING?(o1 o2 a1 a2 refo)
- LESS-COMPELLING?(o1 o2 a1 a2 refo)
- EQUALLY-OR-LESS-COMPELLING?(o1 o2 a1 a2 refo)

MORE-OR-EQUALLY-DIFFERENT?(o1 o2 a1 a2)
- MORE-DIFFERENT?(o1 o2 a1 a2)
- EQUALLY-DIFFERENT?(o1 o2 a1 a2)
- LESS-DIFFERENT?(o1 o2 a1 a2)
- EQUALLY-OR-LESS-DIFFERENT?(o1 o2 a1 a2)

MORE-OR-EQUALLY-IMPORTANT?(o1 o2 refo)
- MORE-IMPORTANT?(o1 o2 refo)
- LESS-IMPORTANT?(o1 o2 refo)
- EQUALLY-IMPORTANT?(o1 o2 refo)
- EQUALLY-OR-LESS-IMPORTANT?(o1 o2 refo)

4.3.2 Abstraction Concepts

Abstraction concepts take continuous-valued reformulation-concept results into a discrete space of qualitative values called a *quantity space*. *Absolute abstraction concepts* take numbers to symbols in a *context-insensitive* fashion, independent of the particular set of related numbers under consideration. *Contextual abstraction concepts* take numbers to symbols in a *context-sensitive* fashion, strictly depending on the particular set of related numbers under consideration.

4.3.2.1 Absolute Abstraction Concepts

Absolute abstraction concepts take numbers to symbols in a *context-insensitive* fashion, independent of the particular set of related numbers under consideration. IVA includes absolute abstraction concepts for ABSOLUTE-QUALITY and for RELATIVE-QUALITY. There is no notion of an absolute abstraction concept for COMPELLINGNESS or for IMPORTANCE, since these reformulation concepts are defined only within the context of a particular population of objectives.

Abstract-Absolute-Quality.   ABSTRACT-ABSOLUTE-QUALITY(a o) maps continuous intervals of ABSOLUTE-QUALITY(a o) into a discrete quantity space, such as {*good, mediocre, poor*}. ABSTRACT-ABSOLUTE-QUALITY(a o) answers questions such as, "Is a a good alternative?" and "Does a provide good o?"
Numbers are mapped to quantity-space symbols according to absolute thresh-

olds,[87] and an arbitrary number of symbols corresponding to an exhaustive and mutually exclusive set of subintervals of [0,1] can be defined.

For notational consistency, we can redundantly express abstraction concepts as predicates; for example, we define GOOD? to test for membership in *good*. If GOOD? corresponds to the interval α, then we define

Definition: GOOD?(a o) returns
- T if ABSOLUTE-QUALITY(a o) $\in \alpha$
- NIL otherwise ■

The quantity spaces have a value-theoretic interpretation. Recall that ABSOLUTE-QUALITY(a o) = RELATIVE-QUALITY(a WORST o). Thus, the quantity space encodes an ordering of value differences that is meaningful in measurable value theory.

Abstract-Relative-Quality. ABSTRACT-RELATIVE-QUALITY(a1 a2 o) maps continuous intervals of RELATIVE-QUALITY(a1 a2 o) into a discrete quantity space of differences, such as {*MuchBetter LittleBetter EQUAL LittleWorse MuchWorse*}. ABSTRACT-RELATIVE-QUALITY(a o) answers questions such as, "Is **a1** much better than **a2**?" and "Does **a1** provide much worse o than **a2** does?"

Numbers are mapped to quantity-space symbols according to absolute thresholds, and an arbitrary number of symbols corresponding to an exhaustive and mutually exclusive set of subintervals of $[-1,0) \cup (0, +1)]$ can be defined, with 0 mapping to the special symbol *EQUAL*.

Again, we can express these concepts as predicates; for example, we define MUCH-WORSE? to test for membership in *MuchWorse*. If MUCH-WORSE? corresponds to the interval α then we define

Definition: MUCH-WORSE?(a1 a2 o) returns
- T if RELATIVE-QUALITY(a1 a2 o) $\in \alpha$
- NIL otherwise ■

These quantity spaces have a value-theoretic interpretation. A quantity space encodes an ordering over intervals of RELATIVE-QUALITY that is meaningful in measurable value theory.[88]

The discrete bounds chosen for ABSTRACT-RELATIVE-QUALITY must be

---

[87]As shall be described, bounds for discretization must be consistent with analogous bounds chosen for ABSTRACT-RELATIVE-QUALITY.

[88]Again, the remarks of section 4.2 regarding negative difference structures apply when employ symbols such as *MuchWorse*.

consistent with those chosen for ABSTRACT-ABSOLUTE-QUALITY. In particular, there are two conditions that we would reasonably expect any such combination of bounds to satisfy:[89]

1. If ABSOLUTE-QUALITY(a1 o) ∈ MAX(ABSTRACT-ABSOLUTE-QUALITY(a o)), and ABSOLUTE-QUALITY(a2 o) ∈ MIN(ABSTRACT-ABSOLUTE-QUALITY(a o)), then RELATIVE-QUALITY(a1 a2 o) ∈ MAX(ABSTRACT-RELATIVE-QUALITY(a1 a2 o))

2. If ABSOLUTE-QUALITY(a1 o), ABSOLUTE-QUALITY(a2 o) ∈ ABSTRACT-ABSOLUTE-QUALITY(a o), and RELATIVE-QUALITY(a1 a2 o) ≠ 0, then RELATIVE-QUALITY(a1 a2 o) ∈ MIN(ABSTRACT-RELATIVE-QUALITY(a1 a2 o) − {*EQUAL*})

Condition 1 requires that, whenever we map **a1** to the highest absolute-valued symbol (e.g., *good*), and **a2** to the lowest absolute-valued symbol (e.g., *bad*), then we must map their difference to the largest-valued difference symbol (e.g., *MuchBetter*). The rationale behind Condition 1 is straightforward: The difference between the largest and smallest qualitative values would reasonably be expected to be the largest qualitative difference. Condition 2 is the dual of Condition 1, requiring that if **a1** and **a2** are not mapped to *EQUAL* (i.e., INDIFFERENT?(a1 a2 o) = NIL), but are mapped to the same absolute-valued symbol, then we must map their difference to the smallest-valued difference symbol (e.g., *LittleBetter*). The rationale behind Condition 2 is also straightforward: The difference between two qualitatively similar values is reasonably expected to be the smallest qualitative difference.

Satisfying Conditions 1 and 2 is straightforward; let

- α be the upper bound on MIN(ABSTRACT-ABSOLUTE-QUALITY(a o))
- β be the lower bound on MAX(ABSTRACT-ABSOLUTE-QUALITY(a o))
- γ be the upper bound on MIN(ABSTRACT-RELATIVE-QUALITY(a o))
- δ be the lower bound on MAX(ABSTRACT-RELATIVE-QUALITY(a o))
- ε be the size of the largest subinterval that corresponds to a symbol in the quantity space of ABSTRACT-ABSOLUTE-QUALITY

Then,

- Condition 1 is satisfied whenever $\delta \leq \beta - \alpha$
- Condition 2 is satisfied whenever $\gamma \geq \varepsilon$

---

[89]Notational note: The lowest-valued symbol in the quantity space for ABSTRACT-ABSOLUTE-QUALITY(a o) is denoted MIN(ABSTRACT-ABSOLUTE-QUALITY(a o)), the highest-valued symbol is denoted MAX, and so on.

Higher Order Absolute Quantity Spaces and Abstraction Concepts.
Systems that employ large quantity spaces (say, five or more symbols) can also employ higher order quantity spaces to discretize further ABSTRACT-ABSOLUTE-QUALITY and ABSTRACT-RELATIVE-QUALITY. For example, *VeryGood*, *Good*, and *Mediocre* might be mapped into *Acceptable*, with *Unacceptable* representing *Bad* and *VeryBad*. Similarly, *EQUAL*, *LittleBetter*, and *LittleWorse* might be mapped to *Similar*, and *MuchBetter* and *MuchWorse* might be mapped to *Different*. Alternatively, quantitative ranges for higher order quantity-space symbols can be defined in isolation, rather than in terms of lower order quantity-space symbols.

4.3.2.2 Contextual Abstraction Concepts

Contextual abstraction concepts take numbers to symbols in a *context-sensitive* fashion, strictly depending on the particular set of related numbers under consideration. All contextual abstraction concepts are defined as variants of the following general definition.

Definition:[90] Let $k > 0$ be a user-defined constant, and X be a population of quantities, $x \geq 0$, $|X| > 2$ with mean μ_X and standard deviation σ_X. NOTABLE?(x) whenever $x > \mu_X + k\sigma_X$ ∎

Informally, a NOTABLE? quantity in a population is an outlier, and k, which is presumed to be user-specific, determines just how much of an outlier the quantity must be to be considered NOTABLE? with respect to that population. The constant k can be interpreted as a measure of conservatism, in that a sufficiently larger k will yield fewer NOTABLE? objects than will a smaller k. For example, one application of NOTABLE? in VIRTUS is to prune objectives from explanations. In this context, k corresponds to terseness: The higher the value of k, the fewer objectives appear in explanations. In VIRTUS, k is adjusted directly by users via a dial on the interface (Fig. 3.2).

This definition of NOTABLE? seems to capture the spirit of the concept for various distributions of objects. For example, if objects are closely clustered in value, then *no* objects are NOTABLE?. As intuition demands, it is impossible for *all* the objects of a population to be NOTABLE?.

NOTABLE? is applicable to any population of objects that is measured on an interval (or more detailed) scale, since, for $a > 0$

NOTABLE?$(ax + b)$
$\equiv ax + b > \mu_{aX+b} + k\sigma_{aX+b}$
$\equiv^{91} ax + b > (a\mu_X + b) + k\sigma_{aX+b}$

---

[90]This definition is reminiscent of z-scores.

[91] $$\mu_{aX+b} = \frac{\sum_X (ax + b)}{n} = \frac{a\sum_X x + nb}{n} = a\frac{\sum_X x}{n} + \frac{nb}{n} = a\mu_X + b$$

$$\equiv^{92} ax + b > (a\mu_x + b) + k(a\sigma_x)$$
$$\equiv \quad ax > a\mu_x + ka\sigma_x$$
$$\equiv \quad x > \mu_x + k\sigma_x$$
$$\equiv \quad \text{NOTABLE?}(x)$$

Contextual-Absolute-Quality.   CONTEXTUAL-ABSOLUTE-QUALITY(a o)
maps continuous intervals of ABSOLUTE-QUALITY(a o) into a discrete quantity space such as {*NotablyGood NotNotablyGoodOrPoor NotablyPoor*}.
CONTEXTUAL-ABSOLUTE-QUALITY(a o) answers questions such as, "Is **a** a notably good alternative?" and "Does **a** provide notably good **o**?"

Numbers are mapped to quantity space symbols according to context-dependent
thresholds that are contextually defined by NOTABLE?. For example,

Definition: NOTABLY-GOOD?(a o) returns
- T if ABSOLUTE-QUALITY(a o) $> \mu_{absolute - quality} + k\sigma_{absolute - quality}$
- NIL otherwise ∎

Unlike ABSTRACT-ABSOLUTE-QUALITY, CONTEXTUAL-ABSOLUTE-QUALITY con-
siders the value of a particular alternative in the context of the population of available alternatives. Thus, in a population where many of the alternatives have a
high ABSOLUTE-QUALITY, a particular alternative **a** might be considered *good* (according to ABSTRACT-ABSOLUTE-QUALITY) but not necessarily *NotablyGood* (according to CONTEXTUAL-ABSOLUTE-QUALITY).

Contextual-Relative-Quality.   CONTEXTUAL-RELATIVE-QUALITY maps
continuous intervals of RELATIVE-QUALITY(a1 a2 o) into a discrete quantity space
of differences such as {*EQUAL NotablySimilar SomewhatDifferent NotablyDiffer-
ent*}. CONTEXTUAL-RELATIVE-QUALITY answers questions like, "Does **a1** provide
o notably different from **a2** relative to other objectives in **opop**?"

Numbers are mapped to quantity-space symbols according to context-dependent
thresholds that are contextually defined by NOTABLE?. For example

---

92

$$\sigma_{aX+b} = \sqrt{\frac{\sum_X (ax + b - \mu_{aX+b})^2}{n}} = \sqrt{\frac{\sum_X (ax + b - a\mu_X - b)^2}{n}} = \sqrt{\frac{\sum_X [a(x - \mu_X)]^2}{n}}$$

$$= \sqrt{\frac{\sum_X a^2(x - \mu_X)^2}{n}} = \sqrt{a^2 \frac{\sum_X (x - \mu_X)^2}{n}} = \sqrt{a^2}\sqrt{\frac{\sum_X (x - \mu_X)^2}{n}} = a\sigma_X$$

Definition: NOTABLY-DIFFERENT?(a1 a2 o opop) returns
- T if ABS(RELATIVE-QUALITY(a1 a2 o))
  $$> \mu_{ABS(relative - quality)} + k\sigma_{ABS(relative - quality)}$$
- NIL otherwise ∎

Contextual-Importance. CONTEXTUAL-IMPORTANCE maps continuous intervals of IMPORTANCE(o refo) into a discrete quantity space such as *{NotablyImportant Unimportant}*. CONTEXTUAL-IMPORTANCE answers questions such as, "Is o a notably important objective, relative to **opop**, in the determination of **refo**?"

Numbers are mapped to quantity-space symbols according to context-dependent thresholds that are contextually defined by NOTABLE?. For example,

Definition: NOTABLY-IMPORTANT?(o opop refo) returns
- T if IMPORTANCE(o refo) $> \mu_{importance} + k\sigma_{importance}$
- NIL otherwise ∎

Contextual-Compellingness. CONTEXTUAL-COMPELLINGNESS maps continuous intervals of COMPELLINGNESS(o a1 a2 refo) into a discrete quantity space such as *{NotablyCompelling Uncompelling INCONSEQUENTIAL}*. CONTEXTUAL-COMPELLINGNESS answers questions such as, "Focusing on **refo**, is o a notably compelling objective in the choice between **a1** and **a2**, relative to other objectives in **opop**?"

Numbers are mapped to quantity-space symbols according to context-dependent thresholds that are contextually defined by NOTABLE?. For example,

Definition: NOTABLY-COMPELLING?(o opop a1 a2 refo) returns
- T if ABS(COMPELLINGNESS(o a1 a2 refo))
  $$> \mu_{ABS(compellingness)} + k\sigma_{ABS(compellingness)}$$
- NIL otherwise ∎

4.3.3 Iteration Over Alternatives

The next class of analysis concepts iterates over the population of available alternatives using the abstraction and ordinal-relation concepts as predicates. The first group of concepts uses the predicates for selecting alternatives. The second group of concepts uses the predicates for sorting alternatives and for selecting from a set of sorted alternatives.

4.3.3.1 Selection

For each of the following subclasses of iterative selection concepts, a primitive concept is defined using $\geq$, and then a set of derived concepts is enumerated.

More-or-Same?   ALTERNATIVES-PROVIDING-MORE-OR-SAME(o a) answers the question, "Which alternatives provide at least as much o as a does?" where o is a leaf objective. More specifically,

> **Definition:** ALTERNATIVES-PROVIDING-MORE-OR-SAME(o a) returns the set of alternatives $\alpha \in A - \{a\}$ such that MORE-OR-SAME?(α a o). ■

The derivatives of ALTERNATIVES-PROVIDING-MORE-OR-SAME are

- ALTERNATIVES-PROVIDING-MORE(o a)
- ALTERNATIVES-PROVIDING-SAME(o a)
- ALTERNATIVES-PROVIDING-LESS(o a)
- ALTERNATIVES-PROVIDING-LESS-OR-SAME(o a)

Preferred-or-Indifferent-To?   PREFERRED-OR-INDIFFERENT-ALTERNA-TIVES(a o) answers the question, "Which alternatives provide at least as good o as a does?" When o = VALUE, this question reduces to the simpler one, "Which alternatives are at least as good as is a?" More specifically,

> **Definition:** PREFERRED-OR-INDIFFERENT-ALTERNATIVES(a o) returns the set of alternatives $\alpha \in A - \{a\}$ such that PREFERRED-OR-INDIFFERENT-TO?(α a o) ■

The derivatives of PREFERRED-OR-INDIFFERENT-ALTERNATIVES are:

- PREFERRED-ALTERNATIVES(a o)
- INDIFFERENT-ALTERNATIVES(a o)
- DISPREFERRED-ALTERNATIVES(a o)
- DISPREFERRED-OR-INDIFFERENT-ALTERNATIVES(a o)

Abstract-Absolute-Quality.   A predicate was defined for each quantity-space symbol defined by ABSTRACT-ABSOLUTE-QUALITY. We can develop an iterative analysis concept for each symbol. For example, ABSOLUTELY-GOOD-ALTERNATIVES(o) answers the question, "Which alternatives provide good o?" When o = VALUE, this question reduces to the simpler one, "Which alternatives are good?" More specifically,

> **Definition:** ABSOLUTELY-GOOD-ALTERNATIVES(o) returns the set of alternatives $\alpha \in A$ such that GOOD?(α o) ■

We could develop an analogous concept for each symbol in the quantity space for ABSTRACT-ABSOLUTE-QUALITY.

Abstract-Relative-Quality. A predicate was defined for each quantity-space symbol defined by ABSTRACT-RELATIVE-QUALITY. We can develop an iterative analysis concept for each symbol. For example, MUCH-BETTER-ALTERNATIVES(a o) answers the question, "Which alternatives provide much better o than a does?" When o = VALUE, this question reduces to the simpler one, "Which alternatives are much better than a?" More specifically,

> **Definition:** MUCH-BETTER-ALTERNATIVES(a o) returns the set of alternatives $\alpha \in A - \{a\}$ such that MUCH-BETTER?(α a o) ∎

We could develop an analogous concept for each symbol in the quantity space for ABSTRACT-RELATIVE-QUALITY.

Contextual-Absolute-Quality. A predicate was defined for each quantity-space symbol defined by CONTEXTUAL-ABSOLUTE-QUALITY. We can develop an iterative analysis concept for each symbol. For example, NOTABLY-GOOD-ALTERNATIVES(o) answers the question, "Which alternatives provide notably good o?" When o = VALUE, this question reduces to the simpler one, "Which alternatives are notably good?" More specifically,

> **Definition:** NOTABLY-GOOD-ALTERNATIVES(o) returns the set of alternatives $\alpha \in A$ such that NOTABLY-GOOD?(α o) ∎

We could develop an analogous concept for each symbol in the quantity space for CONTEXTUAL-ABSOLUTE-QUALITY.

4.3.3.2 Sorting and Selection Over Sorts

The next class of analysis concepts sorts the population of available alternatives and selects alternatives from these sorts. Like the selection concepts, concepts for sorting and selecting from sorts employ as primitive predicates the abstraction and ordinal-relation concepts.

Five concepts are defined for sorting and searching over sorts for each of MORE-OR-SAME? and PREFERRED-OR-INDIFFERENT-TO?.

More-or-Same?

> **Definition:** RANK-ALTERNATIVES-BY-QUANTITY(o) returns A sorted by MORE-OR-SAME?. Alternatives of equal quantity are delineated as subsets. ∎

> **Definition:** NTH-RANKED-ALTERNATIVES-BY-QUANTITY(n o) returns the *n*th set of equal quantities in the sort RANK-ALTERNATIVES-BY-QUANTITY(o). ∎

Definition: ALTERNATIVES-PROVIDING-MOST(o) returns NTH-RANKED-ALTERNATIVES-BY-QUANTITY(1 o). ∎

Definition: ALTERNATIVES-PROVIDING-LEAST(o) returns NTH-RANKED-ALTERNATIVES-BY-QUANTITY(k o), where k is the cardinality of RANK-ALTERNATIVES-BY-QUANTITY(o). ∎

Definition: ALTERNATIVE-POSITION-IN-QUANTITY-RANKING(a o) returns the numerical position of **a** in RANK-ALTERNATIVES-BY-QUANTITY(o). ∎

Preferred-or-Indifferent-To?

Definition: RANK-ALTERNATIVES-BY-QUALITY(o) returns A sorted by PREFERRED-OR-INDIFFERENT-TO?. ∎

Definition: NTH-RANKED-ALTERNATIVES-BY-QUALITY(n o) returns the nth set of alternatives returned by RANK-ALTERNATIVES-BY-QUALITY(o). ∎

Definition: ALTERNATIVES-PROVIDING-BEST(o) returns NTH-RANKED-ALTERNATIVES-BY-QUALITY(1 o). ∎

Definition: ALTERNATIVES-PROVIDING-WORST(o) returns NTH-RANKED-ALTERNATIVES-BY-QUALITY(k o), where k is the cardinality of RANK-ALTERNATIVES-BY-QUALITY(o). ∎

Definition: ALTERNATIVE-POSITION-IN-QUALITY-RANKING(a o) returns the numerical position of **a** in RANK-ALTERNATIVES-BY-QUALITY(o). ∎

4.3.4 Iteration Over Objectives

The next class of analysis concepts iterates over a population of objectives using the abstraction and ordinal-relation concepts as predicates.

4.3.4.1 Pattern Classification

The first set of objective analysis concepts classifies patterns of objectives by iterating ordinal-relation concepts and abstraction concepts.

More-or-Same? In the following definitions, suppose without loss of generality that preferences are monotonically increasing in each $x \in$**opop**.[93]

---

[93]Naturally, we continue to assume that **opop** is a subset of LEAVES(VALUE), because this is the domain of MORE-OR-SAME?.

DOMINATES?(a1 a2 opop) answers the question, "Is **a1** at least as large as **a2** with regard to all objectives in **opop**, and strictly larger with regard to at least one of these objectives?" More specifically,

Definition: DOMINATES?(a1 a2 opop) returns
- T if MORE-OR-SAME?(a1 a2 x) for all x ∈opop and MORE?(a1 a2 x) for at least one x.
- NIL otherwise ■

The dual of DOMINATES? is DOMINATED-BY?, which is defined analogously using LESS-OR-SAME? and LESS?.

STRICTLY-DOMINATES?(a1 a2 opop) answers the question, "Is **a1** strictly larger than **a2** with regard to all objectives in **opop**?" More specifically,

Definition: STRICTLY-DOMINATES?(a1 a2 opop) returns
- T if MORE?(a1 a2 x) for all x ∈opop
- NIL otherwise ■

The dual of STRICTLY-DOMINATES? is STRICTLY-DOMINATED-BY?, which is defined analogously using LESS?.

EQUIVALENT?(a1 a2 opop) answers the question, "Are **a1** and **a2** equal with respect to all objectives in **opop**?" More specifically,

Definition: EQUIVALENT?(a1 a2 opop) returns
- T if SAME?(a1 a2 x) for all x ∈opop
- NIL otherwise ■

TRADEOFFS?(a1 a2 opop) answers the question, "Does choosing **a1** instead of **a2** involve incurring some tradeoffs with respect to **opop**?" More specifically,

Definition: TRADEOFFS?(a1 a2 opop) returns
- T if MORE?(a1 a2 x) for at least one x ∈opop, and LESS?(a1 a2 x) for at least one x.
- NIL otherwise ■

Preferred-or-Indifferent-To? Pattern-classification concepts based on PREFERRED-OR-INDIFFERENT-TO? and its derivatives are similar to those based on MORE-OR-SAME?. The essential semantic difference is that definitions are based on ABSOLUTE-QUALITY, rather than on ABSOLUTE-QUANTITY. We provide a full definition of CARDINALLY-DOMINATES?, and simply list the remaining predicates.

CARDINALLY-DOMINATES?(a1 a2 opop) answers the question, "Is **a1** at least as good as **a2** with regard to all objectives in **opop**, and strictly better with regard to at least one of these objectives?" More specifically,

Definition: CARDINALLY-DOMINATES?(a1 a2 opop) returns
- T if PREFERRED-OR-INDIFFERENT-TO?(a1 a2 x) for all $x \in$ **opop** and PREFERRED?(a1 a2 x) for at least one x
- NIL otherwise ∎

Analogous definitions can be developed in a straightforward fashion for the following predicates:

- CARDINALLY-STRICTLY-DOMINATES?(a1 a2 opop)
- CARDINALLY-DOMINATED-BY?(a1 a2 opop)
- CARDINALLY-STRICTLY-DOMINATED-BY?(a1 a2 opop)
- CARDINALLY-EQUIVALENT?(a1 a2 opop)
- CARDINAL-TRADEOFFS?(a1 a2 opop)

Abstract-Absolute-Quality. Pattern-classification concepts based on ABSTRACT-ABSOLUTE-QUALITY are similar to those based on MORE-OR-SAME?, but employ predicates that test for symbol membership. For example, GOOD-ALL-AROUND?(a opop) answers the question, "Is **a** good with regard to all objectives in **opop**?" More specifically,

Definition: GOOD-ALL-AROUND?(a opop) returns
- T if GOOD?(a x) for all $x \in$ **opop**
- NIL otherwise ∎

We could develop an analogous concept for each symbol in the quantity space for ABSTRACT-ABSOLUTE-QUALITY.

Abstract-Relative-Quality. Pattern-classification concepts based on ABSTRACT-RELATIVE-QUALITY are similar to those based on ABSTRACT-ABSOLUTE-QUALITY, employing a predicate for each quantity-space symbol. For example, MUCH-BETTER-ALL-AROUND?(a1 a2 opop) answers the question, "Is **a1** much better than **a2** with regard to all objectives in **opop**?" More specifically,

Definition: MUCH-BETTER-ALL-AROUND?(a1 a2 opop) returns
- T if MUCH-BETTER?(a1 a2 x) for all $x \in$ **opop**
- NIL otherwise ∎

We could develop an analogous concept for each symbol in the quantity space for ABSTRACT-RELATIVE-QUALITY.

4.3.4.2 Selection

For each of the following subclasses of iterative selection concepts, a concept is defined in detail for the predicate based on $\geq$, and then a set of concepts based on derived predicates is listed.

More-or-Same? MORE-OR-SAME-OBJECTIVES(opop a1 a2) answers the question, "For what leaf objectives in **opop** does **a1** provide as least as much **o** as **a2** does?" More specifically,

> **Definition:** MORE-OR-SAME-OBJECTIVES(opop a1 a2) returns the set of leaf objectives $x \in$**opop** such that MORE-OR-SAME?(a1 a2 x). ∎

Analogously defined concepts based on the derivatives of MORE-OR-SAME? are

- MORE-OBJECTIVES(opop a1 a2)
- SAME-OBJECTIVES(opop a1 a2)
- LESS-OBJECTIVES(opop a1 a2)
- SAME-OR-LESS-OBJECTIVES(opop a1 a2)

Preferred-or-Indifferent-To? PREFERRED-OR-INDIFFERENT-OBJECTIVES (opop al a2) answers the question, "What objectives in **opop** support or are irrelevant to the choice of **a1** over **a2**?" More specifically,

> **Definition:** PREFERRED-OR-INDIFFERENT-OBJECTIVES(opop a1 a2) returns the set of objectives $x \in$**opop** such that PREFERRED-OR-INDIFFERENT-TO?(a1 a2 x). ∎

Analogously defined concepts based on the derivatives of PREFERRED-OR-INDIFFERENT-TO? are

- PREFERRED-OBJECTIVES(opop a1 a2)
- INDIFFERENT-OBJECTIVES(opop a1 a2)
- DISPREFERRED-OBJECTIVES(opop a1 a2)
- DISPREFERRED-OR-INDIFFERENT-OBJECTIVES(opop a1 a2)

More-or-Equally-Different? MORE-OR-EQUALLY-DIFFERENT-OBJECTIVES(o opop al a2) answers the question, "For what objectives in **opop** are **a1** and **a2** at least as different as they are for **o**?" More specifically,

Definition: MORE-OR-EQUALLY-DIFFERENT-OBJECTIVES(o opop a1 a2) returns the set of objectives x ∈opop[94] such that MORE-OR-EQUALLY-DIFFERENT?(x o a1 a2). ∎

Analogously defined concepts based on the derivatives of MORE-OR-EQUALLY-DIFFERENT? are

- MORE-DIFFERENT-OBJECTIVES(o opop a1 a2)
- EQUALLY-DIFFERENT-OBJECTIVES(o opop a1 a2)
- LESS-DIFFERENT-OBJECTIVES(o opop a1 a2)
- LESS-OR-EQUALLY-DIFFERENT-OBJECTIVES(o opop a1 a2)

More-or-Equally-Important?   MORE-OR-EQUALLY-IMPORTANT-OBJECTIVES (o opop refo) answers the question, "What objectives in **opop** are at least as important as **o** with respect to **refo**?" More specifically,

Definition: MORE-OR-EQUALLY-IMPORTANT-OBJECTIVES(o opop refo) returns the set of objectives x ∈opop[94] such that MORE-OR-EQUALLY-IMPORTANT?(x o refo). ∎

Analogously defined concepts based on the derivatives of MORE-OR-EQUALLY-IMPORTANT? are

- MORE-IMPORTANT-OBJECTIVES(o opop refo)
- EQUALLY-IMPORTANT-OBJECTIVES(o opop refo)
- LESS-IMPORTANT-OBJECTIVES(o opop refo)
- LESS-OR-EQUALLY-IMPORTANT-OBJECTIVES(o opop refo)

More-or-Equally-Compelling?   MORE-OR-EQUALLY-COMPELLING-OBJEC-TIVES (o opop a1 a2 refo) answers the question, "What objectives in **opop** are at least as compelling as **o** in the choice between **a1** and **a2** with respect to **refo**?" More specifically,

Definition: MORE-OR-EQUALLY-COMPELLING-OBJECTIVES(o opop a1 a2 refo) returns the set of objectives x ∈opop[94] such that MORE-OR-EQUALLY-COMPELLING?(x o a1 a2 refo). ∎

Analogously defined concepts based on the derivatives of MORE-OR-EQUALLY-COMPELLING? are

- MORE-COMPELLING-OBJECTIVES(o opop a1 a2 refo)
- EQUALLY-COMPELLING-OBJECTIVES(o opop a1 a2 refo)

---

[94]In most applications of this concept, **opop** will exclude o.

- LESS-COMPELLING-OBJECTIVES(o opop a1 a2 refo)
- LESS-OR-EQUALLY-COMPELLING-OBJECTIVES(o opop a1 a2 refo)

Abstract-Absolute-Quality. Iteration using ABSTRACT-ABSOLUTE-QUALITY tests for symbol membership across objectives in a population. For example, ABSOLUTELY-GOOD-OBJECTIVES(opop a) answers the question, "For what objectives in **opop** is **a** good?" More specifically,

> **Definition:** ABSOLUTELY-GOOD-OBJECTIVES(opop a) returns the set of objectives $x \in$ **opop** such that GOOD?(a x). ∎

We could develop an analogous concept for each symbol in the quantity space for ABSTRACT-ABSOLUTE-QUALITY.

Abstract-Relative-Quality. Iteration using ABSTRACT-RELATIVE-QUALITY tests for symbol membership across objectives in a population. For example, MUCH-BETTER-OBJECTIVES(opop a1 a2) answers the question, "For what objectives in **opop** is **a1** much better than **a2** is?" More specifically,

> **Definition:** MUCH-BETTER-OBJECTIVES(opop a1 a2) returns the set of objectives $x \in$ **opop** such that MUCH-BETTER?(a1 a2 x). ∎

We could develop an analogous concept for each symbol in the quantity space for ABSTRACT-RELATIVE-QUALITY.

Contextual-Absolute-Quality. Iterative definitions based on CONTEXTUAL-ABSOLUTE-QUALITY are similar to those based on ABSTRACT-ABSOLUTE-QUALITY. For example, NOTABLY-GOOD-OBJECTIVES(opop a) answers the question, "For what objectives in **opop** is **a** notably good?" More specifically,

> **Definition:** NOTABLY-GOOD-OBJECTIVES(opop a) returns the set of objectives $x \in$ **opop** such that NOTABLY-GOOD?(a x). ∎

We could develop an analogous concept for each symbol in the quantity space for CONTEXTUAL-ABSOLUTE-QUALITY.

Contextual-Relative-Quality. Iterative definitions based on CONTEXTUAL-RELATIVE-QUALITY are similar to those based on ABSTRACT-RELATIVE-QUALITY. For example, NOTABLY-DIFFERENT-OBJECTIVES(opop a1 a2) answers the question, "For what objectives in **opop** are **a1** and **a2** notably different?" More specifically,

Definition: NOTABLY-DIFFERENT-OBJECTIVES(opop a1 a2) returns the set of objectives x ∈**opop** such that NOTABLY-DIFFERENT?(a1 a2 x opop). ∎

We could develop an analogous concept for each symbol in the quantity space for CONTEXTUAL-RELATIVE-QUALITY.

Contextual-Importance. Iteration using CONTEXTUAL-IMPORTANCE tests for symbol membership across objectives in a population. For example, NOTABLY-IMPORTANT-OBJECTIVES(opop refo) answers the question, "What objectives in **opop** are notably important?" More specifically,

Definition: NOTABLY-IMPORTANT-OBJECTIVES(opop refo) returns the set of objectives x ∈**opop** such that NOTABLY-IMPORTANT?(x opop refo). ∎

We could develop an analogous concept for each symbol in the quantity space for CONTEXTUAL-IMPORTANCE.

Contextual-Compellingness. Iteration using CONTEXTUAL-COMPELLING-NESS tests for symbol membership across objectives in a population. For example, NOTABLY-COMPELLING-OBJECTIVES(opop a1 a2 refo) answers the question, "What objectives in **opop** are notably compelling in the choice between **a1** and **a2** with respect to **refo**?" More specifically,

Definition: NOTABLY-COMPELLING-OBJECTIVES(opop a1 a2 refo) returns the set of objectives x ∈**opop** such that NOTABLY-COMPELLING?(x opop a1 a2 refo) ∎

We could develop an analogous concept for each symbol in the quantity space for CONTEXTUAL-COMPELLINGNESS.

4.3.4.3 Sorting and Selection over Sorts

The next class of analysis concepts sorts a population of objectives and selects objectives from these sorts. Because these concepts are similar in structure to the sorting and selection concepts for alternatives, they are simply listed here by the concepts they employ as sorting predicates.

More-or-Equally-Different?

- RANK-OBJECTIVES-BY-RELATIVE-QUALITY(opop a1 a2)
- NTH-RANKED-OBJECTIVES-BY-RELATIVE-QUALITY(n opop a1 a2)

- MOST-DIFFERENT-OBJECTIVES(opop a1 a2)
- MOST-SIMILAR-OBJECTIVES(opop a1 a2)
- OBJECTIVE-POSITION-IN-RELATIVE-QUALITY-RANKING(o opop a1 a2)

More-or-Equally-Important?

- RANK-OBJECTIVES-BY-IMPORTANCE(opop refo)
- NTH-RANKED-OBJECTIVES-BY-IMPORTANCE(n opop refo)
- MOST-IMPORTANT-OBJECTIVES(opop refo)
- LEAST-IMPORTANT-OBJECTIVES(opop refo)
- OBJECTIVE-POSITION-IN-IMPORTANCE-RANKING(o opop refo)

More-or-Equally-Compelling?

- RANK-OBJECTIVES-BY-COMPELLINGNESS(opop a1 a2 refo)
- NTH-RANKED-OBJECTIVES-BY-COMPELLINGNESS(n opop a1 a2 refo)
- MOST-COMPELLING-OBJECTIVES(opop a1 a2 refo)
- LEAST-COMPELLING-OBJECTIVES(opop a1 a2 refo)
- OBJECTIVE-POSITION-IN-COMPELLINGNESS-RANKING(o opop refo)

4.3.5   Intermodel Relations

We can also define predicates to compare decision models. These predicates *do not* perform direct comparisons of decision model components such as ABSOLUTE-QUALITY.

USER-AGREEMENT?(u1 u2 d c) indicates whether two particular users **u1** and **u2** agree on a particular decision **d** in a particular decision context **c**. More specifically,

Definition: USER-AGREEMENT?(u1 u2 d c) returns
- T if ALTERNATIVES-PROVIDING-BEST(VALUE) under **u1, d, c** = ALTERNATIVES-PROVIDING-BEST(VALUE) under **u2, d, c**
- NIL otherwise ■

SIMILAR-DECISIONS?(d1 d2) tests for similarity in the structure of a decision. More specifically,

Definition: SIMILAR-DECISIONS?(d1 d2) returns
- T if CHILDREN(VALUE) under **d1** = CHILDREN(VALUE) under **d2**
- NIL otherwise ■

4.4 SUMMARY

In this chapter, we provided an interpretation of the AMVF that will be shown (in chapters 5 and 6) to facilitate explanation and refinement in value-based systems. The interpretation is based in part on conversations with both decision analysts and nonanalysts. We developed the interpretation in two steps: *Reformulation* takes the AMVF into a provably equivalent model that corresponds more closely to intuition, and *analysis* takes the reformulated model into a set of packaged insights about its operation. The interpretation provides a vocabulary of more than 100 terms for talking about values and value-based choices, called *interpretation concepts*, that serve as the primitives of explanation and refinement, as we describe in the following two chapters.

CHAPTER 5

Explanation

The purpose of explanation is to provide the user with sufficient insight into a model's operation either (a) to become convinced that the chosen alternative is indeed preferred, or (b) to identify for correction a model parameter that deviates from his preferences.

This chapter defines strategies for justifying value-based choices. *Interpretation-concept invocation* (section 5.1) involves providing the user with simple interfaces for arbitrarily invoking interpretation concepts in exploring a decision. *Value-tree pruning and presentation* (section 5.2) involves summarizing a choice between two particular alternatives in a population, guided by the structure of the value tree. *Difference-function traversal* (section 5.3) exposes the details of a choice between two particular alternatives in a population. *Model traversal* (section 5.4) provides an abstract description of how choices are computed.

Together, the explanation strategies provide a space of options that can be implemented in isolation or in combination by knowledge engineers. IVA thus provides a general specification for a variety of explanation systems. Section 5.5 demonstrates how designers can combine explanation strategies to implement common intelligent-system commands such as WHY and HOW, and to produce intuitive reports that describe decisions.

The explanation strategies employ as primitives the interpretation concepts of chapter 4. Because the concepts are defined separately, the output of the explanation strategies is consistent up to the meanings of the concepts. It would be impossible, for example, for an explanation system based on chapter 4 to generate both *DASD is better than EXPENSIVE.PRINTING* and *EXPENSIVE.PRINTING is better than DASD*. In addition, this separation facilitates the definition of the explanation strategies themselves. For example, were we to define an explanation strategy that (foolishly) contrasts two alternatives on the basis of the INCONSEQUENTIAL? factors in a choice between them, we could criticize that strategy specifically for its use of INCONSEQUENTIAL?, rather than of NOTABLY-COMPELLING? or of some other suitable concept. Because the *meanings* of these concepts is addressed separately (in chapter 4), the definitions of explanation strategies are limited to operations such as examining interpretation-concept results and pruning information from explanations accordingly.

Sections 5.1 through 5.5 describe the explanation strategies in more detail, and Section 5.6 provides a summary of these strategies.

5.1   INTERPRETATION-CONCEPT INVOCATION

The interpretation of chapter 4 defines a space of queries that can be made available to the user.[95] Text responses are generated via *interpretation-concept interfaces*, which are simple text templates for displaying interpretation-concept results. An interpretation-concept interface for ABSTRACT-RELATIVE QUALITY, with **a1** = DASD, **a2** = EXPENSIVE.PRINTING, and **o** = VALUE, for instance, produces

> *DASD provides infinitesimally better overall queue space management effectiveness than EXPENSIVE.PRINTING.*

Depending on the value of a global flag, interpretation-concept interfaces can also include a numeric interpretation-concept result, as in the following:

> *DASD provides infinitesimally better (.05) overall queue space management effectiveness than EXPENSIVE.PRINTING.*

In alternative implementations, interpretation-concept interfaces might be selected via a speech-understanding system or by a natural-language parser, and interpretation-concept interfaces might present responses in another natural language, in graphical form, or in the form of generated speech.[96]

Chapters 1 and 3 provided examples of interpretation-concept invocation in the context of JESQ-II, ES-SHELL, and RCTE.

---

[95]In VIRTUS, for example, interpretation concepts and their operands (alternatives and objectives) are selected via mouse and menu. Chapters 3 and 7 describe the VIRTUS interface.

[96]For this reason, the definitions of interpretation-concept interfaces are isolated in VIRTUS. Chapter 7 details the implementation.

5.2 VALUE-TREE PRUNING AND PRESENTATION

Interpretation concepts provide a useful language for talking about choices, but they burden the user with coordinating responses to achieve an understanding of a choice. *Value-tree pruning and presentation* is the first strategy described in this chapter that imposes organization on interpretation-concept results. From a conceptual viewpoint, strategies for value-tree pruning and presentation organize insights into a choice between two alternatives with respect to the sign and magnitude of the COMPELLINGNESS of objectives.

In chapter 4, we observed that a central operation in justifying choices among alternatives is the comparison of two particular alternatives. For realistic choices involving several objectives, the exhaustive display of objectives at a particular level in the value tree represents an impractical approach to explanation, even if we impose some organization on objectives. For example, by grouping objectives according to PREFERRED-OBJECTIVES, DISPREFERRED-OBJECTIVES, and INDIFFERENT-OBJECTIVES, and by ranking objectives by COMPELLINGNESS within groups, VIRTUS produces the following explanation for LEAVES(VALUE) in the domain of RCTE:

> *Treatment assignment process, equivalence of dropout rates, equivalence of prior treatment history, equivalence of side effect rates, performance of blindfolding monitoring, randomization within sites, handling of patients for whom mortality data is unavailable, and stopping appropriateness are reasons to prefer RCT7 over RCT2 with regard to credibility. Success of blindfolding monitoring, quality of actual treatment assignment, adherence to original assignment with respect to analysis, distance of assigner from patient, inclusion of all deaths, handling of non-compliant patients with respect to analysis, and statistical techniques are reasons not to prefer RCT7 over RCT2. Equivalence of demographic factors not related to disease, equivalence of disease severity, equivalence of comorbidity factors, equivalence of prognostic factors, respect for denominator boundaries, P-value, adjustments due to subgroups, and subgroup analysis plan do not at all impact the choice between RCT7 and RCT2.*

The verbosity of such explanations motivates the development of strategies for pruning objectives from the value tree.

The problem of summarizing a comparison of two alternatives can be decomposed into two distinct subproblems. First, the explanation facility must determine a desirable level of abstraction for talking about objectives by *vertically pruning* the value tree to eliminate related detailed objectives that can be summarized by a higher-level objective. Second, the explanation facility must determine the most pertinent objectives to display at a given level of abstraction in the value tree by *horizontally pruning* the value tree to eliminate some set of objectives from a population of siblings. The following two sections describe vertical- and horizontal-pruning techniques.

5.2.1 Vertical Pruning

Vertical-pruning strategies limit the *depth* of the value tree by eliminating value subtrees. There are two component problems in vertical pruning:

1. How can we systematically prune uninteresting subtrees?
2. What properties render a subtree interesting?

Regarding the first problem, top-down traversal (i.e., starting at the root) will fail, since an arbitrarily deep set of subtrees will be pruned without examination whenever a higher level subtree is pruned, even though these subtrees may play a central role in the choice. Thus, a bottom-up strategy is required, starting at the parent of the deepest leaf. The following algorithm takes a value tree of arbitrary depth with root **refo** and two alternatives **a1** and **a2**, and produces a population of objectives if anything about the tree is interesting, and **refo** otherwise.

1. Let **o** = PARENT(deepest leaf in the subtree with root **refo**)
2. If **interesting?**(a1 a2 CHILDREN(o)), then mark **o** as deleted;[97] otherwise, mark CHILDREN(o) as deleted (and retain **o**).
3. If **o** = **refo**, then return the remains of the tree; otherwise, repeat.

The answer to the second question, of when a value subtree is interesting (e.g., when **o** has **interesting?** children), is a matter of taste; the pattern-classification concepts of chapter 4 provide a space of options. In VIRTUS, only subtrees involving tradeoffs are considered interesting, with the rationale that subtrees involving some form of dominance or equivalence would not merit an analysis were **a1** and **a2** the only alternatives under consideration. The VIRTUS vertical-pruning algorithm is thus

1. Let **o** = PARENT(deepest leaf in the subtree with root **refo**)
2. If CARDINAL-TRADEOFFS?(a1 a2 CHILDREN(o)), then mark **o** as deleted; otherwise, mark CHILDREN(o) as deleted (and retain **o**).
3. If **o** = **refo**, then return the remains of the tree; otherwise, repeat.

Vertical pruning is particularly useful for explaining choices that are based on large value trees. Fig. 5.1 shows the RCTE value tree produced by vertical

---

[97]Implementation note: Physical deletion of the objective is impractical, requiring that the original value tree be reinstantiated for each explanation.

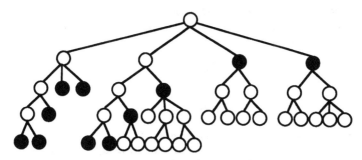

FIG. 5.1. Vertical pruning in RCTE.

pruning, in which the retained nodes are darkened. This collapsed value tree provides the basis for the following explanation:

> *Equivalence of care, distance of assigner from patient, equivalence at study outset, endpoint assessment, and adjustments due to subgroups are reasons to prefer RCT8 over RCT9 with regard to credibility. Blinded assignment design, quality of actual treatment assignment, stopping appropriateness, and subgroup analysis plan are reasons not to prefer RCT8 over RCT9. P-value and statistical techniques do not at all impact the choice between RCT8 and RCT9.*

Although more terse than an exhaustive display, this explanation is still somewhat verbose. The essential problem is that limiting the depth of the value tree still allows for arbitrary breadth. This problem provides the motivation for developing horizontal-pruning strategies.

5.2.2 Horizontal Pruning

Horizontal-pruning strategies limit the *breadth* of the value tree by eliminating objectives from a population. Rational populations of objectives include, for example, CHILDREN(VALUE), LEAVES(VALUE), and the leaves of a vertically-pruned tree.

Like vertical-pruning strategies, horizontal-pruning strategies are limited when used in isolation. When applied to CHILDREN(refo), horizontal pruning produces explanations that are arbitrarily abstract, potentially hiding important trade-offs deeper in the value tree. When applied to LEAVES(refo), horizontal pruning produces explanations that are arbitrarily detailed, failing to exploit the hierarchical nature of objectives for presentation. These problems provide the motivation for the vertical-pruning strategies presented in the previous section.

Strategies for displaying a population of objectives are presented in the following sections, in order of increasing sophistication.[98]

---

[98]Some of the less effective strategies are similar to strategies that have been employed in other systems. Chapter 8 describes these systems in detail, in the context of an evaluation of IVA.

Pruning of Inconsequential Objectives. An obvious strategy for horizontal pruning is to omit objectives that are INCONSEQUENTIAL? in a choice. For example, VIRTUS produces the following explanation for LEAVES(VALUE) in the domain of RCTE, in which objectives are ranked by COMPELLINGNESS within PREFERRED-OBJECTIVES and DISPREFERRED-OBJECTIVES:

> *Treatment assignment process, equivalence of dropout rates, equivalence of prior treatment history, equivalence of side effect rates, performance of blindfolding monitoring, randomization within sites, handling of patients for whom mortality data is unavailable, and stopping appropriateness are reasons to prefer RCT7 over RCT2 with regard to credibility. Success of blindfolding monitoring, quality of actual treatment assignment, adherence to original assignment with respect to analysis, distance of assigner from patient, inclusion of all deaths, handling of non-compliant patients with respect to analysis, and statistical techniques are reasons not to prefer RCT7 over RCT2.*

Apparently, this strategy is somewhat impractical for large value trees, admitting an arbitrary volume of objectives in explanations. This verbosity necessitates more sophisticated strategies for horizontal pruning.

Counterbalanced Objectives. Displaying counterbalanced objectives involves displaying just enough PREFERRED-OBJECTIVES to counterbalance the DISPREFERRED-OBJECTIVES underlying a choice, in increasing order of COMPELLINGNESS. This strategy yields the essential set of reasons that supports the preferred alternative, in the sense that the choice would have been the same were the pruned PREFERRED-OBJECTIVES INDIFFERENT-OBJECTIVES instead.

Applying this strategy to LEAVES(VALUE) in RCTE yields the following explanation:

> *Treatment assignment process, equivalence of dropout rates, equivalence of prior treatment history, equivalence of side effect rates, and performance of blindfolding monitoring are reasons to prefer RCT7 over RCT2 with regard to credibility. Success of blindfolding monitoring, quality of actual treatment assignment, adherence to original assignment with respect to analysis, distance of assigner from patient, inclusion of all deaths, handling of non-compliant patients with respect to analysis, and statistical techniques are reasons not to prefer RCT7 over RCT2.*

The following PREFERRED-OBJECTIVES are pruned because the choice would be the same were they INDIFFERENT-OBJECTIVES:

- Randomization within sites
- Handling of patients for whom mortality data is unavailable
- Stopping appropriateness

The following objectives are pruned because they are INDIFFERENT?:

- Equivalence of demographic factors not related to disease
- Equivalence of disease severity
- Equivalence of comorbidity factors
- Equivalence of prognostic factors
- Respect for denominator boundaries
- P-value
- Adjustments due to subgroups
- Subgroup analysis plan

Although more manageable than previously-presented explanations, this explanation is still somewhat verbose. In cases where several relatively uncompelling PREFERRED-OBJECTIVES together outweigh the COMPELLINGNESS of the DISPREFERRED-OBJECTIVES, it may turn out that *no* PREFERRED-OBJECTIVES are pruned. Thus, this strategy, too, admits an arbitrary volume of objectives in explanations.

Fixed Number of Objectives.   One approach to limiting the volume of objectives in explanations is simply to impose an a priori limitation. For example, we can display, say, the two most compelling PREFERRED-OBJECTIVES and DISPREFERRED-OBJECTIVES via NTH-RANKED-OBJECTIVES-BY-COMPELLINGNESS, yielding the following explanation for LEAVES(VALUE) in RCTE:

> *Treatment assignment process and equivalence of dropout rates are reasons to prefer RCT7 over RCT2. Success of blindfolding monitoring and quality of actual treatment assignment are reasons not to prefer RCT7 over RCT2.*

Several obvious variations are possible. Although these explanations are relatively terse, they are somewhat arbitrary, and they may fail to provide insight into the choice. For example, if the second most compelling objective differs infinitesimally from the third, and we limit the number of objectives to two, then omitting the third lacks intuitive justification. Similarly, the second most compelling objective may differ relatively largely from the first, rendering the second's inclusion questionable. The strategy described in the next section avoids this sort of arbitrariness, while still limiting the volume of objectives that is retained in explanations.

Contextual Pruning.   Contextual pruning involves eliminating objectives on the basis of CONTEXTUAL-COMPELLINGNESS. This strategy works equally well for large and small value trees. Applying the strategy to LEAVES(VALUE) in RCTE yields the following explanation:

Treatment assignment process and equivalence of dropout rates are reasons to prefer
RCT7 over RCT2. Success of blindfolding monitoring, quality of actual treatment
assignment, and adherence to original assignment with respect to analysis are rea-
sons not to prefer RCT7 over RCT2.

Contextual pruning limits the volume of objectives mentioned in explanations on
the basis of their contextual relationships to the population of objectives as a whole.
Recall from chapter 3 that users can adjust the terseness of explanations by turn-
ing a dial on VIRTUS's interface at any point during a session. This dial controls
the value of k in the definition of NOTABLY-COMPELLING?, which in turn affects
the behavior of NOTABLY-COMPELLING-OBJECTIVES, which in turn determines the
objectives mentioned in explanations.

Pattern Classification.   Pattern classification involves explaining a choice
on the basis of patterns of objectives defined by the pattern-classification concepts of chapter 4. For example, VIRTUS generates the following explanation
for CHILDREN(VALUE) in JESQ-II:

DASD is at least as good as COPY regarding all objectives that underlie the
choice with respect to overall queue space management effectiveness.

Because pattern classification does not depend on the number of objectives in
a population, the strategy works equally well for large and small value trees. By
itself, pattern classification is useful only for summarizing choices that involve
no trade-offs for the two alternatives in question, since the following explanation
provides little insight:

DASD and EXPENSIVE.PRINTING involve tradeoffs of value with regard to
overall queue space management effectiveness.

5.2.3 Combined Pruning Strategies

In constructing an explanation facility, a knowledge engineer can include one
or more of the strategies presented in this section and can construct combinations
of them. Applying both pattern classification and contextual pruning, for example, to CHILDREN(VALUE) in JESQ-II yields the following explanation:

DASD is at least as good as COPY regarding all objectives that underlie the
choice with respect to overall queue space management effectiveness. Additional
operator time and problem resolution time provide the most compelling reasons.

Vertical pruning can be performed prior to the application of any horizontal-
pruning strategy. Combining vertical pruning with contextual horizontal pruning

yields a powerful capability for generating summary comparisons. For example, applying vertical pruning and contextual pruning, embellished with a statement of ABSTRACT-RELATIVE-QUALITY, yields the following explanation for VALUE in JESQ-II:

> *EXPENSIVE.PRINTING provides infinitesimally better overall queue space management effectiveness than CHEAP.PRINTING. Compelling reasons to prefer CHEAP.PRINTING, such as additional cost, are outweighed by considerations of overall user satisfaction, along with less compelling reasons that recommend EXPENSIVE.PRINTING.*

Applying the same combined strategy to VALUE in RCTE produces the following explanation:

> *RCT8 provides only marginally better credibility than RCT9. Equivalence of care, distance of assigner from patient, and equivalence at study outset provide the most compelling reasons.*

These explanations are short and to the point, capturing the most compelling objectives for the choice at an appropriate level of abstraction.

5.3 DIFFERENCE-FUNCTION TRAVERSAL

Strategies for value-tree pruning and presentation organize insights into a choice between two alternatives with respect to the sign and magnitude of the COMPELLINGNESS of objectives. Although these methods are useful for providing rough summaries of choices, they provide little insight into the details of how parameters such as IMPORTANCE and ABSOLUTE-QUALITY combine to determine such choices. This level of granularity is required for more complete explanations, and particularly for refinement, because the user needs to understand how parameters combine in order to modify them effectively. *Difference-function-traversal* strategies provide this level of detail by generating step-by-step expositions of how choices between two alternatives are computed by the difference function.

5.3.1 Approach

Difference-function traversal employs a decompositional approach to explanation, explaining the computation of a difference function in terms of interactions among its component computations. Variants of this general approach have been employed to explain the behavior of physical systems (e.g., see de Kleer & Brown, 1984), for example, and to explain recommendations in the context of rule-based systems (Davis, 1976). In terms of the physical-systems analogy, difference-function traversal reflects a view of the difference function as a composite "device" that comprises more primitive devices, with the decomposition terminating at the operators of the difference function. Each operator is associated with an *operation explainer* that generates an intuitive explanation of the relationship between its operands and its result.[99] Operation explainers are described in more detail in section 5.3.2.

Operation explainers are arranged in a *device topology* according to the arithmetic precedence of the associated operators in the difference function. Because the topology provides an explicit representation of the operation-by-operation computation of the difference function, it provides a logical organization for the explanations generated by operation explainers. The structure of topologies is described in section 5.3.3.

With the operation explainers and topologies defined, *control strategies* generate explanations by traversing a topology and concatenating the explanations generated by operation explainers. *Backward chaining* over a topology provides an account of how the final result is derived from intermediate results, and of how intermediate results are derived from primitive inputs. Certain devices can be pruned from the explanation when their outputs are uninteresting. *Forward chaining* provides an account of how a particular parameter determines an intermediate result, which in turn ultimately determines the final result. *Interactive traversal* permits the user to forward and backward chain over the topology interactively. Control strategies are described in section 5.3.4.

Difference-function traversal provides the user with a medium for exploring the details of a choice. Because the *meaning* of a parameter is essentially that parameter's effect on the final result (chapter 3), difference-function traversal also provides support for refinement by showing how user-defined inputs combine to determine a choice. In particular, difference-function traversal provides a basis for performing what-if-style analyses in the spirit of a spreadsheet program by permitting users to alter parameter values and to observe the step-by-step effect of particular parameter values on the final result in the context of an intuitive justification for a choice. Chapter 6 describes refinement strategies that are based on difference-function traversal.

5.3.2 Operation Explainers

Each difference-function operator is associated with an *operation explainer* that generates an intuitive explanation of that operation's computational behavior. In addition to their central role in difference-function traversal, operation explainers may be invoked directly by the user, in the spirit of interpretation-concept

---

[99]Section 4.1.3 provided a sketch of these relationships in the context of conversations about value-based choices.

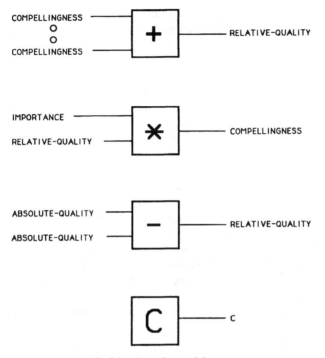

FIG. 5.2. Operation explainers.

invocation.[100] IVA's operation explainers are shown in Fig. 5.2.

An *addition explainer* (+) explains the relationships among COMPELLING-NESS(k a1 a2 o), $k \in$ CHILDREN(o), and RELATIVE-QUALITY(a1 a2 o). A *multiplication explainer* (*) explains the relationships among IMPORTANCE(o PARENT(o)), RELATIVE-QUALITY(a1 a2 o), and COMPELLINGNESS(o a1 a2 PARENT(o)). A *subtraction explainer* (−) explains the relationships among ABSOLUTE-QUALITY(a1 o), ABSOLUTE-QUALITY(a2 o), and RELATIVE-QUALITY(a1 a2 o). A *constant explainer* (c) explains a parameter, which can be viewed as the output of a parameter-specific operator that takes no inputs.[101]

---

[100]The dialogs of chapter 3 provided examples of this capability, including responses to questions such as "Why is price a compelling factor in the choice between SHELL.C and SHELL.B with regard to overall value?" This question is answered by a multiplication explainer.

[101]This organization formalizes the notion that a parameter is associated with the (sole) carrier of an implicit model of another representation (e.g., RELATIVE-QUALITY in *R**). When we speak of "integrating the AMVF with other representations," we refer (less precisely), in part, to the process of making explicit the (implicit) models for computing parameters of the AMVF. The other instance of "integrating the AMVF with other representations" involves including the AMVF as an explicit model of another representation, as we have proposed in the context of JESQ with respect to the computation of rule priorities (chapters 2 and 3). Klein and Finin (1987) elaborated this viewpoint.

Although operation explainers employ qualitative values in explanations, it is important to note that IVA does not include a qualitative calculus of value; rather, operation explainers employ qualitative values to *summarize the results* of operations in a quantitative calculus (i.e., value theory). Professional decision analysts employ a similar strategy to interpret AMVF results for clients (chapter 4).

The role of such explanations varies by operational context. Whenever quantitative values are included in explanations, such explanations provide the user with a *multilevel view* of a computation: Qualitative statements facilitate the identification of quantitative statements that merit closer inspection. This view is essential, for example, in the context of refinement (chapter 6), in which the quantitative values of interpretation-concept results are included unconditionally in explanations, because the user needs to know these values exactly to understand computations in their entirety. Whenever quantitative values are excluded from explanations, these explanations do not provide users with a sufficient basis to understand computations in their entirety; rather, these explanations provide users with a step-by-step feel for why the computation turned out as it did. Recall from section 5.1 that quantitative values can be included in explanations at the user's discretion, so explanations can be set to satisfy the requirements of the operational context at hand.

The following sections describe operation explainers in more detail.

Addition Explainer.   An *addition explainer* is associated with addition, which takes COMPELLINGNESS(k a1 a2 o), $k \in$ CHILDREN(o), and returns RELATIVE-QUALITY(a1 a2 o). An addition explainer answers questions such as, "Why is **a1** much better than **a2** with regard to **o**?" when **o** is a nonleaf objective.[102]

Explaining the output of addition, RELATIVE-QUALITY, is straightforward. RELATIVE-QUALITY can be described intuitively by a number of interpretation concepts, including[103]

- ABSTRACT-RELATIVE-QUALITY
- PREFERRED?, INDIFFERENT?, DISPREFERRED?
- CONTEXTUAL-RELATIVE-QUALITY
- OBJECTIVE-POSITION-IN-RELATIVE-QUALITY-RANKING

The knowledge engineer's choice of interpretation concepts (and combinations thereof) is a matter of taste, not an analytical issue. VIRTUS employs ABSTRACT-RELATIVE-QUALITY in the context of explaining a sum, yielding explanation fragments such as

---

[102]When o is a leaf, a subtraction explainer answers such questions, as shall be described.

[103]CONTEXTUAL-RELATIVE-QUALITY and OBJECTIVE-POSITION-IN-RELATIVE-QUALITY-RANKING are not applicable when o = VALUE.

DASD provides somewhat worse overall user satisfaction than EXPEN-SIVE.PRINTING.

Explaining the operands of addition is more complex. Because addition delimits objectives in the value tree, summarizing its operands is a task of horizontal objective pruning, and all the strategies of section 5.2.2 are candidates for this task. VIRTUS employs the combined pattern-classification and contextual-pruning algorithm of section 5.2.3 to summarize the operands of addition.

Multiplication Explainer. A *multiplication explainer* is associated with multiplication, which takes IMPORTANCE(o PARENT(o)) and RELATIVE-QUALITY(a1 a2 o), and returns COMPELLINGNESS(o a1 a2 PARENT(o)). A multiplication explainer answers questions such as, "Why is o a compelling reason to prefer **a1** over **a2** (in the context of PARENT(o))?"

Several interpretation concepts potentially support the explanation of multiplication output, the COMPELLINGNESS of the associated objective, including

- CONTEXTUAL-COMPELLINGNESS
- MORE-OR-EQUALLY-COMPELLING-OBJECTIVES
- MORE-COMPELLING-OBJECTIVES
- EQUALLY-COMPELLING-OBJECTIVES
- LESS-COMPELLING-OBJECTIVES
- LESS-OR-EQUALLY-COMPELLING-OBJECTIVES
- OBJECTIVE-POSITION-IN-COMPELLINGNESS-RANKING

Again, the knowledge engineer's choice of interpretation concepts (and combinations thereof) is a matter of taste. VIRTUS employs CONTEXTUAL-COMPELLINGNESS, yielding the following sort of explanation fragment:

Additional cost is a compelling factor favoring DASD over EXPENSIVE.PRINTING.

The explanation of the operands employs the following strategy. Recall from chapter 4 that IMPORTANCE and RELATIVE-QUALITY are essentially specializations of COMPELLINGNESS. The higher the IMPORTANCE of an objective, the greater the COMPELLINGNESS of that objective in the choice between any two alternatives; similarly, the greater the magnitude of the RELATIVE-QUALITY of two alternatives with regard to an objective, the higher its COMPELLINGNESS.

In isolation, IMPORTANCE is intuitively described by

- CONTEXTUAL-IMPORTANCE
- OBJECTIVE-POSITION-IN-IMPORTANCE-RANKING

- MORE-OR-EQUALLY-IMPORTANT-OBJECTIVES
- MORE-IMPORTANT-OBJECTIVES
- EQUALLY-IMPORTANT-OBJECTIVES
- LESS-IMPORTANT-OBJECTIVES
- LESS-OR-EQUALLY-IMPORTANT-OBJECTIVES

In the context of explaining a product, VIRTUS employs CONTEXTUAL-IMPORTANCE.

RELATIVE-QUALITY is intuitively described by a number of interpretation concepts, including

- ABSTRACT-RELATIVE-QUALITY
- PREFERRED?, INDIFFERENT?, DISPREFERRED?
- CONTEXTUAL-RELATIVE-QUALITY
- OBJECTIVE-POSITION-IN-RELATIVE-QUALITY-RANKING

In the context of explaining a product, VIRTUS employs CONTEXTUAL-RELATIVE-QUALITY.

A multiplication explainer establishes an intuitive relationship between the inputs and the output of multiplication. There are nine input-output combinations that we need to consider. First, we consider the special situation in which IMPORTANCE is irrelevant: Whenever the two alternatives are INDIFFERENT?, RELATIVE-QUALITY alone determines COMPELLINGNESS, and the relevant objective is *INCONSEQUENTIAL* in the choice. Thus, no explanation of the inputs is required; the result is obvious from the output.

Second, we consider the case in which neither of the inputs is NOTABLE?, and the output is not NOTABLE? either. In this case, the following explanation is appropriate:

> *Problem resolution time is not notably compelling in this particular choice because problem resolution time is not notably important in determining overall queue space management effectiveness, and DASD does not provide notably different problem resolution time from EXPENSIVE.PRINTING relative to other factors.*

Third, we consider the case in which the output is NOTABLE? despite the fact that neither of the inputs is NOTABLE?. This case occurs, for example, when the inputs are both sufficiently near the threshold of notability to make the output just barely NOTABLE?. In this case, the following explanation is provided:

> *While DASD does not provide notably different problem resolution time from COPY relative to other factors, and problem resolution time is not notably important in determining overall queue space management effectiveness, the*

combination of importance and quality difference *together* outweighs the impact of other factors to make problem resolution time notably compelling nonetheless.

Fourth, we consider the case in which IMPORTANCE is not NOTABLE?, and COMPELLINGNESS is not NOTABLE?, despite the notability of RELATIVE-QUALITY. In this case, the following explanation is appropriate:

While COPY provides notably different additional operator time from CARDS relative to other factors, additional operator time is not sufficiently important in determining overall queue space management effectiveness to make additional operator time a notably compelling factor in this particular decision.

Fifth, we consider the case in which RELATIVE-QUALITY is NOTABLE?, and COMPELLINGNESS is NOTABLE?, despite the lack of notability of IMPORTANCE. In this case, VIRTUS generates the following explanation:

While additional operator time is not notably important in determining overall queue space management effectiveness, DASD provides sufficiently different additional operator time from COPY relative to other factors to make additional operator time a notably compelling factor in this particular decision.

Sixth, we consider the case in which RELATIVE-QUALITY is not NOTABLE?, and COMPELLINGNESS is not NOTABLE?, despite the notability of IMPORTANCE. In this case, the following explanation is appropriate:

While overall user satisfaction is notably important in determining overall queue space management effectiveness, DASD does not provide sufficiently different overall user satisfaction from CHEAP.PRINTING relative to other factors to consider overall user satisfaction a notably compelling factor in this particular decision.

Seventh, we consider the case in which IMPORTANCE is NOTABLE?, and COMPELLINGNESS is NOTABLE?, despite the lack of notability of RELATIVE-QUALITY. In this case, VIRTUS provides the following explanation:

While DASD does not provide notably different overall user satisfaction from EXPENSIVE.PRINTING relative to other factors, overall user satisfaction is sufficiently important in determining overall queue space management effectiveness to make overall user satisfaction a notably compelling factor in this particular decision.

Eighth, we consider the case in which COMPELLINGNESS is not NOTABLE?, despite the fact that both the inputs are NOTABLE?. This case occurs, for example, when both inputs barely exceed their respective notability thresholds and a few analogous inputs for other objectives greatly exceed their thresholds. In this case, the following explanation is appropriate:[104]

> *While CARDS provides notably different overall user satisfaction from INSTALL relative to other factors, and overall user satisfaction is notably important in determining overall queue space management effectiveness, this strength of importance and relative quality *together* is outweighed by other factors so that overall user satisfaction fails to be a notably compelling factor in this particular decision nonetheless.*

Finally, we consider the case in which both the inputs are NOTABLE?, and the output is NOTABLE? as well. In this case, the following explanation is appropriate:

> *Overall user satisfaction is notably important in determining overall queue space management effectiveness, and EXPENSIVE.PRINTING provides notably different overall user satisfaction from DELETE relative to other factors, so overall user satisfaction is a notably compelling factor in this particular decision.*

Subtraction Explainer. A *subtraction explainer* is associated with subtraction, which takes ABSOLUTE-QUALITY(a1 o) and ABSOLUTE-QUALITY(a2 o) and returns RELATIVE-QUALITY(a1 a2 o). A subtraction explainer answers questions such as, "Why is **a1** much better than **a2** with regard to **o**?" when **o** is a leaf objective.[105]

Explaining the output of subtraction, RELATIVE-QUALITY, is straightforward, as previously described. VIRTUS employs ABSTRACT-RELATIVE-QUALITY in the context of explaining subtraction, yielding explanation fragments such as

> *DASD provides substantially better additional cost than EXPENSIVE.PRINTING.*

Unlike multiplication and addition, explaining the operands of subtraction, ABSOLUTE-QUALITY (of both alternatives), is straightforward. ABSOLUTE-QUALITY is described intuitively by the following interpretation concepts:

---

[104]This explanation is contrived for exposition and does not reflect the values presented in chapter 2. Although this case did not arise in any of the three VIRTUS applications described in chapter 3, it is theoretically possible, because there is no necessary analytical relationship between the μ or σ of the product of two arbitrary distributions and the μ or σ of either or both of those distributions.

[105]Recall that when **o** is a nonleaf, an addition explainer answers such questions.

- ABSTRACT-ABSOLUTE-QUALITY
- CONTEXTUAL-ABSOLUTE-QUALITY
- ALTERNATIVE-POSITION-IN-QUALITY-RANKING

VIRTUS employs CONTEXTUAL-ABSOLUTE-QUALITY, as in the following example:

DASD provides notably good additional cost in the context of all available alternatives.

Constant Explainers. A *constant explainer* is associated with a particular parameter, which can be viewed as an operator that takes no inputs and returns a constant. A constant explainer answers the question, "What is the value of this parameter?" Recall from chapter 4 that the parameters of the difference function vary with the chosen reformulation algebra.

There is a sense in which constant-explainer outputs are redundant, because the parameters of the difference function are described in explanations of the operands of the lowest-level devices in a difference-function topology. The explanation of IMPORTANCE as a multiplication input, for example, has this form:

While overall user satisfaction is notably important in determining overall queue space management effectiveness,

The interpretation-concept interfaces for these explanations, however, do not expose parameter measurement units and only optionally expose numeric parameter values, whereas refinement requires that both the measurement units and the numeric values be displayed for users to specify modifications.[106] Constant explainers satisfy this requirement; the constant explainer for IMPORTANCE, for example, returns:

Overall user satisfaction accounts for 50% of the determination of overall queue space management effectiveness when JES queue space is at an acceptable level.

This constant explainer mentions IMPORTANCE and its measurement units directly, along with the current decision context (on which IMPORTANCE depends). A refinement facility provides the opportunity to change parameter values, as we describe in chapter 6.

---

[106]As we describe in section 5.3.4, constant explainers are also useful in forward-chaining strategies, which show in a step-by-step fashion how parameters affect intermediate and final results in difference-function computation.

5.3.3 Device Topology

The explanation fragments generated by the operation explainers of section 5.3.2 are combined (by the control strategies defined in section 5.3.4) according to an explicit representation of the difference function called a *device topology*, or *topology* for short. A topology is a set of instances of operation explainers that are connected according to the precedence of arithmetic operators in the difference function.

We can construct systematically the topology for a given difference function by composing the topologies corresponding to individual objectives in the value tree. The reformulation algebras of chapter 4 imply a set of alternative topologies for leaf objectives, each of which employs a progressively restricted subset of the available operation explainers, as shown in Fig. 5.3 (a) through 5.3 (c).

R_1, Fig. 5.3 (a), is probably the most useful topology for most applications, certainly for the applications described in chapter 3. R_1 is sufficiently detailed for refinement, and provides the essential elements of informative explanations. R_2, Fig. 5.3 (b), is also useful for explanation, but is not sufficiently detailed for refinement. In most realistic applications, which may encompass several alternatives and objectives, employing R_2 for refinement would involve capturing a vast number of explicit RELATIVE-QUALITY estimates over pairs of alternatives. R_3, Fig. 5.3 (c), represents the most abstract view, depicting the COMPELLING-NESS of a leaf objective as a constant. R_3 is even less suitable for refinement than is R_2, requiring the user to specify directly the COMPELLINGNESS of every leaf objective for every pair of alternatives. VIRTUS implements R_1, embellishing ABSOLUTE-QUALITY constant-explainer outputs with ABSOLUTE-QUANTITY. In applications concerned solely with explanation, R_2 or R_3 topologies can be used to provide terser explanations.

The topology corresponding to internal objectives is shown in Fig. 5.4, and the topology corresponding to VALUE (the root objective) is shown in Fig. 5.5. These topologies for objectives are composed to form a complete representation of the difference function. Fig. 5.6, for example, depicts the topology for the simple value tree of Fig. 4.1.

5.3.4 Control Strategies

Control strategies traverse a topology and concatenate the explanations produced by operation explainers to produce a justification for a choice between two alternatives. *Backward-chaining strategies* expose the propagation of results from device to device in a backward fashion, starting at the operation explainer corresponding to the last-applied difference-function operator in a topology. Exhaustive backward chaining includes unconditionally all devices in a topology except for constant explainers, which can be included conditionally. Variations on ex-

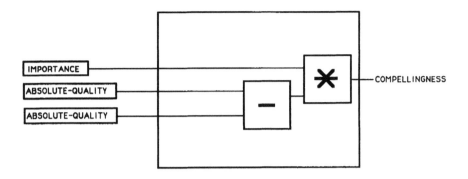

(a) Leaf topology for R₁

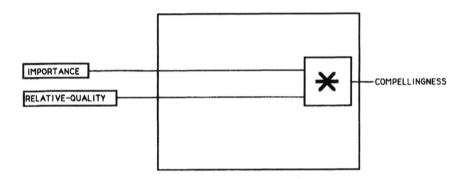

(b) Leaf topology for R₂

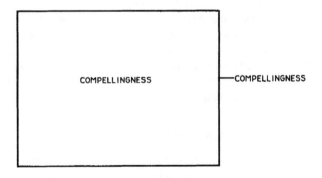

(c) Leaf topology for R₃

FIG. 5.3. Leaf topologies by reformulation algebra.

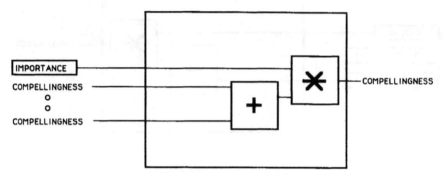

FIG. 5.4. Internal topology.

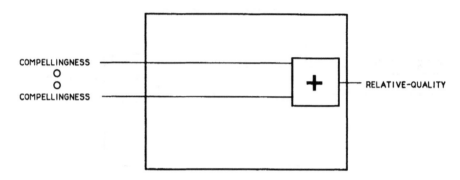

FIG. 5.5. VALUE topology.

haustive backward chaining include pruning uninteresting device outputs from explanations, and restricting backward chaining to particular subtopologies (i.e., topologies corresponding to particular objectives) that are specified by the user. *Forward-chaining strategies* expose the propagation of results from device to device in a forward fashion, starting with a given constant explainer in a topology. Forward chaining can also be restricted to particular subtopologies specified by the user. *Interactive traversal strategies* involve the user-controlled invocation of forward and backward chaining in the context of an interactive facility.

5.3.4.1 Backward Chaining

Backward-chaining strategies expose the propagation of results from device to device in a backward fashion, starting at the operation explainer corresponding to the last-applied difference-function operator in a topology.

In the first variation of backward chaining that we describe, we define and apply iteratively the primitive operation *output-to-input exposition*, which relates

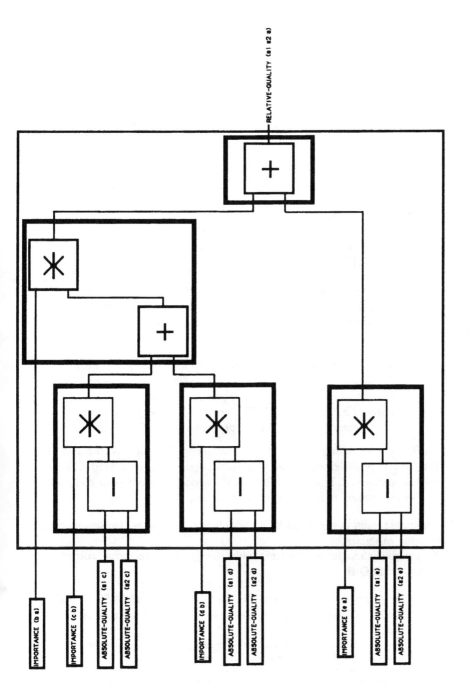

FIG. 5.6. Topology in R_1 for simple value tree.

125

the output of a device to a summary of its inputs.[107] Output-to-input exposition is a process of concatenating the operation explainer's output explanation with that of its input explanation, embellished by enumeration of children objectives for internal and root objectives:

< explanation of output >
< enumeration of children objectives, if applicable >
< explanation of input >

Many variations on this strategy are possible. For example, we may wish to associate inputs and outputs more explicitly by including an adjoining phrase:

< explanation of output >
< enumeration of children objectives, if applicable >
"The following statements support this conclusion:"
< explanation of input >

Because topologies vary for leaf, internal, and root (VALUE) objectives, the result of backward chaining varies by objective topology.[108] Backward chaining over a leaf objective under R_1 yields the following sort of explanation in JESQ-II:

Additional cost is a compelling factor favoring DASD over EXPENSIVE.PRINT-ING. While additional cost is not notably important in determining overall queue space management effectiveness, DASD provides sufficiently different additional cost from EXPENSIVE.PRINTING relative to other factors to make additional cost a notably compelling factor in this particular decision.

DASD provides substantially better additional cost than EXPENSIVE.PRINT-ING. DASD provides notably good additional cost in the context of all available alternatives. EXPENSIVE.PRINTING provides notably poor additional cost in the context of all available alternatives.

The first paragraph is generated by a multiplication explainer, the second by a subtraction explainer.

Backward chaining over an internal objective yields the following sort of explanation in JESQ-II:

Overall user satisfaction is a compelling factor favoring EXPENSIVE.PRINT-ING over DASD. This determination reflects considerations of additional turn-

---

[107]In later sections of this chapter, and in chapter 6, we describe applications of backward chaining that involve exposing only the output explanations of operation explainers.

[108]Recall that explanations for leaf objectives also vary with the knowledge engineer's choice of reformulation algebra (section 5.3.3) and with the conditional inclusion of constant explainers (section 5.3.2). Explanations in this section are generated in R_1 with constant explainers disabled.

around time and similarity to the user's requested form. While DASD does not provide notably different overall user satisfaction from EXPENSIVE.PRINT-ING relative to other factors, overall user satisfaction is sufficiently important in determining overall queue space management effectiveness to make overall user satisfaction a notably compelling factor in this particular decision.

DASD provides somewhat worse overall user satisfaction than EXPEN-SIVE.PRINTING. EXPENSIVE.PRINTING is at least as good as DASD regarding all objectives that underlie the choice with respect to overall user satisfaction. Additional turnaround time provides the most compelling reason.

The first paragraph is generated by a multiplication explainer, the second by an addition explainer.

Backward chaining over the root objective yields the following sort of explanation in JESQ-II:

DASD provide infinitesimally better overall queue space management effectiveness than EXPENSIVE.PRINTING. This determination reflects considerations of additional operator time, additional cost, problem resolution time, and overall user satisfaction. While overall user satisfaction provides a compelling reason to prefer EXPENSIVE.PRINTING, this is outweighed by considerations of additional cost, along with less compelling reasons, that provide motivation for preferring DASD.

This explanation is generated by an addition explainer.

Backward chaining can be applied iteratively to arbitrary portions of a difference-function topology to produce detailed intuitive justifications for choices. The entire topology is employed in exhaustive backward chaining.

Exhaustive Backward Chaining. *Exhaustive backward chaining* unconditionally includes every device in the topology except for constant explainers, which can be included conditionally.[109] For example, exhaustive backward chaining produces the following explanation in JESQ-II:

DASD provides infinitesimally better overall queue space management effectiveness than EXPENSIVE.PRINTING. This determination reflects considerations of additional operator time, additional cost, problem resolution time, and overall user satisfaction. While overall user satisfaction provides a compelling reason to prefer EXPENSIVE.PRINTING, this is outweighed by considerations of additional cost, along with other less compelling reasons, that provide motivation for preferring DASD.

---

[109]For variety, explanations in this section are generated with constant explainers enabled.

Overall user satisfaction is a compelling factor favoring EXPENSIVE.PRINT-ING over DASD. This determination reflects considerations of additional turn-around time and similarity to the user's requested form. While DASD does not provide notably different overall user satisfaction from EXPENSIVE.PRINT-ING relative to other factors, overall user satisfaction is sufficiently important in determining overall queue space management effectiveness to make overall user satisfaction a notably compelling factor in this particular decision. DASD provides somewhat worse overall user satisfaction than EXPENSIVE.PRINT-ING. EXPENSIVE.PRINTING is as least as good as DASD regarding all ob-jectives that underlie the choice with respect to overall user satisfaction. Additional turnaround time provides the most compelling reason. Overall user satisfaction accounts for 50.0 percent of the determination of overall queue space management effectiveness when JES queue space is at an acceptable level.

Additional turnaround time is a compelling factor favoring EXPENSIVE.PRINT-ING over DASD in determining overall user satisfaction. While additional turn-around time is not notably important in determining overall user satisfaction, DASD provides sufficiently different additional turnaround time from EXPEN-SIVE.PRINTING relative to other factors to make additional turnaround time a notably compelling factor in this particular decision. DASD provides sub-stantially worse additional turnaround time than EXPENSIVE.PRINTING. DASD provides neither notably good nor poor additional turnaround time in the context of all available alternatives. EXPENSIVE.PRINTING provides nota-bly good additional turnaround time in the context of all available alterna-tives. Since EXPENSIVE.PRINTING involves 0 minutes of additional turnaround time, EXPENSIVE.PRINTING rates 10 on a scale from 0 to 10. Since DASD involves 32.1 minutes of additional turnaround time, DASD rates 4.0 on a scale from 0 to 10. Additional turnaround time accounts for 50.0 percent of the determination of overall user satisfaction when JES queue space is at an acceptable level.

Similarity to the user's requested form is an inconsequential factor in the choice between DASD and EXPENSIVE.PRINTING in determining overall user satis-faction. DASD provides no better or worse similarity to the user's requested form than EXPENSIVE.PRINTING. DASD provides notably good similarity to the user's requested form in the context of all available alternatives. EX-PENSIVE.PRINTING provides notably good similarity to the user's requested form in the context of all available alternatives. Since EXPENSIVE.PRINT-ING involves 1 subjective unit of similarity to the user's requested form, EX-PENSIVE.PRINTING rates 10 on a scale from 0 to 10. Since DASD involves 1 subjective unit of similarity to the user's requested form, DASD rates 10 on a scale from 0 to 10. Similarity to the user's requested form accounts for 50.0 percent of the determination of overall user satisfaction when JES queue space is at an acceptable level.

Additional cost is a compelling factor favoring DASD over EXPENSIVE. PRINT-ING. While additional cost is not notably important in determining overall queue space management effectiveness, DASD provides sufficiently different additional cost from EXPENSIVE. PRINTING relative to other factors to make additional cost a notably compelling factor in this particular decision. DASD provides substantially better additional cost than EXPENSIVE. PRINTING. DASD provides notably good additional cost in the context of all available alternatives. EXPENSIVE. PRINTING provides notably poor additional cost in the context of all available alternatives. Since EXPENSIVE. PRINTING involves 100 dollars of additional cost, EXPENSIVE. PRINTING rates 4.0 on a scale from 0 to 10. Since DASD involves .5 dollars of additional cost, DASD rates 10 on a scale from 0 to 10. Additional cost accounts for 20.0 percent of the determination of overall queue space management effectiveness when JES queue space is at an acceptable level.

Problem resolution time is a factor favoring DASD over EXPENSIVE. PRINT-ING, although not a compelling one. Problem resolution time is not notably compelling in this particular choice because problem resolution time is not notably important in determining overall queue space management effectiveness, and DASD does not provide notably different problem resolution time from EXPENSIVE. PRINTING relative to other factors. DASD provides reasonably better problem resolution time than EXPENSIVE. PRINTING. DASD provides notably good problem resolution time in the context of all available alternatives. EXPENSIVE. PRINTING provides neither notably good nor poor problem resolution time in the context of all available alternatives. Since EX-PENSIVE. PRINTING involves 25 minutes of problem resolution time, EXPEN-SIVE. PRINTING rates 6.0 on a scale from 0 to 10. Since DASD involves 1 minute of problem resolution time, DASD rates 10 on a scale from 0 to 10. Problem resolution time accounts for 20.0 percent of the determination of overall queue space management effectiveness when JES queue space is at an acceptable level.

Additional operator time is an inconsequential factor in the choice between DASD and EXPENSIVE. PRINTING. DASD provides no better or worse additional operator time than EXPENSIVE. PRINTING. DASD provides neither notably good nor poor additional operator time in the context of all available alternatives. EXPENSIVE. PRINTING provides neither notably good nor poor additional operator time in the context of all available alternatives. Since EX-PENSIVE. PRINTING involves .1 minutes of additional operator time, EXPEN-SIVE. PRINTING rates 10 on a scale from 0 to 10. Since DASD involves .1 minutes of additional operator time, DASD rates 10 on a scale from 0 to 10. Additional operator time accounts for 10.0 percent of the determination of overall queue space management effectiveness when JES queue space is at an acceptable level.

Although informative, exhaustive backward chaining is cumbersome. Exhaustive backward chaining is appropriate for generating detailed explanations that might appear, for example, as the final section or appendix of a report about a decision. The VIRTUS report described in section 5.5 employs this strategy.

Backward Chaining with Local Device Pruning.   *Backward chaining with local device pruning* involves backward chaining on only the outputs of operation explainers, and eliminating those that are uninteresting. This strategy yields a summary of the computation that is more detailed than are the value-tree-level summaries of section 5.2, yet less detailed than is exhaustive backward chaining.

The pruning process starts with the multiplication explainers associated with CHILDREN(VALUE), because the output of the root addition explainer (i.e., the final result) is assumed to be interesting to the user unconditionally. Constant explainers are enabled, because device inputs are excluded. Whenever a device output is pruned (i.e., its output is not interesting), it does not need to be justified, so the devices that compute its inputs are pruned as well.

The definition of "interesting" can vary by explanation facility with the knowledge engineer's choice of interpretation concepts. VIRTUS employs the following definitions:

- Addition explainer: NOTABLY-DIFFERENT?
- Multiplication explainer: NOTABLY-COMPELLING?
- Subtraction explainer: NOTABLY-DIFFERENT?
- Constant explainer for IMPORTANCE: NOTABLY-IMPORTANT?
- Constant explainer for ABSOLUTE-QUALITY: NOTABLY-GOOD? or NOTABLY-POOR?

Compare the following explanation generated by backward chaining with local device pruning with that generated by exhaustive backward chaining:

DASD provides infinitesimally better overall queue space management effectiveness than EXPENSIVE.PRINTING.

Overall user satisfaction is a compelling factor favoring EXPENSIVE.PRINTING over DASD. Overall user satisfaction accounts for 50.0 percent of the determination of overall queue space management effectiveness when JES queue space is at an acceptable level. Additional turnaround time is a compelling factor favoring EXPENSIVE.PRINTING over DASD in determining overall user satisfaction. DASD provides substantially worse additional turnaround time than EXPENSIVE.PRINTING. Since EXPENSIVE.PRINTING involves 0 minutes of additional turnaround time, EXPENSIVE.PRINTING rates 10 on a scale from 0 (worst) to 10 (best).

Additional cost is a compelling factor favoring DASD over EXPENSIVE.PRINT-ING. DASD provides substantially better additional cost than EXPEN-SIVE.PRINTING. Since EXPENSIVE.PRINTING involves 100 dollars of additional cost, EXPENSIVE.PRINTING rates 4.0 on a scale from 0 (worst) to 10 (best). Since DASD involves .5 dollars of additional cost, DASD rates 10 on a scale from 0 (worst) to 10 (best).

The explanation is more focused, but retains the flavor of exhaustive backward chaining. Consider the traversal of *additional turnaround time*:

Additional turnaround time is a compelling factor favoring EXPENSIVE.PRINT-ING over DASD in determining overall user satisfaction. DASD provides sub-stantially worse additional turnaround time than EXPENSIVE.PRINTING. Since EXPENSIVE.PRINTING involves 0 minutes of additional turnaround time, EXPENSIVE.PRINTING rates 10 on a scale from 0 (worst) to 10 (best).

First, note that *additional turnaround time* is included because its multiplication explainer output is interesting. The constant-explainer output of IMPORTANCE is pruned from the explanation, since *additional turnaround time* is not NOTABLY-IMPORTANT? in determining *overall user satisfaction*, but ABSTRACT-RELATIVE-QUALITY is mentioned because of its CONTEXTUAL-RELATIVE-QUALITY. EXPEN-SIVE.PRINTING's ABSOLUTE-QUALITY is mentioned because it is NOTABLY-GOOD?, but DASD's is not mentioned because it is neither NOTABLY-GOOD? nor NOTABLY-POOR?.

Backward chaining with local device pruning may be useful for generating a summary prior to presenting the results of exhaustive backward chaining. The VIRTUS report described in section 5.5 employs this strategy.

Details of an Objective. A designer may also include commands for back-ward chaining on selected portions of the value tree (i.e., subtopologies). VIR-TUS's **detail** command, for example, presents an output-to-input exposition for a given objective, along with an output-to-input exposition for that objective's children, as in the following example:

Overall user satisfaction is a compelling factor favoring EXPENSIVE.PRINT-ING over DASD. This determination reflects considerations of additional turn-around time and similarity to the user's requested form. While DASD does not provide notably different overall user satisfaction from EXPENSIVE.PRINT-ING relative to other factors, overall user satisfaction is sufficiently important in determining overall queue space management effectiveness to make overall user satisfaction a notably compelling factor in this particular decision. DASD provides somewhat worse overall user satisfaction than EXPENSIVE.PRINT-

ING. EXPENSIVE.PRINTING is as least as good as DASD regarding all objectives that underlie the choice with respect to overall user satisfaction. Additional turnaround time provides the most compelling reason.

Additional turnaround time is a compelling factor favoring EXPENSIVE.PRINTING over DASD in determining overall user satisfaction. While additional turnaround time is not notably important in determining overall user satisfaction, DASD provides sufficiently different additional turnaround time from EXPENSIVE.PRINTING relative to other factors to make additional turnaround time a notably compelling factor in this particular decision. DASD provides substantially worse additional turnaround time than EXPENSIVE.PRINTING. DASD provides neither notably good nor poor additional turnaround time in the context of all available alternatives. EXPENSIVE.PRINTING provides notably good additional turnaround time in the context of all available alternatives.

Similarity to the user's requested form is an inconsequential factor in the choice between DASD and EXPENSIVE.PRINTING in determining overall user satisfaction. DASD provides no better or worse similarity to the user's requested form than EXPENSIVE.PRINTING. DASD provides notably good similarity to the user's requested form in the context of all available alternatives. EXPENSIVE.PRINTING provides notably good similarity to the user's requested form in the context of all available alternatives.

Other Strategies.   A variety of backward-chaining strategies might be implemented in the context of the representation defined in this section; we have provided some examples here. For instance, we might combine **detail** with local device pruning. Because the topology, the operation explainers, the interpretation, and the control strategies are isolated from one another, the synthesis of new strategies is a self-contained task.

5.3.4.2 Forward Chaining

Forward chaining provides an account of how a particular parameter determines an intermediate result, which in turn ultimately determines the final result. Forward chaining exposes the propagation of results from device to device, starting with a given constant explainer in a topology.

The primitive operation of forward chaining is *input-to-output exposition*, which relates the inputs of a device to its output, starting with a particular input:[110]

---

[110]As with output-to-input exposition, the knowledge engineer may implement stylistic variations of input-to-output exposition. VIRTUS, for example, omits repetition of the focal input across iterations of input-to-output exposition, as is demonstrated in the context of *semiexhaustive forward chaining* in the next section.

<explanation of focal input>
"Since it's also true that:"
<explanation of sibling inputs>
"It follows that, in toto:"
<explanation of output>

For example, VIRTUS produces the following explanation of multiplication, starting at the constant explainer for IMPORTANCE:

Additional cost accounts for 20 percent of the determination of overall queue space management effectiveness when JES queue space is at an acceptable level.

Since it's also true that:
* *DASD provides substantially better additional cost than EXPEN-SIVE.PRINTING.*
It follows that, in toto:

Additional cost is a compelling factor favoring DASD over EXPENSIVE.PRINT-ING.

Because topologies vary for leaf, internal, and root (VALUE) objectives, the results of forward chaining vary by objective type, as in backward chaining.[111]

Semiexhaustive Forward Chaining. *Semiexhaustive forward chaining* involves traversing the path through the topology from a given device to the root addition explainer, concatenating input-to-output expositions for each device along the path. The strategy is "semiexhaustive" in that the computations supporting inputs not lying along this path are pruned from the explanation. For example, the following explanation is produced to show the effect on the final result of the IMPORTANCE of *additional cost*, which includes the traversal of leaf objective *additional cost* and of VALUE:

Additional cost accounts for 20 percent of the determination of overall queue space management effectiveness when JES queue space is at an acceptable level.

Since it's also true that:
* *DASD provides substantially better additional cost than EXPENSIVE.PRINT-ING.*
It follows that, in toto:

Additional cost is a compelling factor favoring DASD over EXPEN-SIVE.PRINTING.

---

[111]The nature of the variation should be apparent from section 5.3.4.1.

Since it's also true that:
- *Additional operator time is an inconsequential factor in the choice between EXPENSIVE.PRINTING and DASD.*
- *Problem resolution time is a factor favoring DASD over EXPENSIVE.PRINT-ING, although not a compelling one.*
- *Overall user satisfaction is a compelling factor favoring EXPENSIVE.PRINT-ING over DASD.*

It follows that, in toto:

DASD provides infinitesimally better overall queue space management effectiveness than EXPENSIVE.PRINTING.

Relevance of an Objective.   **Relevance** is the forward-chaining analog of **detail**. **Relevance** relates a given objective and its siblings to its parent objective in the context of a particular choice; for example,

Overall user satisfaction is a compelling factor favoring EXPENSIVE.PRINT-ING over DASD.

Since it's also true that:
- *Additional operator time is an inconsequential factor in the choice between EXPENSIVE.PRINTING and DASD.*
- *Additional cost is a compelling factor favoring DASD over EXPEN-SIVE.PRINTING.*
- *Problem resolution time is a factor favoring DASD over EXPENSIVE.PRINT-ING, although not a compelling one.*

It follows that, in toto:

DASD provides infinitesimally better overall queue space management effectiveness than EXPENSIVE.PRINTING.

5.3.4.3   Interactive Traversal

Interactive traversal provides the user with a medium for invoking forward and backward chaining interactively. Consider, for example, the following VIR-TUS dialog:

Overall user satisfaction is a compelling factor favoring EXPENSIVE.PRINT-ING over DASD. This determination reflects considerations of additional turn-around time and similarity to the user's requested form. While DASD does not provide notably different overall user satisfaction from EXPENSIVE.PRINT-ING relative to other factors, overall user satisfaction is sufficiently important in determining overall queue space management effectiveness to make overall user satisfaction a notably compelling factor in this particular decision.

Select a statement for further exploration, R(elevance), or Q(uit):

1. *Overall user satisfaction accounts for 50.0 percent of the determination of overall queue space management effectiveness when JES queue space is at an acceptable level.*

2. *DASD provides somewhat worse overall user satisfaction than EXPEN-SIVE.PRINTING.*

> **2**

DASD provides somewhat worse overall user satisfaction than EXPEN-SIVE.PRINTING. EXPENSIVE.PRINTING is as least as good as DASD regarding all objectives that underlie the choice with respect to overall user satisfaction. Additional turnaround time provides the most compelling reason.

Select a statement for further exploration, R(elevance), or Q(uit):

1. *Similarity to the user's requested form is an inconsequential factor in the choice between DASD and EXPENSIVE.PRINTING in determining overall user satisfaction.*

2. *Additional turnaround time is a compelling factor favoring EXPEN-SIVE.PRINTING over DASD in determining overall user satisfaction.*

{And so on}

This strategy is implemented in VIRTUS by proceeding from device to device as directed by the user, invoking the current operation explainer and offering a menu of options for further exploration.

5.4 MODEL TRAVERSAL

Every explanation system must address at least two classes of questions:

1. Questions about the results of the underlying model for a particular case
2. Questions about the model itself

The previous sections of this chapter all address questions of the first type. To respond to questions of the second type, VIRTUS provides simple textual descriptions of the value tree. These descriptions include the components of a decision model that are independent of any two particular alternatives in the population at hand: the structure of the value tree, the IMPORTANCE of objectives, and the current decision context. In a more elaborate implementation, these textual explanations might be embellished with graphical displays of the hierarchy.[112]

---

[112]Chapter 9 describes potential extensions to VIRTUS in more detail.

Analogs of the control strategies introduced to explain the difference between two alternatives can be employed to describe the value tree.

Details of an Objective.   The alternative-dependent version of **detail** describes the immediate children of an objective in the objectives hierarchy, sorted by RANK-OBJECTIVES-BY-IMPORTANCE. For example, VIRTUS produces the following explanation regarding *overall queue-space-management effectiveness*:

> *Evaluating the overall queue space management effectiveness of an alternative involves considerations of overall user satisfaction, problem resolution time, additional cost, and additional operator time. Overall user satisfaction accounts for 50.0 percent of the determination of overall queue space management effectiveness when JES queue space is at an acceptable level. Problem resolution time accounts for 20.0 percent. Additional cost accounts for 20.0 percent. Additional operator time accounts for 10.0 percent.*

Relevance of an Objective.   **Relevance** describes the siblings and parent of an objective in the objectives hierarchy. For example, VIRTUS produces the following explanation regarding the relevance of *additional turnaround time*:

> *Additional turnaround time is a determining factor of overall user satisfaction, along with similarity to the user's requested form. Additional turnaround time accounts for 50.0 percent of the determination of overall user satisfaction when JES queue space is at an acceptable level. Similarity to the user's requested form accounts for 50.0 percent.*

Backward Chaining.   Backward chaining traverses the value tree from a given objective to the leaves. For example, VIRTUS produces the following explanation regarding *overall queue-space-management effectiveness*:

> *Evaluating the overall queue space management effectiveness of an alternative involves considerations of overall user satisfaction, problem resolution time, additional cost, and additional operator time. Overall user satisfaction accounts for 50.0 percent of the determination of overall queue space management effectiveness when JES queue space is at an acceptable level. Problem resolution time accounts for 20.0 percent. Additional cost accounts for 20.0 percent. Additional operator time accounts for 10.0 percent.*

> *Evaluating the overall user satisfaction of an alternative involves considerations of similarity to the user's requested form and additional turnaround time.*

*Similarity to the user's requested form accounts for 50.0 percent of the deter-
mination of overall user satisfaction when JES queue space is at an acceptable level. Additional turnaround time accounts for 50.0 percent.*

Forward Chaining.   Forward chaining traverses the value tree from a given
objective to the root. For example, VIRTUS produces the following explanation
regarding *similarity to the user's requested form*:

*Similarity to the user's requested form is a determining factor of overall user
satisfaction, along with additional turnaround time. Similarity to the user's
requested form accounts for 50.0 percent of the determination of overall user
satisfaction when JES queue space is at an acceptable level. Additional turnaround time accounts for 50.0 percent.*

*Overall user satisfaction is a determining factor of overall queue space manage-
ment effectiveness, along with problem resolution time, additional cost, and
additional operator time. Overall user satisfaction accounts for 50.0 percent
of the determination of overall queue space management effectiveness when
JES queue space is at an acceptable level. Problem resolution time accounts
for 20.0 percent. Additional cost accounts for 20.0 percent. Additional operator time accounts for 10.0 percent.*

Interactive Traversal.   Interactive traversal allows the user to ascend and
descend the value tree in the context of an interactive dialog. For example, VIR-
TUS supports the following interaction:

*Evaluating the overall queue space management effectiveness of an alterna-
tive involves considerations of overall user satisfaction, problem resolution
time, additional cost, and additional operator time. Overall user satisfaction
accounts for 50.0 percent of the determination of overall queue space management effectiveness when JES queue space is at an acceptable level. Problem
resolution time accounts for 20.0 percent. Additional cost accounts for 20.0
percent. Additional operator time accounts for 10.0 percent.*

Select an objective for further exploration, R(elevance), or Q(uit):
1. Additional operator time
2. Additional cost
3. Problem resolution time
4. Overall user satisfaction

> **4**

*Evaluating the overall user satisfaction of an alternative involves considera-
tions of similarity to the user's requested form and additional turnaround time.*

Similarity to the user's requested form accounts for 50.0 percent of the determination of overall user satisfaction when JES queue space is at an acceptable level. Additional turnaround time accounts for 50.0 percent.

Select an objective for further exploration, R(elevance), or Q(uit):
1. Additional turnaround time
2. Similarity to the user's requested form

{And so on}

5.5   CONSTRUCTION OF EXPLANATION FACILITIES

The strategies introduced in previous sections can be combined in a variety of ways to yield explanation facilities that reflect the tastes of particular knowledge engineers and the requirements of particular applications. Explanation systems might vary, for example, with the particular interpretation concepts associated with operation explainers, with the particular horizontal-pruning strategies that are implemented and, more generally, with the *classes* of strategies that are included: For instance, an engineer might reasonably exclude difference-function traversal or value-tree pruning and presentation from the design of a particular explanation system. The following sections outline the implementation of common interactive commands in intelligent systems and of facilities for generating reports.

5.5.1   Common Interactive Commands

Intelligent systems typically provide simple interactive commands, such as WHY and HOW, as an interface to an explanation facility. In the context of explaining value-based choices, such questions are underconstrained, allowing several reasonable interpretations. To free the user from having to know about multiple interpretations of WHY, for example, the system designer can construct a menu-driven facility to detail the possible interpretations. For example, consider the following dialog:

DASD is the best with regard to overall queue space management effectiveness.

> WHY

By WHY, which of the following interpretations do you mean?

1. What is notably good about DASD?
2. How does DASD compare with the next best choice, EXPEN-
SIVE.PRINTING?

3. What are DASD's close contenders?
4. How does DASD compare with its close contenders?
5. . . .

> 1

DASD provides notably good additional cost and problem resolution time.

Questions such as (1) are answered directly by interpretation concepts. Responses to questions such as (2), on the other hand, might employ more elaborate strategies, such as value-tree pruning and presentation (section 5.2) or difference-function traversal (section 5.3). Alternatively, the designer can combine interpretations of WHY to formulate a response that draws on the variety of the techniques presented in previous sections: An elaborate implementation of this strategy is demonstrated in the generation of a report (section 5.5.2), which can be viewed as an extended response to WHY.

Because question (2) represents a common interpretation of WHY (chapter 4), the designer might include an explicit WHY-NOT command in an explanation facility: "WHY-NOT a?" would be interpreted, "Why not choose alternative a instead of the chosen alternative?" The designer can, in addition, provide a HOW command that invokes strategies for model traversal (section 5.4).

5.5.2 Reports

Explanation facilities can also be combined to generate an intuitive report about a decision. VIRTUS generates the report that appears in the Appendix, which is organized as follows.

1. *Problem statement* describes the choice at hand, drawing on canned interfaces to describe the available alternatives and the problem that motivates a decision.

2. *Solution summary* presents a high-level summary of the choice:

   - ALTERNATIVES-PROVIDING-BEST is invoked to identify the chosen alternative(s).

   - NOTABLY-GOOD-OBJECTIVES and NOTABLY-POOR-OBJECTIVES are invoked to display the particular strengths and weaknesses of the chosen alternative with respect to the population of alternatives.

   - Iteration over user profiles using USER-AGREEMENT? identifies other users who would make the same choice under the same circumstances.[113]

---

[113]This function, along with SIMILAR-DECISIONS?, was not implemented in VIRTUS due to difficulties concerning naming conflicts in the implementation environment, so the corresponding text in the report is canned. The implementation is conceptually trivial, however, as should be apparent from the definitions of chapter 4.

- Iteration of CONTEXTUAL-ABSOLUTE-QUALITY delimits the alternatives into qualitative classes.
- SIMILAR-ALTERNATIVES identifies the close contenders of the chosen alternative.

3. *The decision-making process* exposes the value tree, abstractly communicating how choices are computed via backward-chaining model-traversal. In addition, an analogy is made with other problems, if any, using SIMILAR-DECISIONS?.

4. *Brief analysis of the decision* provides more detail than does section 2, but still summarizes the choice at a relatively high level. This section employs the following explanation facilities:

- RANK-ALTERNATIVES-BY-QUALITY shows the ranking of alternatives in order of preference.
- SIMILAR-ALTERNATIVES identifies the close contenders of the chosen alternative.
- A combined vertical- and horizontal-pruning strategy (section 5.2.3) provides a summary comparison of the chosen alternative with alternatives that are close contenders.
- Repeated application of ABSTRACT-RELATIVE-QUALITY provides an enumeration of the relative quality of the chosen alternative and of each of the others with respect to VALUE.

5. *Brief analysis of close contenders* provides a more detailed comparison than does section 4 using backward chaining with local device pruning.

6. *Detailed analysis of close contenders* provides a still more detailed comparison than does section 5 using exhaustive backward chaining with quantitative values and constant explainers enabled.

5.6   SUMMARY

In this chapter we defined strategies for justifying value-based choices. *Interpretation-concept invocation* involves providing the user with simple interfaces for arbitrarily invoking interpretation concepts in exploring a decision. *Value-tree pruning and presentation* involves summarizing a choice between two particular alternatives in a population, guided by the structure of the value tree. *Difference-function traversal* exposes the details of a choice between two particular alternatives in a population. *Model traversal* provides an abstract description of how choices are computed.

Together, the explanation strategies provide a space of options that can be implemented in isolation or in combination by knowledge engineers. IVA thus provides a general specification for a variety of explanation systems. Section 5.5 demonstrated how designers can combine explanation strategies to implement common intelligent-system commands such as WHY and HOW, and to produce intuitive reports that describe decisions.

CHAPTER 6

Refinement

The purpose of refinement is twofold. First, a refinement facility provides a basis for capturing insights that are gained from the exercise of acquisition. Second, a refinement facility provides the means with which to modify a model to reflect changing preferences over time. There are several reasons that a model of choice may require repairs, including changes in the attitudes of users over time and changes in the decision-making situation (Zeleny, 1982). In short, refinement is a tool for incremental model correction.

This chapter describes strategies for refinement. Recall from chapters 3 and 5 that refinement is coupled strongly with explanation: An explanation system provides a window into the computation of choices, and a refinement system provides an opportunity to repair iteratively the underlying model until the system generates convincing justifications (Davis, 1976). Refinement strategies thus build on the interpretation of chapter 4 and on the explanation strategies of chapter 5. In the context of refinement, explanations impose a high-level organization on the computation taking place in the underlying calculus (value theory).[114]

Refinement strategies comprise a set of modular components. *Parameter assessors* (section 6.1.1) implement strategies for capturing individual parameters; parameter assessors are invoked whenever the user indicates that a parameter value must be modified. *Sensitivity analyzers* (section 6.1.2) indicate threshold values for individual parameters that will result in a change of preference between two alternatives; sensitivity analyzers are invoked prior to the modification of a parameter value to give the user a summary-level understanding of the

---

[114]For this reason, the numeric values for interpretation concepts are included unconditionally in explanations during refinement: The user needs to know these numbers exactly to modify them.

final result's sensitivity to that parameter value.[115] *Parameter-integrity checkers* (section 6.1.3) implement value-theoretic and heuristic tests on user inputs; parameter-integrity checkers are invoked to verify parameter-value changes.

Refinement strategies organize these component refinement operations. *Interactive diagnosis and repair* (section 6.2.1) guides the user through the computation of the difference function and provides the user with an opportunity to identify, modify, and verify the correction of a faulty parameter value. *Diagnosis* employs difference-function traversal in an interactive, backward-chaining mode to help the user to identify a potentially faulty parameter. Whenever the user identifies a faulty parameter, *repair* initiates a parameter assessor and invokes difference-function traversal in a forward-chaining mode to demonstrate the step-by-step effect of the new parameter value on the final result. Interactive diagnosis and repair is potentially useful for resolving perceived inconsistencies with reality in an existing model of value. *Direct parameter modification* (section 6.2.2) allows the user to initiate repair directly. Under this strategy, the user decides on his own to modify a parameter, without performing interactive diagnosis. Direct parameter modification initiates the appropriate parameter assessor to capture the new parameter and shows how the new parameter affects the final result via difference-function traversal in a forward-chaining mode. This facility is potentially useful when a change in an environment (e.g., a corporate directive to reduce costs) necessitates a corresponding change to an existing model of value, but the appropriate degree of change is unclear. Finally, *parameter suggestion* (section 6.2.3) is a set of heuristic strategies for presenting candidate parameters for modification. The user might initiate parameter suggestion to identify logical parameters to investigate.

This chapter is organized as follows. Section 6.1 describes refinement components. Section 6.2 describes refinement strategies. Section 6.3 describes the integration of acquisition techniques (for capturing new objectives and their subhierarchies) with refinement techniques. Section 6.4 provides a summary of this chapter.

6.1 REFINEMENT COMPONENTS

Refinement strategies comprise a set of modular components that includes parameter assessors, sensitivity analyzers, and parameter-integrity checkers.

6.1.1 Parameter Assessors

Parameter assessors implement strategies for capturing individual parameters. Parameter assessors are invoked by refinement strategies whenever the user indicates that a parameter value must be modified. Some parameter assessors em-

---

[115]Recall from chapter 5 that semiexhaustive forward chaining addresses the same goal but proceeds in a step-by-step fashion.

ploy heuristics that are designed to reduce the volume of information that must be captured from users. VIRTUS's IMPORTANCE assessors, for example, infer the IMPORTANCE of the remaining objectives in a population whenever the user changes the IMPORTANCE of a particular objective.

The following sections describe VIRTUS's parameter assessors. Note that, because the definitions of parameter assessors are isolated in VIRTUS, a knowledge engineer can substitute other parameter assessors for these modules according to taste, or can provide redundant parameter assessors to check for consistency.

New Alternatives.   Recall from chapter 2 that a central reason for including explicit models of choice in intelligent systems is to facilitate the integration of new alternatives with an existing population of alternatives. Under VIRTUS, the capture of new alternatives is a trivial task of capturing descriptive strings and values for attributes.[116] Consider the following dialog, in which an operations manager adds a new alternative, called SCREEN:[117]

Enter the name of the new alternative:

> **SCREEN**

Enter a description of SCREEN:

> **routing the user's output to his terminal screen**

What is the correct number of minutes of additional turnaround time involved in performing SCREEN?

> **0**

What is the correct number of minutes of problem resolution time involved in performing SCREEN?

> **.1**

What is the correct number of minutes of additional operator time involved in performing SCREEN?

> **.1**

{And so on}

---

[116]This task is more complex in systems that employ initial attribute ranges that reflect only a subset of the potentially feasible alternatives in an application domain: Whenever new alternatives that exceed these ranges are introduced, the relevant ABSOLUTE-QUALITY and IMPORTANCE values need to be reassessed. Von Winterfeldt and Edwards (1986) provided a general description of options for attribute-range selection and of the associated implications for assessment.

[117]In this dialog, VIRTUS captures only instances of the data selector ABSOLUTE-QUANTITY, because the corresponding ABSOLUTE-QUALITY values already have been recorded in JESQ-II.

The AMVF integrates these values to establish the overall value of the new alternative relative to the existing population.

Importance. Researchers have developed several techniques for capturing a set of IMPORTANCE values; VIRTUS implements two such techniques. The first technique involves capturing IMPORTANCE values as percentages (Stillwell & Edwards, 1979). When a single IMPORTANCE percentage is modified in refinement, VIRTUS infers values for the remaining objectives by distributing the total remaining weight among these objectives such that the ratios among them are preserved. VIRTUS then verifies the inferred weights with the user, as we demonstrate in the following dialog fragment:

What is the correct percentage?

> **10**

OK. The statement has been changed to:

Additional cost accounts for 10.0 percent of the determination of overall queue space management effectiveness when queue space is at an acceptable level.

Note that with this change:

1. *Additional operator time accounts for 11.25 percent of the determination of overall queue space management effectiveness when queue space is at an acceptable level.*
2. *Additional cost accounts for 10.0 percent of the determination of overall queue space management effectiveness when queue space is at an acceptable level.*
3. *Problem resolution time accounts for 22.5 percent of the determination of overall queue space management effectiveness when queue space is at an acceptable level.*
4. *Overall user satisfaction accounts for 56.25 percent of the determination of overall queue space management effectiveness when queue space is at an acceptable level.*

Does this seem reasonable?

> **YES**

Whenever the new distribution of IMPORTANCE measures seems incorrect to the user, he can effect additional modifications. Note that the current decision context is mentioned along with IMPORTANCE values, because these values vary by decision context.

The second implementation of IMPORTANCE capture involves collecting ratios among IMPORTANCE values from the user and computing the corresponding IMPORTANCE values (Edwards, 1977):

Assuming JES queue space is at an acceptable level, select the LEAST important overall queue space management effectiveness-related factor from the following:

1. *overall user satisfaction*
2. *problem resolution time*
3. *additional cost*
4. *additional operator time*

> **4**

Assuming JES queue space is at an acceptable level, how many times more important is additional cost than additional operator time?

> **2**

Assuming JES queue space is at an acceptable level, how many times more important is problem resolution time than additional operator time?

> **2**

Assuming JES queue space is at an acceptable level, how many times more important is overall user satisfaction than additional operator time?

{And so on}

As in the previous method, a single ratio involving the value to be altered can be captured, and the remaining IMPORTANCE measures can be inferred.

A number of additional techniques for assessing IMPORTANCE has been developed;[118] the knowledge engineer can implement any of these techniques in an IMPORTANCE assessor.

Absolute-Quality. Researchers have developed several techniques for capturing component value and utility functions, including direct rating, category estimation, curve drawing, difference standard sequence, and others.[119] Some of these techniques have been implemented in interactive computer programs (Keeney & Sicherman, 1976; Klein et al., 1982; Nair & Sicherman, 1979; Novick et al., 1980; Schlaifer, 1971; Seo et al., 1978; von Nitzsch & Weber, 1988; Weber, 1985). VIRTUS captures new ABSOLUTE-QUALITY measures using a combination of simple direct rating and difference verification, as we demonstrate in the following dialog fragment:[120]

---

[118]Von Winterfeldt and Edwards (1986) provided a review of these techniques.

[119]Farquhar and Keller (1988) and von Winterfeldt and Edwards (1986) reviewed techniques for value-function construction.

[120]This dialog reflects refinement in R_1, embellished with the capture of data selector ABSOLUTE-QUANTITY (chapter 4). Alternatively, a designer can implement indifference techniques to capture

CARDS involves 20 minutes of addition time expended by the user.

Now an evaluation of this level of additional time expended by the user must be captured.

As reference points, recall that:

1. *On a scale from 0 (worst) to 10 (best), COPY rates 10.0 with regard to additional time expended by the user.*

2. *On a scale from 0 (worst) to 10 (best), FICHE rates 0 with regard to additional time expended by the user.*

Now, on this same scale from 0 to 10, how would you rate the 20 minutes of additional time expended by the user involved in performing CARDS?

> 5

OK. You should now be able to agree with the following statement:

On a scale from 0 (worst) to 10 (best), CARDS rates 5.0 with regard to additional time expended by the user.

Note that with this change:

1. *CARDS provides substantially worse (−.5) additional time expended by the user than INSTALL.*

2. *CARDS provides substantially worse (−.5) additional time expended by the user than EXPENSIVE.PRINTING.*

3. *CARDS provides substantially worse (−.5) additional time expended by the user than DASD.*

4. *CARDS provides substantially worse (−.5) additional time expended by the user than CHEAP.PRINTING.*

5. *CARDS provides substantially worse (−.5) additional time expended by the user than COPY.*

6. *CARDS provides substantially better (.5) additional time expended by the user than DELETE.*

7. *CARDS provides substantially better (.5) additional time expended by the user than FICHE.*

Does this seem reasonable?

> YES

OK

ABSTRACT-QUALITY over the range of ABSOLUTE-QUANTITY measures; some decision theorists would argue that these techniques are more formally appropriate. In applications that do not involve a mapping from a natural scale to a value scale, references to ABSOLUTE-QUANTITY can be omitted entirely.

Were the user to disagree with the resulting RELATIVE-QUALITY assessments, he could reassess ABSOLUTE-QUALITY, and examine the results again.

6.1.2 Sensitivity Analyzers

Sensitivity analyzers calculate values for parameters that will result in a change of preference between two alternatives, or *break-even values*. The sensitivity analyzer for IMPORTANCE, for example, returns the break-even value for IMPORTANCE(o refo) in a choice between two particular alternatives **a1** and **a2**:

> *With no other modifications, you must lower the importance of additional cost to less than 12.72 percent in order to prefer EXPENSIVE.PRINTING over DASD.*

Analogous sensitivity analyzers can be developed for other parameters.

The information provided by sensitivity analyzers is valuable, for example, to users who are refining the underlying basis for a choice for the purpose of explaining that choice to other users. Sensitivity analyzers are invoked by refinement strategies, and can also be invoked by users directly.

6.1.3 Parameter-Integrity Checkers

Parameter-integrity checkers implement value-theoretic and heuristic tests on user inputs, and are invoked to verify parameter-value changes. Parameter-integrity checkers alert the user to erroneous or suspicious semantic relationships. In VIRTUS, for example, component value functions are assumed to be monotonic, and VIRTUS alerts the user to violations of this assumption, as in the following dialog fragment:

> *As reference points, recall that:*
> * *On a scale from 0 (worst) to 10 (best), DELETE rates 10 with regard to additional cost.*
> * *On a scale from 0 (worst) to 10 (best), INSTALL rates 0 with regard to additional cost.*
>
> *Now, on this same scale from 0 to 10, how would you rate the 80 dollars of additional cost involved in performing EXPENSIVE.PRINTING?*

> **> 3**

> *This doesn't make sense. It is assumed that the less additional cost, the better. Yet, you have entered the following:*

- *80 dollars of additional cost rates 3.0 on a scale from 0 to 10.*
- *100 dollars of additional cost rates 4.0 on a scale from 0 to 10.*

An analogous parameter-integrity checker could be implemented to test for difference independence (chapter 2).[121] A knowledge engineer can also define heuristic integrity checkers that alert the user to refinements that may have marginal effects, as in the case of adding a new attribute that fails to produce a difference in preference. An even less conservative strategy is to flag refinements that fail to produce qualitative changes in particular local outputs, such as a change from UNCOMPELLING? to NOTABLY-COMPELLING?.

6.2   REFINEMENT STRATEGIES

Refinement strategies combine parameter assessors, sensitivity analyzers, parameter-integrity checkers, and explanation strategies to provide an interactive framework for refining the AMVF.

6.2.1   Interactive Diagnosis and Repair

Interactive diagnosis and repair guides the user through the computation of the difference function, and provides the user with an opportunity to identify, modify, and verify the correction of a faulty parameter value. This strategy is potentially useful for resolving perceived inconsistencies with reality in an existing model of value.

Diagnosis employs difference-function traversal in an interactive, backward-chaining mode (chapter 5) to help the user to identify potentially faulty parameters for modification. Diagnosis begins at the addition explainer for VALUE. Whenever the user disagrees with the output of an operation explainer, he is asked either to identify one of the operation explainer's inputs as incorrect, or (at an objective break) to specify that an objective is missing.[122] This interactive verification process continues until the user identifies a faulty parameter (constant-explainer output).[123]

Whenever the user identifies a faulty parameter, the *repair* process is initiated. Repair, in turn, initiates the appropriate parameter assessor (section 6.1.1)

---

[121]A number of authors describe such tests (e.g., Dyer & Sarin, 1979; von Winterfeldt & Edwards, 1986).

[122]Section 6.3 describes a view of missing objectives as implicit objectives with IMPORTANCE = 0.

[123]This style of diagnosis is reminiscent of, for example, fault diagnosis in qualitative reasoning about physical systems (Davis, 1984; Genesereth, 1984), but is fundamentally different in the following sense: Diagnosis algorithms in qualitative reasoning search for a faulty component *device* in a composite device (under the assumption that the inputs are defined correctly), whereas IVA's diagnosis algorithm searches for a faulty primitive *input* to a composite device (under the assumption that the *devices*—decision theory, the interpretation of chapter 4, and the operation-explainer definitions—are defined correctly).

and invokes difference-function traversal in a forward-chaining mode (chapter 5) to demonstrate the step-by-step effect of the new parameter value on the final result.

We demonstrate interactive diagnosis and repair in the following VIRTUS dialog. In this dialog, an operations manager is suspicious of the system's preference for DASD over EXPENSIVE.PRINTING, and he employs VIRTUS to guide him through the computation of this choice. Ultimately, the manager decides that *minimize additional cost* is being considered too strongly in the installation's operational policy, and he corrects the corresponding IMPORTANCE value.

Interactively diagnose and repair the choice between DASD and EXPEN-SIVE.PRINTING.

DASD provides infinitesimally better (.05) overall queue space management effectiveness than EXPENSIVE.PRINTING.

If you disagree with this statement, then you must disagree with at least one of the statements that supports it: With which of the following statements are you least comfortable?

1. *Additional operator time is an inconsequential (0.0) factor in the choice between DASD and EXPENSIVE.PRINTING.*

2. *Additional cost is a compelling (.12) factor favoring DASD over EXPEN-SIVE.PRINTING.*

3. *Problem resolution time is a factor favoring DASD over EXPEN-SIVE.PRINTING, although not a compelling one (.08).*

4. *Overall user satisfaction is a compelling (−.15) factor favoring EXPEN-SIVE.PRINTING over DASD.*

5. *The above represents a complete list of factors underlying the determination of overall queue space management effectiveness.*

> **2**

You selected:

Additional cost is a compelling (.12) factor favoring DASD over EXPEN-SIVE.PRINTING.

If you disagree with this statement, then you must disagree with at least one of the statements that supports it: With which of the following statements are you least comfortable?

1. *DASD provides substantially better (.6) additional cost than EXPEN-SIVE.PRINTING.*

2. *Additional cost accounts for 20.0 percent of the determination of overall queue space management effectiveness when queue space is at an acceptable level.*

> **2**

You selected:

Additional cost accounts for 20.0 percent of the determination of overall queue space management effectiveness when queue space is at an acceptable level.

This is a primitive statement that you can modify directly. Do you want to change it?

> **YES**

With no other modifications, you must lower the importance of additional cost to less than 12.72 percent in order to prefer EXPENSIVE.PRINTING over DASD.

What is the correct percentage?

> **10**

OK. The statement has been changed to:

Additional cost accounts for 10.0 percent of the determination of overall queue space management effectiveness when queue space is at an acceptable level.

Note that with this change:

1. *Additional operator time accounts for 11.25 percent of the determination of overall queue space management effectiveness when queue space is at an acceptable level.*
2. *Additional cost accounts for 10.0 percent of the determination of overall queue space management effectiveness when queue space is at an acceptable level.*
3. *Problem resolution time accounts for 22.5 percent of the determination of overall queue space management effectiveness when queue space is at an acceptable level.*
4. *Overall user satisfaction accounts for 56.25 percent of the determination of overall queue space management effectiveness when queue space is at an acceptable level.*

Does this seem reasonable?

> **YES**

OK. The choice is now argued for as follows:

Additional cost accounts for 10.0 percent of the determination of overall queue space management effectiveness when queue space is at an acceptable level.

Since it's also true that:

- *DASD provides substantially better (.6) additional cost than EXPEN-SIVE.PRINTING.*

It follows that, in toto:

Additional cost is a factor favoring DASD over EXPENSIVE.PRINTING, although not a compelling one (.06).

Since it's also true that:

1. *Additional operator time is an inconsequential (0.0) factor in the choice between DASD and EXPENSIVE.PRINTING.*
2. *Problem resolution time is a factor favoring DASD over EXPEN-SIVE.PRINTING, although not a compelling one (.09).*
3. *Overall user satisfaction is a compelling (−.17) factor favoring EXPEN-SIVE.PRINTING over DASD.*

It follows that, in toto:

DASD provides infinitesimally worse (−.02) overall queue space management effectiveness than EXPENSIVE.PRINTING.

Although the current VIRTUS implementation demonstrates the essential characteristics of our approach, it could be embellished in several ways. For example, a form of regression testing might be implemented to expose discrepancies between the original ranking and the modified ranking of a small set of sample alternatives. Another straightforward embellishment involves eliminating the interactive verification of parameters that have already been verified by the user earlier in a particular VIRTUS session.

6.2.2 Direct Parameter Modification

Direct parameter modification involves the direct initiation of repair. This strategy provides the user with an opportunity to change parameters directly, without first being guided by the diagnosis process. Direct parameter modification is potentially useful when a change in an environment necessitates a corresponding change to an existing model of value, but the appropriate degree of change is unclear.

Suppose, for example, that a data-center manager's budget is increased, causing him to lower the IMPORTANCE of *minimize additional cost*. The user might examine the implications of this change in the context of two particular alternatives — say, the (current) best alternative (DASD) and an alternative that is characterized by an extreme value for the altered objective (e.g., EXPENSIVE.PRINTING). The following VIRTUS dialog, a portion of the dialog of section 6.2.1, demonstrates this strategy.

With no other modifications, you must lower the importance of additional cost to less than 12.72 percent in order to prefer EXPENSIVE.PRINTING over DASD.

What is the correct percentage?

> 10

OK. The statement has been changed to:

Additional cost accounts for 10.0 percent of the determination of overall queue space management effectiveness when queue space is at an acceptable level.

Note that with this change:

1. *Additional operator time accounts for 11.25 percent of the determination of overall queue space management effectiveness when queue space is at an acceptable level.*

2. *Additional cost accounts for 10.0 percent of the determination of overall queue space management effectiveness when queue space is at an acceptable level.*

3. *Problem resolution time accounts for 22.5 percent of the determination of overall queue space management effectiveness when queue space is at an acceptable level.*

4. *Overall user satisfaction accounts for 56.25 percent of the determination of overall queue space management effectiveness when queue space is at an acceptable level.*

Does this seem reasonable?

> YES

OK. The choice is now argued for as follows:

Additional cost accounts for 10.0 percent of the determination of overall queue space management effectiveness when queue space is at an acceptable level.

Since it's also true that:

• *DASD provides substantially better (.6) additional cost than EXPENSIVE.PRINTING.*

It follows that, in toto:

Additional cost is a factor favoring DASD over EXPENSIVE.PRINTING, although not a compelling one (.06).

Since it's also true that:

1. *Additional operator time is an inconsequential (0.0) factor in the choice between DASD and EXPENSIVE.PRINTING.*

2. *Problem resolution time is a factor favoring DASD over EXPEN-SIVE.PRINTING, although not a compelling one (.09).*

3. *Overall user satisfaction is a compelling (−.17) factor favoring EXPEN-SIVE.PRINTING over DASD.*

It follows that, in toto:

DASD provides infinitesimally worse (−.02) overall queue space management effectiveness than EXPENSIVE.PRINTING.

The user can examine the new ranking of alternatives to verify the global effects of the modification.

EXPENSIVE.PRINTING (.85) is the best alternative with regard to overall queue space management effectiveness. DASD (.83) is the next best. CHEAP.PRINTING (.75) is the next best. COPY (.73) is the next best. FICHE (.44) is the next best. DELETE (.4375) is the next best. CARDS (.434) is the next best. INSTALL (.28) is the next best.

When the user disagrees with this ranking, he can again initiate direct parameter modification or invoke the diagnosis-and-repair process in the context of a mis-ranked pair of alternatives.

6.2.3 Parameter Suggestion

Parameter suggestion encodes heuristic strategies for presenting candidate parameters for modification. The user might initiate parameter suggestion to iden-tify logical parameters to investigate.

One form of parameter suggestion involves organizing the results of a sensi-tivity analysis, as in the following VIRTUS example:

In order of smallest changes first, your options for changing the choice are:

1. *With no other modifications, you must raise the importance of overall user satisfaction from 50 percent to more than 57.143 percent in order to prefer EXPENSIVE.PRINTING over DASD.*

2. *With no other modifications, you must lower the importance of additional cost from 20 percent to less than 12.73 percent in order to prefer EXPEN-SIVE.PRINTING over DASD.*

3. *With no other modifications, you must lower the importance of problem resolution time from 20 percent to less than 8.57 percent in order to prefer EXPENSIVE.PRINTING over DASD.*

4. *No modification of additional operator time alone will alter the choice between DASD and EXPENSIVE.PRINTING.*

Another strategy is to present parameters in order of recency of modification;
the rationale behind this strategy is that recently modified parameters are less
likely to be tuned properly than are older ones, which have been scrutinized by
the user in the context of previous explanations.

6.3. ACQUISITION IN A REFINEMENT CONTEXT

Recall from section 6.2.1 that new objectives can be added to the value tree in
the context of refinement. The dynamic addition of new objectives necessitates
the capture of a value subtree, of alternative attributes, and of other parameters.
Thus, a complete refinement facility includes an acquisition facility as a subset.

We can view a value tree as a structure with infinite breadth: The value tree
contains an unbounded number of implicit objectives with IMPORTANCE $= 0$. In
the context of refinement, acquisition can be viewed as a process of making explicit the implicit objectives in a value tree. The following VIRTUS dialog fragment illustrates the capture of a new value subtree in the context of interactive
diagnosis and repair. We begin at the point in the dialog where the user disagrees
with VIRTUS's choice with respect to *maximize user satisfaction.*

*If you disagree with this statement, then you must disagree with at least one
of the statements that supports it: With which of the following statements are
you least comfortable?*

1. *Additional turnaround time is an inconsequential (0.0) factor in the choice
   between CARDS and FICHE in determining overall user satisfaction.*
2. *Similarity to the user's requested form is a compelling ($-.05$) factor favoring FICHE over CARDS in determining overall user satisfaction.*
3. *The above represents a complete list of factors underlying the determination of overall user satisfaction.*

> 3

*Enter the name of the factor that has been omitted in the assessment of overall
user satisfaction.*

> **USER.TIME**

Enter a short name for USER.TIME:

> **additional time expended by the user**

Which is preferred: MORE additional time expended by the user or LESS?

> **LESS**

{Next, VIRTUS captures the IMPORTANCE of the new objective for each known context. VIRTUS assumes that the current IMPORTANCE value is zero.}

The statement to be changed is:

Additional time expended by the user accounts for 0.0 percent of the determination of overall user satisfaction when JES queue space is at a dangerously low level.

No modification of additional time expended by the user alone will alter the choice between FICHE and CARDS.

What is the correct percentage?

> **30**

OK. The statement has been changed to:

Additional time expended by the user accounts for 30.0 percent of the determination of overall user satisfaction when JES queue space is at a dangerously low level.

{The IMPORTANCE distribution heuristic of section 6.1.1 is employed to compute the remaining values.}

Note that with this change:

1. *Additional time expended by the user accounts for 30.0 percent of the determination of overall user satisfaction when JES queue space is at a dangerously low level.*
2. *Additional turnaround time accounts for 35.0 percent of the determination of overall user satisfaction when JES queue space is at a dangerously low level.*
3. *Similarity to the user's requested form accounts for 35.0 percent of the determination of overall user satisfaction when JES queue space is at a dangerously low level.*

Does this seem reasonable?

> **YES**

OK

{VIRTUS proceeds to the next decision context.}

The statement to be changed is:

Additional time expended by the user accounts for 0.0 percent of the determination of overall user satisfaction when JES queue space is at an acceptable level.

No modification of additional time expended by the user alone will alter the choice between FICHE and CARDS.

What is the correct percentage?

> **30**

OK. The statement has been changed to:

Additional time expended by the user accounts for 30.0 percent of the determination of overall user satisfaction when JES queue space is at an acceptable level.

Note that with this change:

1. *Additional time expended by the user accounts for 30.0 percent of the determination of overall user satisfaction when JES queue space is at an acceptable level.*
2. *Additional turnaround time accounts for 35.0 percent of the determination of overall user satisfaction when JES queue space is at an acceptable level.*
3. *Similarity to the user's requested form accounts for 35.0 percent of the determination of overall user satisfaction when JES queue space is at an acceptable level.*

Does this seem reasonable?

> **YES**

OK

{Next, VIRTUS captures the value subtree for the new objective.}

Select the most convenient method for measuring additional time expended by the user:

1. *In terms of more detailed factors*
2. *Making qualitative judgements about particular levels of additional time expended by the user*

> **2**

{The user has indicated that the new objective is a leaf. Had the user selected option 1, VIRTUS would recursively capture new objectives.}

Enter the units in which additional time expended by the user is measured:

> **minutes**

{VIRTUS captures the value of the new attribute for all known alternatives.}

Which alternative involves the most additional time expended by the user?

> **FICHE**

What is the correct number of minutes of additional time expended by the user pertaining to FICHE?

> **60**

OK. It is now recorded that:

FICHE involves 60 minutes of additional time expended by the user.

Which alternative involves the least additional time expended by the user?

> **DASD**

What is the correct number of minutes of additional time expended by the user pertaining to DASD?

> **0**

OK. It is now recorded that:

DASD involves 0 minutes of additional time expended by the user.

What is the correct number of minutes of additional time expended by the user pertaining to INSTALL?

> **0**

OK. It is now recorded that:

INSTALL involves 0 minutes of additional time expended by the user.

What is the correct number of minutes of additional time expended by the user pertaining to EXPENSIVE.PRINTING?

> **0**

OK. It is now recorded that:

EXPENSIVE.PRINTING involves 0 minutes of additional time expended by the user.

What is the correct number of minutes of additional time expended by the user pertaining to CHEAP.PRINTING?

> **0**

OK. It is now recorded that:

CHEAP.PRINTING involves 0 minutes of additional time expended by the user.

What is the correct number of minutes of additional time expended by the user pertaining to COPY?

> 0

OK. It is now recorded that:

COPY involves 0 minutes of additional time expended by the user.

What is the correct number of minutes of additional time expended by the user pertaining to DELETE?

> 60

OK. It is now recorded that:

DELETE involves 60 minutes of additional time expended by the user.

What is the correct number of minutes of additional time expended by the user pertaining to CARDS?

> 20

OK. It is now recorded that:

CARDS involves 20 minutes of additional time expended by the user.

Now an evaluation of this level of additional time expended by the user must be captured.

As reference points, recall that:

1. *On a scale from 0 (worst) to 10 (best), COPY rates 10.0 with regard to additional time expended by the user.*
2. *On a scale from 0 (worst) to 10 (best), FICHE rates 0 with regard to additional time expended by the user.*

Now, on this same scale from 0 to 10, how would you rate the 20 minutes of additional time expended by the user involved in performing CARDS?

> 5

OK. You should now be able to agree with the following statement:

On a scale from 0 (worst) to 10 (best), CARDS rates 5.0 with regard to additional time expended by the user.

Note that with this change:

1. *CARDS provides substantially worse (−.5) additional time expended by the user than INSTALL.*

2. *CARDS provides substantially worse (−.5) additional time expended by the user than EXPENSIVE.PRINTING.*

3. *CARDS provides substantially worse (−.5) additional time expended by the user than DASD.*

4. *CARDS provides substantially worse (−.5) additional time expended by the user than CHEAP.PRINTING.*

5. *CARDS provides substantially worse (−.5) additional time expended by the user than COPY.*

6. *CARDS provides substantially better (.5) additional time expended by the user than DELETE.*

7. *CARDS provides substantially better (.5) additional time expended by the user than FICHE.*

Does this seem reasonable?

> YES

OK

Note that the user need not describe these parameter values with complete reliability in the context of the acquisition portion of a session: The user may initiate interactive diagnosis and repair again to refine the new value subtree's associated parameter values.

6.4 SUMMARY

In this chapter, we described strategies for refinement. Refinement strategies comprise a set of modular components: *Parameter assessors* implement strategies for capturing individual parameters; *sensitivity analyzers* indicate threshold values for individual parameters that will result in a change of preference between two alternatives; and *parameter-integrity checkers* implement value-theoretic and heuristic tests on user inputs. Refinement strategies organize these component refinement operations: *Interactive diagnosis and repair* guides the user through the computation of the difference function and provides the user with an opportunity to identify, modify, and verify the correction of a faulty parameter value; *direct parameter modification* allows the user to initiate repair directly; and *parameter suggestion* presents candidate parameters for modification. Component refinement operations are also employed in an integration of acquisition and refinement techniques for capturing new objectives and their subhierarchies.

CHAPTER 7

Implementation

Chapters 4 through 6 presented the details of IVA in an implementation-independent fashion. This chapter describes the implementation of VIRTUS and of VIRTUS applications.[124] VIRTUS, JESQ-II, RCTE, and ES-SHELL were completed largely at Stanford University, in a Xerox environment under Interlisp-D (Koto) and KEE 3.0. Additional VIRTUS components were developed at IBM's Thomas J. Watson Research Center (Yorktown Heights, New York) under Common Lisp. FORECASTER, which includes the ES-SHELL knowledge base, was implemented at IBM in a System/370 VM environment under KnowledgeTool 1.0 and SAS. In the Stanford implementation, which we detail here, VIRTUS data structures are implemented in KEE frames and in INTERLISP structures, and VIRTUS algorithms are implemented in KEE control structures (inheritance, demons, etc.) and in INTERLISP procedures.

VIRTUS comprises the following components. *Application Knowledge Bases (KBs)* (section 7.1) contain all the essential information that defines decision problems, including descriptions of alternatives, objectives, attributes, and other objects in IVA. The *Services KB* (section 7.2) includes most of the code for VIRTUS processing, including interpretation concepts (chapter 4), explanation strategies (chapter 5), refinement and acquisition strategies (chapter 6), and interface management (chapter 3). The *Device KB* and the *Topology KB* (section 7.3) implement the device-centered representation of the difference function (chapter 5). The *Presentation KB* (section 7.4) implements interpretation-concept interfaces (chapter 5).

---

[124]Non-computer-scientists may want to skip this chapter, which assumes familiarity with computer representations and techniques such as object-oriented programming, frame-based reasoning, and applicative programming.

Sections 7.1 through 7.4 describe these KBs in more detail. Section 7.5 provides a summary of this chapter.

7.1 APPLICATION KBs

Application KBs contain all the essential information that defines decision problems, including descriptions of alternatives, of objectives, of attributes, and of other objects in IVA. Application KBs are isolated from interpretation-concept interfaces, from interpretation concepts, from explanation facilities, and from refinement facilities.

Figure 7.1 depicts a KEE-generated graph of the JESQ-II KB; note the hierarchical portion's (MANAGE.QUEUE.SPACE and forward) similarity to the value tree of chapter 2. Application-KB objects include alternatives (e.g., CARDS), objectives (e.g., MINIMIZE.ADDITIONAL.COST), attributes (e.g., ADDITIONAL.COST), and decision contexts (e.g., QUEUE.SPACE.IS.FINE). Objectives, attributes, and decision contexts inherit their respective structures from generic frames in the Services KB (which is described in section 7.2). The structure of alternatives consists of one slot per decision-specific attribute, and a slot that stores a text description of the alternative. Alternative instances inherit their values from a decision-specific PROTOTYPE.ALTERNATIVE frame such as that shown in Fig. 7.2; an instance of PROTOTYPE.ALTERNATIVE, DASD, is shown in Fig. 7.3.[125]

Application KBs are organized by user, by decision, and by decision context (chapter 4), with each decision represented in an isolated KEE KB. A CONTEXT.IMPORTANCE.MAP slot is associated with each OBJECTIVE frame to specify the IMPORTANCE of that objective for each decision context known to VIRTUS.

7.2 SERVICES KB

The *Services KB* houses the essential code for VIRTUS processing and interface management. The Services KB is implemented as a KEE KB and a file of INTERLISP functions. The primary objects include

- User-interface structures (implemented in ACTIVEIMAGES), such as icons, windows, and menus
- Control facilities, such as demons (implemented in ACTIVEVALUES)
- Interpretation concepts

---

[125]Frame descriptions in this chapter include only those slots that are necessary to understand the implementation; KEE-generated slots and low-level data structures are omitted.

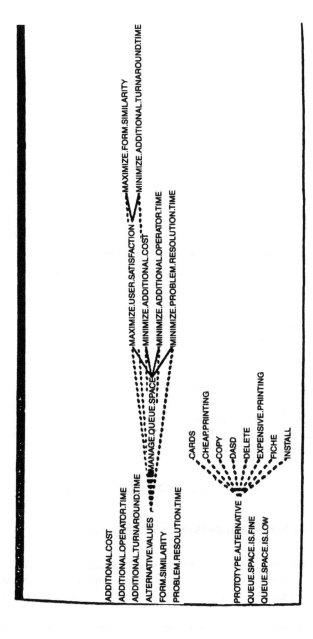

FIG. 7.1.　JESQ-II KB.

ADDITIONAL.COST
ADDITIONAL.OPERATOR.TIME
ADDITIONAL.TURNAROUND.TIME
PROBLEM.RESOLUTION.TIME
FORM.SIMILARITY
DESCRIPTION

FIG. 7.2.   PROTOTYPE.ALTERNATIVE frame from JESQ-II.

ADDITIONAL.COST .5
ADDITIONAL.OPERATOR.TIME .1
ADDITIONAL.TURNAROUND.TIME 32.1
PROBLEM.RESOLUTION.TIME 1
FORM.SIMILARITY 1
DESCRIPTION "transferring the user's dataset to his private disk storage"

FIG. 7.3.   DASD frame from JESQ-II.

- Explanation strategies
- Refinement strategies
- Context-management functions
- Value-tree-traversal functions
- Value-tree-computation functions
- Schemata for Application-KB objects
- Global variables and management functions
- Device-topology-traversal functions
- Statistical functions

The following sections elaborate the principal objects and their interactions.

7.2.1   Object-Oriented Value-Function Computation

Because subexpressions of the AMVF are accessed frequently in VIRTUS, some values are cached. Cached values include decision-context-dependent IMPORTANCE values and ABSOLUTE-QUALITY values for all objectives across all alternatives.

The value tree is implemented in an object-oriented representation that is based on KEE frames, with OBJECTIVE frames serving as primitive objects. A set of demons (implemented in ACTIVEVALUES) implements logical dependencies among objective values, and cached values are recomputed automatically whenever the values on which they depend are altered. When the IMPORTANCE of an objective is changed, for example, that objective sends a message to the objective's parent in the value tree to update ABSOLUTE-QUALITY values across all alternatives, which in turn triggers a message to the parent's parent, and so on. This explicit representation of logical dependencies enables VIRTUS to avoid recomputing any unaffected values.

7.2.2 Global Session Variables

The Services KB also manages the global session variables shown in Fig. 7.4. ALTERNATIVE.TERSENESS and OBJECTIVE.TERSENESS are the current settings of the terseness dials on VIRTUS's interface. Recall that the dials control the values of k in definitions that are based on NOTABLE? (chapter 4), which, in turn, determine the volumes of alternatives and objectives that are included in explanations. SIMILAR.THRESHOLD and DIFFERENT.THRESHOLD are thresholds that are employed in the corresponding interpretation concepts. Although only two such thresholds dials appear on the interface, an entire panel could be implemented to allow users to dial thresholds for other interpretation concepts as well.

PARAMETERS? is a flag that controls the conditional inclusion of constant-explainer outputs in explanations. NUMBERS? is a flag that controls the conditional inclusion of quantitative values for interpretation concepts in explanations. VIRTUS facilities can set these flags automatically; VIRTUS's refinement facili-

```
ALTERNATIVE.TERSENESS .75
OBJECTIVE.TERSENESS .5
SIMILAR.THRESHOLD .1
DIFFERENT.THRESHOLD .4

PARAMETERS? NIL
NUMBERS? NIL

CURRENT.CONTEXT QUEUE.SPACE.IS.FINE
CURRENT.DECISION MANAGE.QUEUE.SPACE
CURRENT.USER JEFF

USER.PROFILES
  ((JEFF ((MANAGE.QUEUE.SPACE JESQ)
          (MANAGE.HARDWARE.ERRORS HDWRE))
   (JOHN ((MANAGE.QUEUE.SPACE JESQJ)
          (MANAGE.HARDWARE.ERRORS HDWREJ))
   (DAVE ((PICK.BEST.SHELL FC)
          (PICK.BEST.STUDY REF)))
```

FIG. 7.4.   GLOBAL.SESSION.VARIABLES frame.

```
ATTRIBUTE
PSEUDO.ATTRIBUTE
DIRECTION
CONTEXT.IMPORTANCE.MAP
IMPORTANCE
STATUS
UPDATE.VX
GET.IMPORTANCE
```

FIG. 7.5.   OBJECTIVE frame.

ties, for example, include quantitative values unconditionally in all interpretation-concept displays.

7.2.3   Schemata for Application-KB Objects

The Services KB also houses the generic schemata for Application-KB objects. Whenever refinement facilities create new Application-KB objects, the structure of these objects is inherited from these schemata.

The generic structure of OBJECTIVEs is shown in Fig. 7.5; an instance of OBJECTIVE, MINIMIZE.ADDITIONAL.COST, is shown in Fig. 7.6.

ATTRIBUTE is a pointer to the associated ATTRIBUTE frame for leaf objectives, and is set to NIL for internal objectives and for VALUE. PSEUDO.ATTRIBUTE is a string of text that identifies the objective in explanations,

```
ATTRIBUTE ADDITIONAL.COST
PSEUDO.ATTRIBUTE "additional cost"
DIRECTION LESS
CONTEXT.IMPORTANCE.MAP ((QUEUE.SPACE.IS.FINE .2)
                        (QUEUE.SPACE.IS.LOW .1))
IMPORTANCE .2
STATUS PRESENT
UPDATE.VX
GET.IMPORTANCE

BEST 1
CARDS .8
CHEAP.PRINTING 1
COPY 1
DASD 1
DELETE 1
EXPENSIVE.PRINTING .4
FICHE .6
INSTALL 0
WORST 0
```

FIG. 7.6.   MINIMIZE.ADDITIONAL.COST frame.

```
MEASURED.OBJECTIVE
MEASUREMENT.UNITS

VALUE.FUNCTION
VALUE.FUNCTION.TYPE
VALUE.FUNCTION.RESULT
```

FIG. 7.7.   ATTRIBUTE frame.

```
MEASURED.OBJECTIVE MINIMIZE.ADDITIONAL.COST
MEASUREMENT.UNITS "dollars"

VALUE.FUNCTION ((0 1) (.5 1) (1 1) (20 .8) (70 .6) (100 .4) (5000 0))
VALUE.FUNCTION.TYPE DISCRETE
VALUE.FUNCTION.RESULT
```

FIG. 7.8.   ADDITIONAL.COST frame.

such as "additional cost" for MINIMIZE.ADDITIONAL.COST. DIRECTION indicates the direction of preference (*more is better* or *less is better*) for the objective. CONTEXT.IMPORTANCE.MAP captures the IMPORTANCE of the objective indexed by decision context, and the IMPORTANCE under the CURRENT.CONTEXT is cached in IMPORTANCE. STATUS records the logical status (PRESENT or ELIMINATED) of the objective in the context of vertical pruning (chapter 5), and value-tree-traversal functions (e.g., CHILDREN, PARENT) examine STATUS to provide a logical view of the value tree. This implementation strategy is employed as an alternative to deleting objectives in the context of vertical pruning; deleting objectives is impractical, requiring that the original value tree be reinstantiated for each explanation. UPDATE.VX and GET.IMPORTANCE are methods that update cached values upon receiving messages from the demons described in section 7.2.1. Along with these slots, a slot for each alternative is inherited by OBJECTIVE frames to store the cached value of ABSOLUTE-QUALITY for the alternative with respect to the objective in question.

The structure of attributes is shown in Fig. 7.7; an instance of ATTRIBUTE, ADDITIONAL.COST, is shown in Fig. 7.8. MEASURED.OBJECTIVE is a pointer to the attribute's associated leaf objective. MEASUREMENT.UNITS is a text string that describes the units of measurement for the attribute when a natural scale is employed. VALUE.FUNCTION is a representation of the component value function associated with the attribute, which depends on VALUE.FUNC-TION.TYPE. VIRTUS implements value-function computation over continuous, discrete, and interval domains.[126] VALUE.FUNCTION.RESULT is a method

---

[126]However, we have implemented parameter assessors only for discrete functions in VIRTUS, assuming a mapping from a natural scale to a value scale.

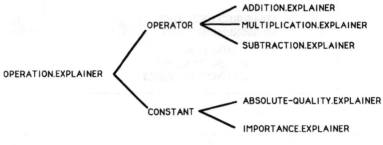

FIG. 7.9. Device KB.

for value-function computation that assists in the object-oriented scheme described in section 7.2.1.

7.2.4 VIRTUS Interface

The Services KB also houses KEE code and structures for managing the VIR-TUS interface, which is shown in Fig. 3.2 (chapter 3). The user operates VIR-TUS from the interface as follows. To begin, the user loads an Application KB by mousing on and typing into the USER, DECISION, and DECISION CON-TEXT windows. Next, the user mouses on either the EXPLAIN or the REFINE icon to display a menu of explanation or refinement facilities. Mousing the EX-PLAIN icon, for example, initiates a pop-up menu of interpretation concepts and explanation strategies (chapter 5). The user then selects the desired explanation (e.g., ALTERNATIVES-PROVIDING-BEST), and VIRTUS displays the appropriate menu(s) of parameter values (e.g., the set of objectives concerning the current decision problem) for selection. When the user is done selecting parameter values, VIRTUS paraphrases the user's explanation or refinement request in the large blank window, and then displays the requested explanation or conducts the re-quested refinement session (as described throughout chapters 5 and 6) in this win-dow. At any time during a VIRTUS session, the user can change threshold values for interpretation concepts by mousing on the dials on the VIRTUS interface (sec-tion 7.2.2).

7.3 DEVICE KB AND TOPOLOGY KB

The device-centered representation introduced in chapter 5 is implemented in an object-oriented fashion using KEE frames. The Device KB defines operation ex-plainers, and the Topology KB implements objective topologies. The Device KB is shown in Fig. 7.9.[127]

---

[127]This figure is simplified for exposition: There are actually two explainers associated with ABSOLUTE-QUALITY in our implementation (one for each alternative operand), but this design reflects parameter-passing restrictions in our implementation environment and is not of conceptual interest.

```
                        INTERESTING.OUTPUT?
                        INPUT.EXPLAINER
                        OUTPUT.EXPLAINER
```

FIG. 7.10.   OPERATION.EXPLAINER frame.

The generic OPERATION.EXPLAINER frame shown in Fig. 7.10 defines a set of slots that is inherited by OPERATOR and CONSTANT frames. Particular instances of OPERATOR and of CONSTANT (such as ADDITION.EXPLAINER and IMPORTANCE.EXPLAINER, respectively), in turn, inherit these slots, which are inherited ultimately by instances of these frames (e.g., particular ADDITION.EXPLAINERs) in the Topology KB.

INTERESTING.OUTPUT? is a lambda expression that returns T if the device's output is interesting (chapter 5) and NIL otherwise. INPUT.EXPLAINER and OUTPUT.EXPLAINER are lambda expressions that explain the inputs and outputs of operation explainers by concatenating interpretation-concept interfaces for inclusion in explanations (chapter 5).

CONSTANT explainers contain an additional slot, called REFINER. REFINER is a lambda expression that invokes the parameter assessor (chapter 6) that is associated with the parameter in question.

Rather than maintaining a fully enumerated device topology for the entire difference function, the Topology KB represents explicitly the generic device topologies (chapter 5) for leaf objectives, for internal objectives, and for VALUE, as shown in Fig. 7.11 (a)–7.11 (c). In the course of explanation and refinement, VIRTUS refers to the value tree in the current Application KB to determine the position of an objective and instantiates dynamically the associated topology as required. Maintaining a fully enumerated device topology would be computation-

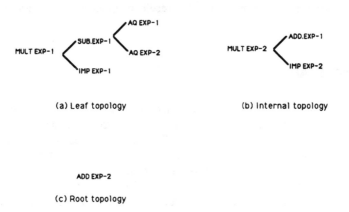

(a) Leaf topology   (b) Internal topology

(c) Root topology

FIG. 7.11. Topology KB.

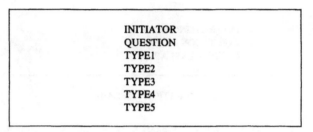

FIG. 7.12.   INTERPRETATION.CONCEPT.INTERFACE frame.

intensive, because adding objectives during the refinement process would require regenerating the entire topology dynamically.

7.4   PRESENTATION KB

The *Presentation KB* houses a set of interpretation-concept interfaces (chapter 5). Recall that interpretation-concept interfaces provide for the direct invocation of interpretation concepts, and are also invoked by OPERATION.EXPLAINERs, INPUT.EXPLAINERs, and OUTPUT.EXPLAINERs. The structure of these interfaces is inherited from a schema in the Services KB, which is shown in Fig. 7.12.

INITIATOR is a lambda expression that prompts for the arguments of the interpretation-concept interface via mouse and menu, following the receipt of a message from the VIRTUS interface. QUESTION is a lambda expression that displays a paraphrase of the question that the interface is intended to answer, with parameters instantiated (chapters 1 and 3). TYPEi is a text template that is instantiated with interpretation-concept results. Several TYPE slots can be defined to provide slight rewordings that result in smoother prose in various explanatory contexts.

7.5   SUMMARY

Chapters 4 through 6 presented the details of IVA in an implementation-independent fashion. In this chapter, we described the implementation of VIRTUS and of VIRTUS applications. VIRTUS data structures are implemented in KEE frames and in INTERLISP structures, and VIRTUS algorithms are implemented in KEE control structures (inheritance, demons, etc.) and in INTERLISP procedures. More specifically, VIRTUS comprises the following components. *Application KBs* contain all the essential information that defines decision problems, including descriptions of alternatives, of objectives, of attributes, and of other objects in IVA. The *Services KB* includes most of the code for VIRTUS processing, including interpretation concepts (chapter 4), explanation strategies (chapter 5), refinement and acquisition strategies (chapter 6), and interface management (chapter 3). The *Device KB* and the *Topology KB* implement the device-centered representation of the difference function (chapter 5). The *Presentation KB* implements interpretation-concept interfaces (chapter 5).

CHAPTER 8

Evaluation, Experience, and Observations

This chapter provides an evaluation of IVA and describes observations concerning IVA's construction. Section 8.1 presents an analytical evaluation of IVA, contrasting IVA with previous value-based systems in AI and in DA. In section 8.2, we document the development of IVA and VIRTUS, providing an anecdotal empirical evaluation and outlining the potential structure of more rigorous evaluation studies. Section 8.3 provides observations regarding the relationship between formality and transparency and discusses the potential generality of the approach that underlies the construction of IVA, with an eye toward the development of analogous frameworks to support other formal models. Section 8.4 provides a summary of this chapter.

8.1 ANALYTICAL EVALUATION

In this section, we elucidate the advantages of IVA in the context of previous value-based systems, with respect to formality and to transparency. Naturally, the limitations of previous systems need to be interpreted in an appropriate context: In examining previous heuristic models of value, it is important to note that their designers were *not* seeking a general foundation for value-based systems, as we are in this work; rather, they developed frameworks to support reasoning and explanation in particular domains, and they were not concerned with refinement. In examining previous systems that are based on decision theory, we should bear in mind that these systems, too, reflect goals that differ significantly from ours: Generally speaking, the designs of DA tools reflect an assumed audience of trained decision analysts, whereas we are concerned with tools for the intelligent-system user who may not have such training. We expose the limitations of previous value-based systems in the following sections only to demonstrate the relative advantages of IVA in the context of particular examples.

8.1.1 Formality

Chapter 2 provided a characterization of *formality* in models of value; because IVA is based on value theory, IVA is formal in this regard. In particular, we can have confidence in the results of IVA-based applications as long as we can agree with the assumptions described in chapter 2, and we can distinguish appropriate applications of IVA from inappropriate ones by observing whether these assumptions are violated systematically. These characteristics provide advantages over value-based systems that are designed to model choices in particular domains.

For example, models of value that are constructed to satisfy the requirements of particular domains sometimes lack a representation of general value-related concepts, rendering some of their results ambiguous. Consider MYCIN's revised therapy-selection algorithm (Clancey, 1984), which can be viewed as machinery for computing multiattribute choices under certainty. The following objectives are considered in various portions of the algorithm:

- Maximize drug effectiveness
- Minimize volume of drugs
- Maximize organism coverage
- Minimize redundant drug effects
- Minimize harmful reactions to drugs

In the first step of the selection algorithm, heuristic rules sort an initial list of drugs to which the organisms being considered are sensitive, to incorporate patient-specific drug-sensitivity information. This step classifies the component drugs of a candidate therapy into FIRST-, SECOND-, and THIRD-RANK drugs. The second step of the algorithm generates possible recommendations by comparing therapies according to a set of *instructions*.[128] From a value-theoretic viewpoint, each instruction can be viewed as a three-attribute alternative, with x_1 = number of FIRST-RANK drugs, x_2 = number of SECOND-RANK drugs, and x_3 = number of THIRD-RANK drugs. The set of instructions encodes a preference ordering over the universe of possible alternatives:

(1 0 0)
(2 0 0)

---

[128]The algorithm also includes a third step that is not particularly relevant to this analysis.

(1 1 0)
(1 0 1)
. . .

The earlier an alternative appears in the ordering, the greater the value of that alternative. In this list, for example, one FIRST-RANK drug is preferred to two, because (1 0 0) appears before (2 0 0).

Clancey's system performed well in the context of the cases that were tested; however, the system can produce unclear results for certain cases. Because IM-PORTANCE is not represented in the system, for example, there is no way to represent trade-offs among competing objectives, so preferences can be arbitrary: Although preference for lower-numbered (i.e., preferred) drug classes justifies a preference of, say, (1 0 0) over (0 1 0), and drug minimization justifies a prefer-ence of (1 0 0) over (2 0 0), there is no identifiable rationale to support a choice between (0 2 0) and (1 0 1). In addition, the model lacks a representation of ordi-nal relations on alternatives such as INDIFFERENT?: There is no way to express, for example, that $(x\ x\ x)$ is no better or worse than $(y\ y\ y)$. Another potential limitation is that, without sufficient representational support, explanations imply a strength of preference interpretation: Statements such as "RECOMMENDATION-2 is *substantially inferior* to RECOMMENDATION-1" are produced by the explana-tion system,[129] whereas the instructions specify only *ordinal* relationships among alternatives, and the required foundation for computing differences among alter-natives is omitted. The lack of an underlying theory raises questions of confi-dence in the model's results for such cases. There is also the question of whether these are the *only* potential anomalies; because the model was not developed from first principles, there may exist additional cases that are open to question, but we lack a systematic method for identifying them.

Because IVA is based on value theory, it represents explicitly notions that are implicit in or omitted from some heuristic value-based systems, and in a modular fashion that provides practical benefits. Should the omission of subtle notions be discovered in IVA at a later time, for example, chapter 4 could be embel-lished with additional interpretation concepts, and we could verify their consistency with existing concepts systematically by requiring the specification of a value-theoretic interpretation. In contrast, it is not clear how, in a straightforward fashion, we might embellish MYCIN with an explicit representation of trade-offs.

A related problem of heuristic value-based systems concerns the inclusion of case-specific machinery. QBKG (Ackley & Berliner, 1983; Berliner & Ackley, 1982), for example, selects among competing moves in the backgammon domain based on a directed, acyclic graph of *concepts*, called a *Judgement Structure*.[130] Concepts can be viewed roughly as objectives, and the Judgement Structure can

---

[129]Italics have been added.

[130]Following the authors, we retain the British spelling of *judgement* in describing this work.

be viewed as a value tree in which an objective can appear an arbitrary number of times.[131] In *portions* of QBKG's choice-making machinery, an AMVF-like weighted sum is computed; for example,[132]

Heur = −CostWgt*DollarValue + CalWgt*CalorieValue
DollarValue = PricePerOrange*OrangeCount + PricePerApple*AppleCount
CalorieValue = 100*OrangeCount + 150*AppleCount

Although these calculations bear syntactic similarity to the AMVF, we cannot impose a value-theoretic interpretation on them: The repetition of concepts in the Judgement Structure disallows the use of the additive form, because such repetition violates the preferential-independence assumption (chapter 2). We can speculate that this deviation from value theory led the authors to embellish *nonuniformly* the computation of concept scores with higher-order polynomial terms such as squares and cubes, and with conditionals such as

if AppleCount < 10 then PieWgt*AppleCount else Factors

Because the assumptions of the AMVF are violated, case-specific deviations from the additive form are required to offset the effects of the violations. From a pragmatic perspective, we need to be concerned that some compensatory subexpressions may have been omitted from the computation (specifically, those that failed to arise during testing), and therefore that some of QBKG's results may be questionable.[133] This potential problem might account for the fact that, "QBKG will occasionally make the wrong move in a position, or make the right move for the wrong reasons. . . ." (Berliner & Ackley, 1983, p. 47).

The same problem characterizes the original implementation of the REFEREE system (Haggerty, 1984),[134] which includes rules to compensate for preferential dependence such as

IF it is known whether the paper statistics were bad
THEN it is definite (1.0) that the following are irrelevant:
        the list of quality measures inferred by the program
        the flaws of the current paper inferred by the program

---

[131]Equivalently, the authors describe the Judgement Structure in terms of concepts with multiple parents.

[132]Here, we follow Ackley and Berliner (1983), which employs these examples rather than examples from the backgammon domain.

[133]The compensatory subexpressions also impede transparency, as is described in the next section.

[134]Recall from chapter 1 that REFEREE is a system for evaluating medical research, and that RCTE represents an attempt to resolve difficulties in REFEREE. Chapter 3 provided a detailed description of RCTE.

Because IVA is based on value theory, which specifies explicitly the required relationships among attributes, IVA-based applications require no such case-specific machinery.

In summary, IVA addresses explicitly the complexity of value-based choices in a formal fashion, providing potential pragmatic advantages. There exists an abstract argument to support the results of IVA-based models that increases the designer's confidence in such models regarding cases beyond those that have been tested empirically. In particular, the designer does not need to be concerned about including special functions (as in QBKG) or rules (as in REFEREE) to compensate for preferential dependence among objectives, and he can address the inclusion and substantiation of central value-based notions as a separate question (as in chapter 4) to avoid potential omissions of the sort exhibited by MYCIN's revised therapy-selection algorithm.

8.1.2 Transparency

Chapter 2 provided a detailed characterization of *transparency* in models of value; IVA is transparent in this regard. First, IVA defines a rich set of symbols for responding to users' queries, including a variety of interpretation concepts over alternatives and objectives (chapter 4). Second, IVA provides a natural set of operations that helps users to understand how symbols are combined in reaching conclusions (chapters 4 and 5): Addition[135] relates COMPELLINGNESS with RELATIVE-QUALITY, multiplication relates RELATIVE-QUALITY and IMPORTANCE with COMPELLINGNESS, and so on. Finally, IVA provides a natural and informative set of strategies for relating symbols that assists users in understanding model results and in modifying primitive model symbols: Interpretation-concept invocation provides the capability to inspect elements of a choice arbitrarily; combined vertical- and horizontal-pruning strategies provide a mechanism for generating concise summaries of a choice at an appropriate level of abstraction; model traversal provides the capability to inspect the choice-making machinery itself; and difference-function traversal permits inspection of a choice at a sufficient level of detail for refinement, providing the basis for interactive diagnosis and repair and for direct parameter modification. These facilities provide transparency-related advantages over previous value-based systems.

The explanation and refinement facilities of automated DA tools, for example, are limited generally to numerical and graphical displays of model values, and to primitive functions (e.g., add, modify, delete) for modifying parameters.

---

[135]Operations in the difference function should not be confused with operations of the same name in the AMVF, because their respective roles in the computation of choices are different. Addition under AMVF computation, for example, combines quantities $w_i v_i(x_i)$ (which are derivable from but not defined in IVA) to produce ABSOLUTE-QUALITY.

Lightyear (Lightyear, Inc.), for example, includes "criteria" (objectives), alternatives, and weights on objectives. The explanation component provides a "summary evaluation" that is a display of $v(a)$ for all alternatives, and a "detailed evaluation" that is a display of $v_i(a_i)$ for a selected alternative. The refinement facility is limited to the unaided modification of raw values and the addition and deletion of criteria and of alternatives. In particular, Lightyear omits pruning strategies, traversal strategies, notions of objective abstraction, consistency checking, and other central components in IVA that assist users in interpreting and modifying models of value.

IVA also provides transparency-related advantages over previous heuristic value-based systems. First, we are not aware of any heuristic value-based systems that provide a refinement component in the spirit of chapter 6; moreover, we can speculate that existing heuristic value-based systems could not easily be extended for refinement because of the lack of precision with which primitive and composite symbols are defined: Because the meanings of the symbols are open to question, and because symbols in some systems are often combined nonuniformly, explanation and refinement strategies such as computation traversal and interactive diagnosis and repair would be difficult to provide. It is unclear, for example, how QBKG's higher order polynomials (which appear in only some of the concept-score computations) should be explained or refined, because there is no analytical basis for their inclusion.

Second, the explanation facilities of heuristic value-based systems generally provide a relatively small space of user queries, such as WHY. Because these systems contain no analog of the interpretation of chapter 4 (nor of interpretation-concept invocation), users cannot arbitrarily explore a choice from multiple points of view, or at various levels of granularity.

Third, the explanation strategies of previous value-based systems generally reflect domain-specific assumptions about the potential volume of information that underlies choices. BLAH (Weiner, 1980), for example, displays exhaustively all the objectives that a user specifies; ExAct (Schulman & Hayes-Roth, 1987) displays graphically all objectives, and highlights those that are not INDIFFERENT?. Chapter 5 demonstrated that such strategies are impractical for objective populations of realistic size.

Fourth, some heuristic models fail to account for the *component differences* among alternatives, whereas empirical data (chapter 4) suggest that comparing differences is a central function in explaining choices. The original implementation of REFEREE (Haggerty, 1984), for example, describes alternatives in isolation (e.g., *This paper is good*) rather than contrasting them (e.g., *This paper is much better than that paper*). Because only isolated evaluations can be explored in more depth under REFEREE, the user cannot gain insight into how component differences are combined to yield composite differences. "The VIRTUS implementation performs better because it does a comparison and explains it well" (Lehmann, REFEREE project, personal communication, 1988).

Finally, IVA provides greater transparency than do some heuristic value-based systems because richer relationships among objectives and alternatives are represented explicitly. For example, because IVA includes notions such as IN-DIFFERENT? and IMPORTANCE explicitly, these notions are available for explanation, whereas this is not the case under systems such as MYCIN's revised therapy-selection algorithm.

In summary, IVA provides transparency-related advantages over previous value-based systems. Previous DA tools have not provided an intuitive framework for explaining choices, nor for refining them. Previous heuristic value-based systems have provided neither a general, well-formed vocabulary for talking about choices (such as the interpretation of chapter 4), nor a basis for systematic refinement (chapter 6), and many of these systems provide explanation strategies that reflect implicit domain-specific expectations about the volume of and relationships among values (unlike the strategies presented in chapter 5).

8.2 DEVELOPING AND INFORMALLY EVALUATING IVA

The development of IVA was motivated initially by the need for an explainable, maintainable conflict-resolution algorithm (in the context of the JESQ application described in chapter 2). Following current thinking (chapter 2), we first assumed that a mathematical model would fail to fulfill JESQ's transparency-related requirements, so we turned to the task of designing a specialized representation of preferences that could meet those requirements. Decision theorists pointed out that the resulting representation was similar in spirit to decision theory, although comparatively poor in rigor. This observation seemed to contradict our earlier assumption: How could decision theory be similar "in spirit" to a model developed expressly for transparency, yet be opaque, as AI researchers had warned? This inconsistency prompted a closer look at decision theory.

We found that, indeed, the essential elements of our specialized representation were present in decision theory, although somewhat obscured. This observation triggered a change in approach: Rather than devising a new model to achieve transparency, we directed our attention to explaining and refining an existing decision-theoretic model. We hoped to inherit the formality and generality of decision theory, while embellishing the theory to achieve transparency. The choice of decision-theoretic model was obvious: The AMVF was the model most often used in practice, and measurable value theory in particular supported many of the notions that we thought would be intuitively appealing. Dialogs collected from both computer operators and decision analysts confirmed this hypothesis (chapter 4).

Our initial approach to explanation was to instantiate decision-theoretic results in large chunks of canned text. We implemented this approach in a preliminary version of VIRTUS (called UTIL), using JESQ's domain as a vehicle for experimentation. Experience with computer operators was encouraging—the explanations made sense to them—but a number of problems remained. First, we found that operators wanted answers to questions that either had been omitted, or were buried in some larger response; it became apparent that a *vocabulary*, separate from the text that included it, was required. Second, we found ourselves inventing new quantities (e.g., COMPELLINGNESS), and it was necessary to ensure the consistency of their semantics with respect to previously defined terms (e.g., RELATIVE-QUALITY). Third, it became clear that the large chunks of text could not satisfactorily support refinement; a decompositional approach to explanation would be required to support refinement, as had been demonstrated in the context of rule-based systems and in qualitative physics (chapters 2 and 5).

In our next implementation of VIRTUS, we viewed explanation as a task of composing small units of text (interpretation-concept interfaces), which in turn were designed to reference decision-theoretic quantities (interpretation concepts) via function calls. We came to view refinement as a process of interrupting explanations and changing primitive statements. This approach evolved to the work reported in chapters 4 through 6.

We continued to work with the JESQ domain in building VIRTUS; conveniently, we had the benefit of verifying VIRTUS's explanations with YES/MVS project members. We searched for additional projects to facilitate our verification of the domain-independence of VIRTUS and to establish that VIRTUS would perform effectively in the context of more complicated decision problems (i.e., larger value trees). REFEREE (chapter 3) was ideal in this respect: The REFEREE project had been going on for some time at Stanford, and a value-theoretic approach seemed appropriate. Concurrently, we began the FORECASTER project at IBM, which employed what became the ES-SHELL knowledge base (chapter 3). The results in all three domains were positive: JESQ-II received a favorable evaluation from researchers and from managers on the YES/MVS project, RCTE was viewed as progressive by experts involved with earlier versions of REFEREE, and ES-SHELL seemed to impress members of the FORECASTER project.

Although encouraging, these anecdotal evaluations naturally lack the persuasiveness of more formal evaluations. A central experimental hypothesis of this work is that VIRTUS produces convincing justifications. This hypothesis might be verified formally by presenting participants with justifications composed by VIRTUS and by human experts and asking participants to identify the more convincing justification. Alternatively, we might observe the number of situations in which VIRTUS's advice, rather than that of a colleague, is followed, whenever these recommendations differ. Another experimental hypothesis of the work is that users will converge on a set of preferences in a reasonable amount of time. Convergence might be verified empirically by presenting a uniform population of users with an initial model (say, IMPORTANCE $= 1/n$, ABSOLUTE-QUALITY $=$ 0.5 except for BEST and WORST) and timing the refinement process. Another potential experiment involves providing a given user with multiple models of a particular decision and verifying that the user refines each of these models to arrive at roughly the same set of preferences. Naturally, the experimenter would be challenged by the need to control a plethora of independent variables in each of these studies.

8.3 OBSERVATIONS

In this section, we provide observations regarding the relationship between formality and transparency; then, we discuss the potential generality of the approach that underlies the construction of IVA, with an eye toward the development of analogous frameworks to support other formal models.

8.3.1 The Synergy Between Formality and Transparency

Chapter 2 described varying emphases on formality and transparency in previous value-based systems: Value-theoretic models stress formality, with transparency as a secondary goal; heuristic models of value stress transparency, with formality as a secondary goal. IVA provides a framework for value-based systems that is both formal and transparent by embellishing the transparency of a formal model of value. Observations derived from the experience of developing IVA suggest that formality and transparency are synergistic properties of representations.

First, a formal model provides a basis for defining the semantics of intermediate results, and these definitions permit the decompositional approach to explanation that facilitates interactive refinement. IVA is the only value-based system of which we are aware, for example, that defines explicitly a notion such as COMPELLING-NESS, and chapter 4 showed that fundamental decision-theoretic notions such as IMPORTANCE and RELATIVE-QUALITY can be viewed as specializations of COM-PELLINGNESS. This analysis provided the necessary conceptual link for defining strategies such as difference-function traversal.[136] Conversely, when primitive symbols are given only an intuitive semantics (without reference to a more encompassing theory), the meaning of their composition can be unclear, and intermediate results can become more difficult to interpret as the number of combining operations that determines them is increased. In the limit, a level of ambiguity may be reached where computation traversal becomes infeasible, thereby disallowing the style of refinement explored in chapter 6. In this sense, formality promotes transparency.

Second, a formal model provides a framework for addressing issues of transparency. The interpretation of every model bottoms out at the parameters; thus,

---

[136]In the case of relating COMPELLINGNESS with IMPORTANCE and RELATIVE-QUALITY, we are providing a basis for defining a multiplication explainer.

there is room for debate with regard to the interpretations of parameters that seem most natural with respect to the operations that combine these parameters. The more specific is a model in its definition, the more focused (and productive) these debates can be, because questions concerning the semantics of parameters and questions concerning the naturalness of parameters can be addressed separately. For example, debates concerning various scales of value measurement (chapters 2 and 4) focus on the relative naturalness of parameters under these scales, not on the theoretical validity of the associated results. In contrast, issues of meaning and of naturalness are ordinarily fused under heuristic models; for example, at one time, there was considerable discussion in the AI community regarding both the meaning and naturalness of certainty factors (Shortliffe & Buchanan, 1975). When Shortliffe and his colleagues later elaborated the relationship of certainty factors to utilities (Langlotz et al., 1986) and to likelihood ratios (Heckerman, 1986), however, the semantics of certainty factors were clarified, and so, knowledge engineers were provided with a basis for identifying applications in which certainty factors would likely be natural quantities for users to specify. Thus, debates about the naturalness of parameters are more focused under models that have a formal semantics. In this sense, formality promotes transparency by providing a framework for addressing issues of transparency.

Third, formality promotes transparency by providing for semantic consistency in explanations. The interpretation of chapter 4, for example, defines over 100 value-related concepts, and the mutual consistency of this volume of definitions might well be open to question were the concepts not defined with respect to a common theory. Because the substance of explanations is defined solely in terms of interpretation concepts, with interpretation-concept interfaces specifying the relationship between local form and substance (i.e., how individual interpretation-concept results are presented), and with explanation strategies specifying the relationship between global form and substance (i.e., how individual interpretation-concept interfaces are concatenated), explanations communicate consistent results, and are therefore more meaningful to users than would be explanations that might admit subtle inconsistencies. In this sense, too, does formality promote transparency.

The converse also is true: There is a sense in which transparency permits formal models to fulfill their promise. Recall from chapter 2 that the benefits of formal models can be realized only when primitive symbols are captured accurately from users. The accuracy of symbol capture relies, to a large extent, on the user's understanding of what a symbol means—that is, of how it affects the final result. Strategies such as difference-function traversal make this effect apparent by providing a step-by-step account of difference-function computation. These strategies clarify the meaning of parameters, and they therefore potentially increase the likelihood that parameters will be captured accurately. In this sense, transparency promotes the employment of formal models.

Because transparency promotes the capture of formal models, and because formality promotes the provision of transparency, we are inclined to view formality and transparency as synergistic properties of representations.

8.3.2 The Potential Generality of Our Approach

Although IVA focuses on the explanation and refinement of decision-theoretic choices, the approach underlying IVA's development may be applicable to other formal models as well.

In the context of a given model, a knowledge engineer may need to develop an alternative interpretation that corresponds more closely to intuition than does the model's standard analytical representation. The development of an interpretation might involve rewriting the model in a different form and proving that the rewritten form is equivalent to the original. Next, the designer needs to delimit subexpressions in the reformulated model and to provide each subexpression with an intuitive interpretation and with an analytical interpretation (with respect to the original theory). These subexpressions provide the basis for developing a set of packaged insights into the model that define a space of potential user queries.

A designer then constructs a set of explanation strategies for organizing elements of the interpretation. The explanation strategies may also employ elements of the interpretation in determining the structure and content of explanations. Although a designer is free to implement explanation strategies that are specific to the particular model under consideration (e.g., value-tree pruning and presentation under IVA), the basic strategy of computation traversal has potentially broader application in the context of mathematical models.

Finally, a designer develops a set of refinement strategies that is based on the explanation strategies and on the interpretation. Refinement implements an approach to model construction as iterative argument with a machine, which terminates whenever the machine's argument converges with that of the user. The approach employs computation traversal to provide the user with a step-by-step account of a computation and invokes parameter assessors, sensitivity analyzers, and parameter-integrity checkers whenever the user identifies parameters for modification. Although the definitions of these components are model-specific, their respective roles in refinement might be similar across models.

Because the general organization of IVA seems to be independent of any particular model, we observe that this organization might facilitate the development of analogous frameworks for explaining and refining other formal models in the context of intelligent systems.

8.4 SUMMARY

In this chapter, we provided an evaluation of IVA and described observations concerning IVA's construction. We presented an analytical evaluation of IVA, contrasting IVA with previous value-based systems in AI and in DA, and we concluded that IVA provides practical formality- and transparency-related benefits in the context of value-based systems:

- We can have confidence in IVA-based applications as long as we can agree with the assumptions described in chapter 2
- We can distinguish appropriate applications of IVA from inappropriate ones by observing whether these assumptions are violated systematically in the context of knowledge engineering
- Value theory enjoys a history of application in diverse domains, and IVA inherits the theory's breadth of application
- IVA defines a rich set of symbols for responding to users' queries, including a variety of interpretation concepts over alternatives and objectives
- IVA provides a natural set of operations that helps users to understand how symbols are combined in reaching conclusions
- IVA provides a natural and informative set of strategies for relating symbols that assists users in understanding model results and in modifying primitive model symbols

In short, IVA provides a general foundation for value-based systems that are at once formally justifiable, intelligible, and modifiable.

We also described the development of IVA and VIRTUS, provided an anecdotal empirical evaluation, and described the potential structure of more rigorous evaluation studies. Finally, we reflected on observations regarding the relationship between formality and transparency and discussed the potential generality of the approach that underlies the construction of IVA, with an eye toward the development of analogous frameworks to support other formal models.

CHAPTER 9

Summary, Contributions, and Future Work

This chapter provides a summary of the material presented in this book. Section 9.1 presents a summary of IVA and its applications. Section 9.2 reviews the contributions of the research. Section 9.3 describes opportunities for future work in the context of IVA's and of VIRTUS's limitations. Section 9.4 provides concluding remarks.

9.1 SUMMARY

In this book, we presented *Interpretive Value Analysis (IVA)*, a framework for modeling value-based choices in the context of intelligent systems. The design of IVA reflects empirical observations; interviews with both decision analysts and nonanalysts suggest an intuitive framework for talking about value and value-based choices. This framework provides a basis for developing an alternative *interpretation* for the *additive multiattribute value function (AMVF)* that retains the AMVF's rigor but is more intuitive. The interpretation provides a formal vocabulary of over 100 *interpretation concepts* for talking about value-based choices. We developed the interpretation in two stages: reformulation and analysis. Chapter 4 described the interpretation in detail.

We defined a set of *explanation strategies* based on the vocabulary of interpretation concepts. The purpose of the strategies is to provide the user with sufficient insight into a model's operation either (a) to become convinced that the chosen alternative is indeed preferred, or (b) to identify for correction a model parameter that deviates from his preferences. Interpretation concepts are employed as the primitive elements of explanations and as evaluation functions that guide the organization and content of the explanations.

IVA includes four classes of explanation strategies. *Interpretation-concept invocation* involves providing the user with simple interfaces for arbitrarily invoking interpretation concepts in exploring a decision. *Value-tree pruning and presentation* involves summarizing a choice between two particular alternatives in a population, guided by the structure of the value tree. *Difference-function traversal* exposes the details of a choice between two particular alternatives in a population. *Model traversal* provides an abstract description of how choices are computed. Together, the explanation strategies provide a space of options that can be implemented in isolation or in combination by knowledge engineers. IVA thus provides a general specification for a variety of explanation systems. Chapter 5 described these explanation strategies in detail and demonstrated how designers can combine explanation strategies to implement common intelligent-system commands such as WHY and HOW, and to produce intuitive reports that describe decisions.

We defined a set of *refinement strategies* based on the explanation strategies and on the interpretation. *Interactive diagnosis and repair* guides the user through the computation of the difference function and provides the user with an opportunity to identify, modify, and verify the correction of a faulty parameter value. This strategy is potentially useful for resolving perceived inconsistencies with reality in an existing model of value. *Direct parameter modification* allows the user to initiate repair directly. Under this strategy, the user decides on his own to modify a parameter, without performing interactive diagnosis. Direct parameter modification is potentially useful when a change in an environment (e.g., a corporate directive to reduce costs) necessitates a corresponding change to an existing model of value, but the appropriate degree of change is unclear. Finally, *parameter suggestion* is a set of heuristic strategies for presenting candidate parameters for modification. The user might initiate parameter suggestion to identify logical parameters to investigate. Chapter 6 described these refinement strategies in detail.

Many of the elements of IVA are implemented in VIRTUS, a shell for building value-based systems. VIRTUS is a domain-independent and architecture-independent module that can be used in isolation or in concert with other representations. Three practical value-based systems have been constructed using VIRTUS: JESQ-II is a system that chooses among competing alternative actions in managing a large computer complex; RCTE is a program for evaluating clinical research in medicine; and ES-SHELL is an application for choosing among competing expert-system shells. These systems demonstrate the range of IVA-based applications, underscoring the generality of our approach. Chapter 3 described VIRTUS, JESQ-II, RCTE, and ES-SHELL.

9.2 CONTRIBUTIONS

The work reported in this book addresses open problems in AI and in DA.

9.2.1 Artificial Intelligence

A Formal and Transparent Framework for Value-Based Systems.
IVA provides a general foundation for building value-based systems that are at
once formally justifiable, intelligible, and modifiable. The formality with which
IVA is defined provides confidence in the results of IVA-based applications and
provides a basis for identifying appropriate applications. IVA also is transparent
in its operation, defining a rich set of symbols for responding to users' queries
(chapter 4), a natural set of operations that helps users to understand how symbols are combined in reaching conclusions (chapters 4 and 5), and a natural and
informative set of strategies for relating symbols that assists users in understanding model results and in modifying primitive model symbols (chapters 5 and 6).

*An Approach to Employing Formal Mathematical Models in Intelli-
gent Systems.*   The book outlines an approach to employing formal models
in the context of intelligent systems; chapter 8 provided an abstract characterization of this approach. Because the general organization of IVA seems to be independent of any particular model, this organization might facilitate the
development of analogous frameworks for explaining and refining other formal
models in the context of intelligent systems.

9.2.2 Decision Analysis

A Tool for Justifying Decision-Theoretic Advice in Intuitive Terms.
Several authors have noted that, without the assistance of a trained decision analyst,
it can be difficult for a nonanalyst to interpret the results of a decision analysis
and, hence, to adopt decision-analytic advice (chapter 2). By describing the results
of a decision analysis in intuitive terms, an IVA-based system provides the user
with a justification for its advice that is likely to be more convincing than would
be an abstract extolment of the virtues of DA. IVA potentially provides a basis
for increasing the acceptance of decision-theoretic advice.

A Tool for Managing Bias in Parameter Assessment.   Biases in acquiring decision-theoretic models impede the effectiveness of such models. In
part, such biases are due to users' lack of understanding of the information being
elicited (chapter 2). Under traditional assessment techniques, respondents are required to assess parameters that are employed in (what they perceive to be) a

complex black box (i.e., decision theory). In contrast, IVA allows users to observe the step-by-step effect of a parameter value on the final result. This style of parameter assessment is intended to encourage users to view parameters as knobs that can be turned to influence the final result in a particular way. Because the meaning of parameters is made accessible to users through direct observation and manipulation, parameter elicitation under IVA may be influenced less by the particular fashion in which parameter-assessment questions are posed.

A Tool for Reducing the Cost of Initial Parameter Assessment.
Recall from chapter 3 that IVA encourages the analyst to employ relatively inexpensive parameter-assessment procedures, because IVA provides a vehicle for incremental model repair. Of particular interest are assessment methods that do not require the user to think hard initially about trade-offs among objectives. Whatever acquisition methods are chosen, the existence of a refinement facility permits the capture of only rough approximations of parameters during acquisition because the user is provided with an opportunity to effect subsequent refinements in the context of model operation, when he is already thinking hard about particular choices.

A Tool for Managing Preferences Over Time.   DA techniques have been employed mostly in the context of important, one-time decisions. In contrast, models that are employed for repetitive decision making are evolving entities, and support for their incremental modification is among their principal requirements. IVA addresses this requirement by providing a tool for managing preferences over time.

9.3 LIMITATIONS AND FUTURE WORK

We can identify four classes of opportunities for extending the work presented in this book: extensions to VIRTUS (section 9.3.1), extensions to IVA (section 9.3.2), the integration of IVA with other intelligent-system representations (section 9.3.3), and the development of a comprehensive framework for modeling decisions in intelligent systems (section 9.3.4).

9.3.1 Extensions to VIRTUS

The current implementation of VIRTUS could be enhanced in a number of respects. The current interface is limited, for example, and we might replace VIRTUS's menu-driven input facilities with a more sophisticated front end. One possibility is to parse constrained text that includes tokens such as OBJECTIVE and ALTERNATIVE. More sophisticated text-generation techniques might also be employed, and the resulting text could be embellished with graphical displays. In particular, graphical displays of relevant portions of the value tree (e.g., sub-hierarchy displays) and of attribute values (e.g., bar charts) would be useful, as they are in current DA tools. In addition, the styling of VIRTUS's interpretation-concept interfaces could be improved. Another obvious enhancement is to embellish VIRTUS with more sophisticated parameter assessors. Finally, as we noted in Chapter 8, we would want to perform a more rigorous evaluation of VIRTUS before deploying VIRTUS in a production setting.

9.3.2 Extensions to IVA

IVA's interpretation, its explanation strategies, and its refinement strategies might be extended. Although the interpretation provides over 100 interpretation concepts, for example, it seems likely that this vocabulary could be embellished with additional concepts. There also exists an opportunity to embellish IVA with additional explanation and refinement strategies; with the essential components of the representation (e.g., value tree, operation explainers, difference-function topologies) in place, the development of new strategies is an isolated task. In particular, it would be interesting to explore refinement strategies that reflect the possibility of multiple faults in the difference function; the refinement strategies of chapter 6 reflect a single-fault assumption.[137]

IVA might also be extended in more general ways. First, IVA might be enhanced to accommodate explicitly multiattribute choices under *uncertainty*. Recall from chapter 1 that authors have questioned the distinction between certain and uncertain models of choice (Barron, von Winterfeldt, & Fischer, 1984; Dyer & Sarin, 1979; Sarin, 1982; von Winterfeldt & Edwards, 1986), particularly in the context of repetitive choices; thus, there is a sense in which IVA already addresses multiattribute choices under uncertainty. However, IVA does not address the explicit representation, explanation, and refinement of uncertainty in models of choice.

Another obvious area for extension, although a less pragmatically motivated one, involves accommodating other forms of the value function, such as the multiplicative form. A more interesting endeavor would be to apply the approach to developing IVA (chapters 3 and 8) to formal models from other disciplines, such as queueing theory or linear programming. Obviously, the development of an IVA-like framework for any of these models represents an effort-intensive research task in itself.

9.3.3 Integration of IVA with Other Representations

Another extension to this work concerns the integration of IVA with common intelligent-system representations. Experiments of potential interest abound, such

---

[137]This limitation is not particularly significant, however, because the user can initiate refinement an arbitrary number of times to address multiple potential faults.

as the integration of IVA with analogous facilities for theorem provers and for causal models. Consider, for instance, the integration of VIRTUS's explanation facilities with those of a forward-chaining rule-based system such as JESQ. Recall from chapter 2 that the antecedents of JESQ's rules list the conditions under which the plans encoded in rule consequents are eligible for execution. Explaining the actions of such a system involves explaining not only the system's choice of plan, but also the conditions under which the plan is applicable, and the component steps that constitute the plan. In the context of such rule-based systems, comprehensive explanations might be generated by an explanation supervisor that invokes an explanation routine that is appropriate to the current state of the system: In response to "WHY-NOT alternative **a**?", when **a** is in the conflict set, for example, the supervisor would invoke the WHY-NOT module described in chapter 5; when **a** is not in the conflict set, the supervisor would invoke instead a rule-antecedent explanation routine that describes the conditions under which **a** is applicable, and indicates the antecedent's failed (i.e., unmatched) conditions. In the latter case, it is **a**'s *ineligibility* that prevents its execution, rather than its relative *undesirability*. In a similar fashion, a separate module could be employed to describe the component steps of plans (as listed in the consequents of rules), which are canned in the current implementation of VIRTUS.

9.3.4 Toward an Interpretive Decision Analysis

IVA is limited to computing, explaining, and refining value-based choices. Recall from chapter 3 that IVA requires an initial problem structure that includes the definition of alternatives, as well as a fairly complete value tree. VIRTUS provides no facilities for helping users to structure decision problems, and central model construction tasks require the assistance of a trained decision analyst. Although researchers have made important advances in automating problem structuring (chapter 2), significant work remains.

Ultimately, we might combine IVA, frameworks for automating problem structuring, and frameworks for automating the explanation and refinement of other decision-theoretic models in a unified framework — an *Interpretive Decision Analysis* — for defining, acquiring, executing, explaining, and refining models of choice in an intelligent-system context. The ideal system would access general storehouses of information to help users identify the objectives and alternatives associated with arbitrary problems. The system would select a specific form of utility or value function for the problem at hand and aid in the acquisition of this function. The system would produce concise, convincing explanations for its choices and would make it convenient for users to focus on precisely those portions of decision-theoretic models that need to be repaired. Obviously, significant work will be required before this ideal can be achieved.

9.4 CONCLUDING REMARKS

In this book, we have demonstrated the feasibility of building on a formal model of value to provide a framework for value-based systems that is both formal and transparent. In particular, chapters 4, 5, and 6 demonstrated that IVA increases the transparency of value theory, without compromising its rigor. More generally, our methodology suggests that formal methods from disciplines outside AI can provide a foundation for satisfying the requirements of intelligent systems — sound reasoning, intelligibility, and modifiability — despite the presumed opacity of such methods. Upon closer inspection of presumably opaque models, researchers may often find that problems of transparency can be overcome.

VIRTUS Report

ANALYSIS OF THE QUEUE SPACE DECISION

1. Problem Statement

JES queue space is at an acceptable level, but there is a 1,000,000 line dataset on the queue awaiting a printer that will not be repaired for another 30 minutes. The problem is to maximize overall queue space management effectiveness given the following alternative actions:

1. INSTALL: installing a new printer
2. EXPENSIVE.PRINTING: printing the user's dataset on a fast, high quality printer
3. DASD: transferring the user's dataset to his private disk storage for later printing
4. CHEAP.PRINTING: printing the user's dataset on the slow, low quality printer
5. COPY: transferring the user's dataset to tape for later printing
6. DELETE: deleting the user's dataset
7. FICHE: transferring the user's dataset to microfiche
8. CARDS: transferring the user's dataset to punched cards

2. Solution Summary

DASD is the best with regard to overall queue space management effectiveness. DASD provides notably good additional cost and problem resolution time. Models reflecting the views of shift managers Joe and Tom produce the same choice.

191

EXPENSIVE.PRINTING, DASD, and CHEAP.PRINTING provide notably good overall queue space management effectiveness. Only INSTALL provides notably poor overall queue space management effectiveness. COPY, DELETE, FICHE, and CARDS provide neither notably good nor poor overall queue space management effectiveness. Close contenders of DASD include EXPENSIVE.PRINTING and CHEAP.PRINTING.

3. The Decision-Making Process

In the abstract, choosing among actions to promote overall queue space management effectiveness is similar to choosing actions to promote effective hardware recovery.

Evaluating the overall queue space management effectiveness of an alternative involves considerations of overall user satisfaction, problem resolution time, additional cost, and additional operator time. Overall user satisfaction accounts for 50.0 percent of the determination of overall queue space management effectiveness when JES queue space is at an acceptable level. Problem resolution time accounts for 20.0 percent. Additional cost accounts for 20.0 percent. Additional operator time accounts for 10.0 percent.

Evaluating the overall user satisfaction of an alternative involves considerations of similarity to the user's requested form and additional turnaround time. Similarity to the user's requested form accounts for 50.0 percent of the determination of overall user satisfaction when JES queue space is at an acceptable level. Additional turnaround time accounts for 50.0 percent.

4. Brief Analysis of the Decision

DASD is the best alternative with regard to overall queue space management effectiveness. EXPENSIVE.PRINTING is the next best. CHEAP.PRINTING is the next best. COPY is the next best. DELETE is the next best. CARDS is the next best. FICHE is the next best. INSTALL is the next best.

Close contenders of DASD include EXPENSIVE.PRINTING and CHEAP.PRINTING. DASD, for example, provides infinitesimally better overall queue space management effectiveness than EXPENSIVE.PRINTING. Compelling reasons to prefer EXPENSIVE.PRINTING, such as overall user satisfaction, are outweighed by considerations of additional cost, along with less compelling reasons that recommend DASD. Another example: DASD provides infinitesimally better overall queue space management effectiveness than CHEAP.PRINTING. Compelling reasons to prefer CHEAP.PRINTING, such as additional turnaround time, are outweighed by considerations of problem resolution time, along with less compelling reasons that recommend DASD.

To summarize:

1. DASD provides substantially better overall queue space management effectiveness than INSTALL.

2. DASD provides infinitesimally better overall queue space management effectiveness than EXPENSIVE.PRINTING.

3. DASD provides infinitesimally better overall queue space management effectiveness than CHEAP.PRINTING.

4. DASD provides infinitesimally better overall queue space management effectiveness than COPY.

5. DASD provides reasonably better overall queue space management effectiveness than DELETE.

6. DASD provides reasonably better overall queue space management effectiveness than FICHE.

7. DASD provides reasonably better overall queue space management effectiveness than CARDS.

5. Brief Analysis of Close Contenders

Close contenders of DASD include EXPENSIVE.PRINTING and CHEAP.PRINTING. Supporting analyses follow.

DASD vs. EXPENSIVE.PRINTING

DASD provides infinitesimally better overall queue space management effectiveness than EXPENSIVE.PRINTING.

Overall user satisfaction is a compelling factor favoring EXPENSIVE.PRINTING over DASD. Overall user satisfaction accounts for 50.0 percent of the determination of overall queue space management effectiveness when JES queue space is at an acceptable level. Additional turnaround time is a compelling factor favoring EXPENSIVE.PRINTING over DASD in determining overall user satisfaction. DASD provides substantially worse additional turnaround time than EXPENSIVE.PRINTING. Since EXPENSIVE.PRINTING involves 0 minutes of additional turnaround time, EXPENSIVE.PRINTING rates 10 on a scale from 0 (worst) to 10 (best).

Additional cost is a compelling factor favoring DASD over EXPENSIVE.PRINTING. DASD provides substantially better additional cost than EXPENSIVE.PRINTING. Since EXPENSIVE.PRINTING involves 100 dollars of additional cost, EXPENSIVE.PRINTING rates 4.0 on a scale from 0 (worst) to 10 (best). Since DASD involves .5 dollars of additional cost, DASD rates 10 on a scale from 0 (worst) to 10 (best).

DASD vs. CHEAP.PRINTING

DASD provides infinitesimally better overall queue space management effectiveness than CHEAP.PRINTING.

Problem resolution time is a compelling factor favoring DASD over CHEAP.PRINTING. DASD provides substantially better problem resolution time than CHEAP.PRINTING. Since DASD involves 1 minute of problem resolution time, DASD rates 10 on a scale from 0 (worst) to 10 (best).

6. Detailed Analysis of Close Contenders

Close contenders of DASD include EXPENSIVE.PRINTING and CHEAP.PRINTING. Supporting analyses follow.

DASD vs. EXPENSIVE.PRINTING

DASD provides infinitesimally better (.05) overall queue space management effectiveness than EXPENSIVE.PRINTING. This determination reflects considerations of additional operator time, additional cost, problem resolution time, and overall user satisfaction. While overall user satisfaction $(-.15)$ provides a compelling reason to prefer EXPENSIVE.PRINTING, this is outweighed by considerations of additional cost (.12), along with other less compelling reasons (.08), that provide motivation for preferring DASD.

Overall user satisfaction is a compelling $(-.15)$ factor favoring EXPENSIVE.PRINTING over DASD. This determination reflects considerations of additional turnaround time and similarity to the user's requested form. While DASD does not provide notably different $(-.3)$ overall user satisfaction from EXPENSIVE.PRINTING relative to other factors, overall user satisfaction is sufficiently important (.5) in determining overall queue space management effectiveness to make overall user satisfaction a notably compelling $(-.15)$ factor in this particular decision. DASD provides somewhat worse $(-.3)$ overall user satisfaction than EXPENSIVE.PRINTING. EXPENSIVE.PRINTING is at least as good as DASD regarding all objectives that underlie the choice with respect to overall user satisfaction. Additional turnaround time $(-.3)$ provides the most compelling reason. Overall user satisfaction accounts for 50.0 percent of the determination of overall queue space management effectiveness when JES queue space is at an acceptable level.

Additional turnaround time is a compelling $(-.3)$ factor favoring EXPENSIVE.PRINTING over DASD in determining overall user satisfaction. While additional turnaround time is not notably important (.5) in determining overall user satisfaction, DASD provides sufficiently different $(-.6)$ additional turnaround time from EXPENSIVE.PRINTING relative to other factors to make additional turnaround time a notably compelling ($-.3$) factor in this particular decision. DASD provides substantially worse ($-.6$) additional turnaround time than EXPENSIVE.PRINTING. DASD provides neither notably good nor poor additional turnaround time in the context of all available alternatives. EXPENSIVE.PRINTING provides notably good additional turnaround time in the context of all available alternatives. Since EXPENSIVE.PRINTING involves 0 minutes of additional turnaround time, EXPENSIVE.PRINTING rates 10 on a scale from 0 (worst) to 10 (best). Since DASD involves 32.1 minutes of additional turnaround time, DASD rates 4.0 on a scale from 0 (worst) to 10 (best). Additional turnaround time accounts for 50.0 percent of the determination of overall user satisfaction when JES queue space is at an acceptable level.

Similarity to the user's requested form is an inconsequential (0.0) factor in the choice between DASD and EXPENSIVE.PRINTING in determining overall user satisfaction. DASD provides no better or worse (0.0) similarity to the user's requested form than EXPENSIVE.PRINTING. DASD provides notably good similarity to the user's requested form in the context of all available alternatives. EXPENSIVE.PRINTING provides notably good similarity to the user's requested form in the context of all available alternatives. Since EXPENSIVE.PRINTING involves 1 subjective unit of similarity to the user's requested form, EXPENSIVE.PRINTING rates 10 on a scale from 0 (worst) to 10 (best). Since DASD involves 1 subjective unit of similarity to the user's requested form, DASD rates 10 on a scale from 0 (worst) to 10 (best). Similarity to the user's requested form accounts for 50.0 percent of the determination of overall user satisfaction when JES queue space is at an acceptable level.

Additional cost is a compelling (.12) factor favoring DASD over EXPENSIVE.PRINTING. While additional cost is not notably important (.2) in determining overall queue space management effectiveness, DASD provides sufficiently different (.6) additional cost from EXPENSIVE.PRINTING relative to other factors to make additional cost a notably compelling (.12) factor in this particular decision. DASD provides substantially better (.6) additional cost than EXPENSIVE.PRINTING. DASD provides notably good additional cost in the context of all available alternatives. EXPENSIVE.PRINTING provides notably poor additional cost in the context of all available alternatives. Since EXPENSIVE.PRINTING involves 100 dollars of additional cost, EXPENSIVE.PRINTING rates 4.0 on a scale from 0 (worst) to 10 (best). Since DASD involves .5 dollars of additional cost, DASD rates 10 on a scale from 0 (worst) to 10 (best). Additional cost accounts for 20.0 percent of the determination of overall queue space management effectiveness when JES queue space is at an acceptable level.

Problem resolution time is a factor favoring DASD over EXPENSIVE.PRINTING, although not a compelling one (.08). Problem resolution time is not notably compelling (.08) in this particular choice because problem resolution time is not notably important (.2) in determining overall queue space management effectiveness, and DASD does not provide notably different (.4) problem resolution time from EXPENSIVE.PRINTING relative to other factors. DASD provides reasonably better (.4) problem resolution time than EXPENSIVE.PRINTING. DASD provides notably good problem resolution time in the context of all available alternatives. EXPENSIVE.PRINTING provides neither notably good nor poor problem resolution time in the context of all available alternatives. Since EXPENSIVE.PRINTING involves 25 minutes of problem resolution time, EXPENSIVE.PRINTING rates 6.0 on a scale from 0 (worst) to 10 (best). Since DASD involves 1 minute of problem resolution time, DASD rates 10 on a scale from 0 (worst) to 10 (best). Problem resolution time accounts for 20.0 percent of the determination of overall queue space management effectiveness when JES queue space is at an acceptable level.

Additional operator time is an inconsequential (0.0) factor in the choice between DASD and EXPENSIVE.PRINTING. DASD provides no better or worse (0.0) additional operator time than EXPENSIVE.PRINTING. DASD provides neither notably good nor poor additional operator time in the context of all available alternatives. EXPENSIVE.PRINTING provides neither notably good nor poor additional operator time in the context of all available alternatives. Since EXPENSIVE.PRINTING involves .1 minutes of additional operator time, EXPENSIVE.PRINTING rates 10 on a scale from 0 (worst) to 10 (best). Since DASD involves .1 minutes of additional operator time, DASD rates 10 on a scale from 0 (worst) to 10 (best). Additional operator time accounts for 10.0 percent of the determination of overall queue space management effectiveness when JES queue space is at an acceptable level.

DASD vs. CHEAP.PRINTING

DASD provides infinitesimally better (.07) overall queue space management effectiveness than CHEAP.PRINTING. This determination reflects considerations of additional operator time, additional cost, problem resolution time, and overall user satisfaction. Problem resolution time (.12) provides the most compelling reason.

Problem resolution time is a compelling (.12) factor favoring DASD over CHEAP.PRINTING. While problem resolution time is not notably important (.2) in determining overall queue space management effectiveness, DASD provides sufficiently different (.6) problem resolution time from CHEAP.PRINTING relative to other factors to make problem resolution time a notably compelling (.12) factor in this particular decision. DASD provides substantially better (.6) problem resolution time than CHEAP.PRINTING. DASD provides notably good problem resolution time in the context of all available alternatives. CHEAP.PRINTING provides neither notably good nor poor problem resolution time in the context of all available alternatives. Since CHEAP.PRINTING involves 40 minutes of problem resolution time, CHEAP.PRINTING rates 4.0 on a scale from 0 (worst) to 10 (best). Since DASD involves 1 minute of problem resolution time, DASD rates 10 on a scale from 0 (worst) to 10 (best). Problem resolution time accounts for 20.0 percent of the determination of overall queue space management effectiveness when JES queue space is at an acceptable level.

Overall user satisfaction is a factor favoring CHEAP.PRINTING over DASD, although not a compelling one (−.05). This determination reflects considerations of additional turnaround time and similarity to the user's requested form. While overall user satisfaction is notably important (.5) in determining overall queue space management effectiveness, DASD does not provide sufficiently different (−.1) overall user satisfaction from CHEAP.PRINTING relative to other factors to consider overall user satisfaction a notably compelling (−.05) factor in this particular decision. DASD provides only marginally worse (−.1) overall user satisfaction than CHEAP.PRINTING. Additional turnaround time (−.2) provides the most compelling reason. Overall user satisfaction accounts for 50.0 percent of the determination of overall queue space management effectiveness when JES queue space is at an acceptable level.

Additional turnaround time is a compelling (−.2) factor favoring CHEAP.PRINTING over DASD in determining overall user satisfaction. While additional turnaround time is not notably important (.5) in determining overall user satisfaction, DASD provides sufficiently different (−.4) additional turnaround time from CHEAP.PRINTING relative to other factors to make additional turnaround time a notably compelling (−.2) factor in this particular decision. DASD provides reasonably worse (−.4) additional turnaround time than CHEAP.PRINTING. DASD provides neither notably good nor poor additional turnaround time in the context of all available alternatives. CHEAP.PRINTING provides notably good additional turnaround time in the context of all available alternatives. Since CHEAP.PRINTING involves 10 minutes of additional turnaround time, CHEAP.PRINTING rates 8.0 on a scale from 0 (worst) to 10 (best). Since DASD involves 32.1 minutes of additional turnaround time, DASD rates 4.0 on a scale from 0 (worst) to 10 (best). Additional turnaround time accounts for 50.0 percent of the determination of overall user satisfaction when JES queue space is at an acceptable level.

Similarity to the user's requested form is a factor favoring DASD over CHEAP.PRINTING in determining overall user satisfaction, although not a compelling one (.1). Similarity to the user's requested form is not notably compelling (.1) in this particular choice because similarity to the user's requested form is not notably important (.5) in determining overall user satisfaction, and DASD does not provide notably different (.2) similarity to the user's requested form from CHEAP.PRINTING relative to other factors. DASD provides only marginally better (.2) similarity to the user's requested form than CHEAP.PRINTING. DASD provides notably good similarity to the user's requested form in the context of all available alternatives. CHEAP.PRINTING provides neither notably good nor poor similarity to the user's requested form in the context of all available alternatives. Since CHEAP.PRINTING involves .8 subjective units of similarity to the user's requested form, CHEAP.PRINTING rates 8.0 on a scale from 0 (worst) to 10 (best). Since DASD involves 1 subjective unit of similarity to the user's requested form, DASD rates 10 on a scale from 0 (worst) to 10 (best). Similarity to the user's requested form accounts for 50.0 percent of the determination of overall user satisfaction when JES queue space is at an acceptable level.

Additional cost is an inconsequential (0.0) factor in the choice between DASD and CHEAP.PRINTING. DASD provides no better or worse (0.0) additional cost than CHEAP.PRINTING. DASD provides notably good additional cost in the context of all available alternatives. CHEAP.PRINTING provides notably good additional cost in the context of all available alternatives. Since CHEAP.PRINT-ING involves 0 dollars of additional cost, CHEAP.PRINTING rates 10 on a scale from 0 (worst) to 10 (best). Since DASD involves .5 dollars of additional cost, DASD rates 10 on a scale from 0 (worst) to 10 (best). Additional cost accounts for 20.0 percent of the determination of overall queue space management effectiveness when JES queue space is at an acceptable level.

Additional operator time is an inconsequential (0.0) factor in the choice between DASD and CHEAP.PRINTING. DASD provides no better or worse (0.0) additional operator time than CHEAP.PRINTING. DASD provides neither notably good nor poor additional operator time in the context of all available alternatives. CHEAP.PRINTING provides neither notably good nor poor additional operator time in the context of all available alternatives. Since CHEAP.PRINTING in-volves .1 minutes of additional operator time, CHEAP.PRINTING rates 10 on a scale from 0 (worst) to 10 (best). Since DASD involves .1 minutes of addition-al operator time, DASD rates 10 on a scale from (0) worst to 10 (best). Addition-al operator time accounts for 10.0 percent of the determination of overall queue space management effectiveness when JES queue space is at an acceptable level.

References

Ackley, D., & Berliner, H. (1983). *The QBKG system: Knowledge representation for producing and explaining judgements* (Report CMU-CS-83-116, Dept. of Computer Science). Pittsburgh, PA: Carnegie Mellon University.

Aikens, J. (1980). *Prototypes and production rules: A knowledge representation for computer consultations.* Unpublished doctoral dissertation, Dept. of Computer Science, Stanford University, Stanford, CA.

Astrom, K., Anton, J., & Arzen, K. (1986). Expert control. *Automatica, 22*(3), 1–10.

Barr, A., & Feigenbaum, E. (1981). *The handbook of artificial intelligence* (Vol. 1). Los Altos, CA: William Kaufman Inc.

Barron, H., von Winterfeldt, D., & Fischer, G. (1984). Theoretical and empirical relationships between risky and riskless utility functions. *Acta Psychologica, 56*, 233–244.

Barsalou, T., Chavez, R., & Wiederhold, G. (1989). Hypertext interfaces for decision-support systems: A case study. *Proceedings of MEDINFO* (pp. 126–130). Singapore.

Beinlich, I., Suermondt, H., Chavez, R., & Cooper, G. (1989). *The ALARM monitoring system: A case study with two probabilistic inference techniques for belief networks.* (Memo KSL-88-84, Section on Medical Informatics). Stanford, CA: Stanford University.

Ben-Bassat, M., Carlson, R., Puri, V., Davenport, M., Schriver, J., Latif, M., Smith, R., Portigal, L., Lipnick, E., & Weil, M. (1980). Pattern-based interactive diagnosis of multiple disorders: The MEDAS system. *IEEE Transactions on Pattern Analysis and Machine Intelligence, PAMI-2*(2), 148–160.

Berliner, H., & Ackley, D. (1982). The QBKG system: Generating explanations from a nondiscrete knowledge representation. *Proceedings of AAAI* (pp. 213–216). Pittsburgh, PA:

Birkhoff, G., & Lipson, J. (1970). Heterogeneous algebras. *Journal of Combinatorial Theory, 8*, 115–133.

Bobrow, D. (Ed.). (1985). *Qualitative reasoning about physical systems.* Cambridge, MA: MIT Press.

Chavez, R., & Cooper, G. (1988). *KNET: Integrating hypermedia and Bayesian modelling.* (Report KSL-88-47). Stanford, CA: Knowledge Systems Laboratory, Stanford University.

Chavez, R., & Lehmann, H. (1988). REFEREE: A belief network that helps evaluate the credibility of a randomized clinical trial. *Artificial Intelligence in Medicine Workshop*, Stanford University, p. 18.

Chester, D., Lamb, D., & Dhurjati, P. (1984). Rule based alarm analysis in chemical process plants. *Proceedings of Micro-Delcon* (pp. 22–29). Silver Spring, MD.

Clancey, W. (1981). *Methodology for building an intelligent tutoring system*. (Report STAN-CS-81-894, Dept. of Computer Science). Stanford, CA: Stanford University.

Clancey, W. (1984). Details of the revised therapy algorithm. In B. Buchanan & E. H. Shortliffe (Eds.), *Rule-based expert systems*. Reading, MA: Addison-Wesley.

Cohen, M., & Axelrod, R. (1984). Coping with complexity: The adaptive value of changing utility. *American Economic Review, 74*, 30–42.

Coles, L., Robb, A., Sinclair, P., Smith, M., & Sobek, R. (1973). Decision analysis for an experimental robot with unreliable sensors. *Proceedings of IJCAI* (pp. 749–757). Georgia, USSR.

Cooper, G. (1988a). *An algorithm for computing probabilistic propositions*. (Memo KSL-87-21, Section on Medical Informatics). Stanford, CA: Stanford University.

Cooper, G. (1988b). *Computer-based medical diagnosis using belief networks and bounded probabilities*. (Memo KSL-87-48, Section on Medical Informatics). Stanford, CA: Stanford University.

Cooper, G. (1988c). *Expert systems based on belief networks – Current research directions*. (Memo KSL-87-51, Section on Medical Informatics). Stanford, CA: Stanford University.

Cromarty, A. (1985). What are current expert system tools missing?. *Proceedings of the IEEE Computer Conference* (pp. 411–418). San Francisco, CA.

Cruise, A., Ennis, R., Finkel, A., Hellerstein, J., Klein, D., Loeb, D., Masullo, M., Milliken, K., Van Woerkom, H., & Waite, N. (1986). YES/MVS and the automation of operations for large computer complexes. *IBM Systems Journal, 25*(2), 159–180.

Cruise, A., Ennis, R., Finkel, A., Hellerstein, J., Klein, D., Loeb, D., Masullo, M., Milliken, K., Van Woerkom, H., & Waite, N. (1987). YES/L1: Integrating rule-based, procedural, and real-time programming for industrial applications. *Proceedings of the Third IEEE Conference on Artificial Intelligence Applications* (pp. 134–139). Kissimmee, FL.

Cyert, R., & DeGroot, M. (1975). Adaptive utility. In R. Day & T. Groves (Eds.), *Adaptive economic models*. New York: Academic Press.

Davis, R. (1976). *Teiresias: Applications of meta-level knowledge*. Doctoral dissertation, Dept. of Computer Science, Stanford University, Stanford, CA.

Davis, R. (1980). Meta-rules: Reasoning about control. *Artificial Intelligence, 15*, 179–221.

Davis, R. (1984). Diagnostic reasoning based on structure and behavior. *Artificial Intelligence, 24*, 347–410.

Davis, R., & Buchanan, B. (1977). Meta-level knowledge: Overview and applications. *Proceedings of IJCAI* (pp. 920–927). Cambridge, MA.

DeJong, K. (1983). Intelligent control: Integrating AI and control theory. *IEEE Conference on Trends and Applications* (pp. 158–161). Gaithersburg, MD.

de Kleer, J., & Brown, J. S. (1984). A qualitative physics based on confluences. *Artificial Intelligence, 24*, 7–83.

Druzdzel, M., & Henrion, M. (1990). Qualitative propagation and scenario-based approaches to explanation of probabilistic reasoning. *Proceedings of the Sixth Conference on Uncertainty and Artificial Intelligence* (pp. 10–20). Cambridge, MA.

Dyer, J., & Sarin, R. (1979). Measurable multiattribute value functions. *Operations Research, 27*, 810–822.

Edwards, W. (1977). How to use multiattribute utility theory for social decision making. *IEEE Trans. Syst., Man, Cybern., 7*, 326–340.

Edwards, W. (1980). Reflections on and criticisms of a highly political multiattribute utility analysis. In L. Cobb & R. Thrall (Eds.), *Mathematical frontiers of behavioral and policy sciences*. Boulder, CO: Westview Press.

Edwards, W., & Newman, J. (1982). *Multiattribute evaluation*. Beverly Hills: Sage.

Einhorn, H., & Hogarth, R. (1981). Behavioral decision theory: Processes of judgement and choice. *Annual Review of Psychology, 32*, 52–88.

Elsaesser, C. (1990). *Explanation of Bayesian conditioning for decision support* (Report MP-89W00037). McLean, VA: The MITRE Corporation.

Ennis, R., Griesmer, J., Hong, S., Karnaugh, M., Kastner, J., Klein, D., Milliken, K., Schor, M., & Van Woerkom, H. (1984). YES/MVS: A continuous realtime expert system. *Proceedings of AAAI* (pp. 130–136). Austin, TX.

Ennis, R., Griesmer, J., Hong, S., Karnaugh, M., Kastner, J., Klein, D., Milliken, K., Schor, M., & Van Woerkom, H. (1986a). A continuous realtime expert system for computer operations. *IBM Journal of Research and Development, 30*(1), 14–28.

Ennis, R., Griesmer, J., Hong, S., Karnaugh, M., Kastner, J., Klein, D., Milliken, K., Schor, M., & Van Woerkom, H. (1986b). Automation of MVS operations, an expert systems approach. *Computer Systems Science and Engineering, 1*(2), 119–124.

Ennis, R., Griesmer, J., Hong, S., Karnaugh, M., Klein, D., Milliken, K., Schor, M., & Van Woerkom, H. (1984). A computer operator's expert system. *New World of the Information Society: Proceedings of the Seventh International Conference on Computer Communication* (pp. 812–817). Sydney, Australia.

Farquhar, P. (1984). Utility assessment methods. *Management Science, 30*, 1283–1300.

Farquhar, P. (1986). Applications of utility theory in artificial intelligence research. (Report TR 86-2, Graduate School of Industrial Administration). Pittsburgh, PA: Carnegie Mellon University.

Farquhar, P., & Fishburn, P. (1981). Equivalence and continuity in multivalent preference structures. *Operations Research, 29*, 282–293.

Farquhar, P., & Keller, R. (1988). *Preference intensity measurement.* (Report TR 88-2, Graduate School of Industrial Administration). Pittsburgh, PA: Carnegie Mellon University.

Feldman, J., & Sproull, R. (1975). Decision theory and artificial intelligence II: The hungry monkey. *Cognitive Science, 1*, 158–192.

Ferrante, R. (1985). The characteristic error approach to conflict resolution. *Proceedings of IJCAI* (pp. 331–334). Los Angeles, CA.

Fischer, G. (1972). *Four methods for assessing multiattribute utilities: An experimental validation* (Technical Report). University of Michigan, Engineering Psychology Laboratory. Ann Arbor.

Fischer, G. (1976). Multidimensional utility models for risky and riskless choice. *Organizational Behavior and Human Performance, 17*, 127–146.

Fischer, G. (1977). Convergent validation of decomposed multiattribute utility assessment procedures for risky and riskless decisions. *Organizational Behavior and Human Performance, 18*, 295–315.

Fischer, G. (1979). Utility models for multiple objective decisions: Do they accurately represent human preferences? *Decision Sciences, 10*, 451–479.

Fischhoff, B., Goitein, B., & Shapira, Z. (1982). *The experienced utility of expected utility approaches.* (Technical Report PTR-1091-80-4). Eugene, OR: Decision Research.

Fishburn, P. (1969). Preferences, summation, and social welfare functions. *Management Science, 16*, 179–186.

Fishburn, P. (1970). *Utility theory for decision making.* New York: Wiley.

Fleming, M. (1952). A cardinal concept of welfare. *Quarterly Journal of Economics, 66*, 366–384.

Forbus, K. (1984). Qualitative process theory. *Artificial Intelligence, 24*, 85–168.

Forbus, K., & Stevens, A. (1981). Using qualitative simulation to generate explanations. *Proceedings of the Third Annual Conference of the Cognitive Science Society* (pp. 112–116). Berkeley, CA.

Forgy, C. (1981). *OPS5 user's manual* (Report CMU-CS-81-135, Dept. of Computer Science). Pittsburgh, PA: Carnegie Mellon University.

Forgy, C. (1984). *OPS83 user's manual* (Dept. of Computer Science). Pittsburgh, PA: Carnegie Mellon University.

Friedman, L. (1985). Controlling production rule firing: The FCL language. *Proceedings of IJCAI* (pp. 359–366). Los Angeles, CA.

Gallier, J. (1986). *Logic for computer science: Foundations of automatic theorem proving.* New York: Harper & Row.

Gardiner, P. (1974). *The application of decision technology and Monte Carlo simulation to multiobjective public policy decision making.* Unpublished doctoral dissertation, University of Southern California, Los Angeles.

Genesereth, M. (1984). The use of design descriptions in automated diagnosis. *Artificial Intelligence, 24,* 411–436.

Georgeff, M. (1982). Procedural control in production systems. *Artificial Intelligence, 18,* 175–201.

Goodman, B., Saltzman, M., Edwards, W., & Krantz, D. (1979). Prediction of bids for two outcome gambles in a casino setting. *Organizational Behavior and Human Performance, 29,* 382–399.

Gorn, S. (1965). Explicit definitions and linguistic dominoes. In J. Hart & S. Takasu (Eds.), *Systems and computer science.* Toronto, Canada: University of Toronto Press.

Green, P., & Srinivasan, V. (1978). Conjoint analysis in consumer research: Issues and outlook. *Journal of Consumer Research, 5,* 103–123.

Haggerty, J. (1984). *REFEREE and RULECRITIC: Two prototypes for assessing the quality of a medical paper.* Unpublished master's thesis, Dept. of Computer Science, Stanford University, Stanford, CA.

Hauser, J., & Shugan, S. (1980). Intensity measures of consumer preference. *Operations Research, 28,* 278–320.

Heckerman, D. (1986). Probabilistic interpretations for MYCIN's certainty factors. In L. Kanal & J. Lemmer (Eds.), *Uncertainty in artificial intelligence* (pp. 167–196). Amsterdam, The Netherlands: Elsevier Science Publishers.

Heckerman, D. (1991). *Probabilistic similarity networks.* Cambridge, MA: MIT Press.

Henrion, M., & Cooley, D. (1987). An experimental comparison of knowledge engineering for expert systems and for decision analysis. *Proceedings of AAAI* (pp. 471–476). Seattle, WA: Morgan Kaufmann Publishers.

Hershey, J., Kunreuther, H., & Schoemaker, P. (1982). Sources of bias in assessment procedures for utility functions. *Management Science, 28,* 936–956.

Higgens, P. (1962). Algebras with a scheme of operators. *Eingegangen am, 8*(8), 115–132.

Hogarth, R. (1980). *Judgment and choice: The psychology of decisions.* Chichester, England: Wiley.

Holloway, C. (1979). *Decision making under uncertainty.* Englewood Cliffs, NJ: Prentice-Hall.

Holtzman, S. (1989). *Intelligent decision systems.* Reading, MA: Addison-Wesley.

Hoepfl, R., & Huber, G. (1970). A study of self-explicated utility models. *Behavioral Science, 5,* 408–414.

Horvitz, E. (1987). *A multiattribute utility approach to inference understandability and explanation.* (Memo KSL-87-28, Section on Medical Informatics). Stanford, CA: Stanford University.

Horvitz, E. (1988). Reasoning under varying and uncertain resource constraints. *Proceedings of AAAI* (pp. 111–116). St. Paul, MN.

Horvitz, E., Breese, J., & Henrion, M. (1988). Decision theory in expert systems and artificial intelligence. *Journal of Approximate Reasoning, 2,* 247–302.

Horvitz, E., Heckerman, D., Nathwani, B., & Fagan, L. (1984). Diagnostic strategies in the hypothesis-directed PATHFINDER system. *Proceedings of the First IEEE Conference on Artificial Intelligence Applications* (pp. 630–636). Denver, CO: IEEE Society Publishers.

Howard, R. (1968). The foundations of decision analysis. *IEEE Transactions on Systems, Science, and Cybernetics* SSC-4 (pp. 211–219).

Howard, R., & Matheson, J. (1980). *Influence diagrams* (Technical Report, SRI International). Menlo Park, CA.

Humphreys, P., & Wishuda, A. (1980). *Multiattribute utility decomposition* (Report 72-2/2). Uxbridge, Middlesex, England: Brunel Institute of Organizational and Social Studies, Decision Analysis Unit.

Humphreys, P., & Wishuda, A. (1987). *Methods and tools for structuring and analyzing decision problems* (Vols. 1 and 2, Technical Report). London: London School of Economics and Political Science: Decision Analysis Unit.

Jacobs, W., & Keifer, M. (1973). Robot decisions based on maximizing utility. *Proceedings of IJCAI* (pp. 402–411). Georgia, USSR.

Jimison, H. (1988). *A representation for gaining insight into clinical decision models.* (Memo KSL-88-75, Section on Medical Informatics). Stanford, CA: Stanford University.

John, R. (1984). *Value tree analysis of social conflicts about risky technologies.* Unpublished doctoral dissertation, Dept. of Social Systems Science, University of Southern California, Los Angeles.

Kastner, J. (1983). *Strategies for expert consultation in therapy planning.* Unpublished doctoral dissertation, Dept. of Computer Science, Rutgers University, New Brunswick, NJ.

Keen, P., & Scott Morton, M. (1978). *Decision support systems: An organizational perspective.* Reading, MA: Addison-Wesley.

Keeney, R. (1975). Examining corporate policy using multiattribute utility analysis. *Sloan Management Review, 17,* 63–76.

Keeney, R. (1981). Analysis of preference dependencies among objectives. *Operations Research, 29,* 1105–1120.

Keeney, R. (1982). Decision analysis: An overview. *Operations Research, 30,* 803–838.

Keeney, R. (1986). Value-driven expert systems. *Proceedings: Multi-Attribute Decision Making via OR-Based Expert Systems* (pp. 142–162). Universität Passau, April 1986.

Keeney, R., & Raiffa, H. (1976). *Decisions with multiple objectives: Preferences and value tradeoffs.* New York: Wiley.

Keeney, R., & Sicherman, A. (1976). Assessing and analyzing preferences concerning multiple objectives: An interactive computer program. *Behavioral Science, 21,* 173–182.

Kimbrough, S., & Weber, M. (1989). *An empirical comparison of utility assessment programs* (Report 89-03-03, Dept. of Decision Sciences). Philadelphia, PA: The Wharton School.

Klein, D. A. (1985). *An expert systems approach to realtime, active management of a target resource.* Unpublished master's thesis, Dept. of Computer and Information Science, University of Pennsylvania, Philadelphia, PA.

Klein, D. A. (1988). Integrating expert systems technology into the data processing environment. In M. L. Emrich, A. R. Sadlowe, & L. F. Arrowood (Eds.), *Expert Systems and Advanced Data Processing: Proceedings of the Conference on Expert Systems Technology in the ADP Environment* (pp. 252–265). Amsterdam, The Netherlands: Elsevier Science Publishers.

Klein, D. A., & Finin, T. (1987). On the requirements of active expert systems. *Proceedings of the Seventh International Conference on Expert Systems and Their Applications* (pp. 1199–1207). Avignon, France.

Klein, D. A., & Finin, T. (1989). What's in a deep model? A characterization of knowledge depth in intelligent safety systems. *Applied Artificial Intelligence, 3*(2–3), 129–142.

Klein, D. A., & Milliken, K. (1984). YES/MVS: Managing large installations with expert systems. *Proceedings of SHARE, 63* (pp. 6276–6281).

Klein, D. A. (1991). Integrating artificial intelligence and decision theory to forecast new products. In N. Circone, F. Gardin (Eds.), & G. Valle (Co-ed.), *Computational Intelligence III: Proceedings of the International Conference Computational Intelligence '90* (pp. 97–102). Amsterdam, The Netherlands: Elsevier Science Publishers.

Klein, D. A., Lehmann, H., & Shortliffe, E. H. (1990). A value-theoretic expert system for evaluating randomized clinical trials. *Proceedings Fourteenth Annual Symposium on Computer Applications in Medical Care* (pp. 810–814). Washington, DC.

Klein, D. A., & Shortliffe, E. H. (1990a). Explaining decision-theoretic choices. *Proceedings Eighth Biennial Conference of the Canadian Society for Computational Studies of Intelligence* (pp. 46–53). Ottawa, Canada.

Klein, D. A., & Shortliffe, E. H. (1990b). Integrating artificial intelligence and decision theory in heuristic process control systems. *Proceedings Tenth International Workshop on Expert Systems and Their Applications* (pp. 165–177). Avignon, France.

Klein, D. A., & Shortliffe, E. H. (1991). Interactive diagnosis and repair of decision-theoretic models. *Proceedings Seventh IEEE Conference on Artificial Intelligence Applications* (pp. 289–293). Miami, FL.

Klein, D. A., Weber, M., & Shortliffe, E. H. (in press). Computer-based explanation of multiattribute decisions. *Proceedings of the Ninth International Conference on Multiple Criteria Decision Making*, Fairfax, VA.

Klein, G., Moskowitz, S., & Ravindran, A. (1982). *Simplified assessment of single- and multiattribute utility functions via mathematical programming* (Report 82-7, Dept. of MIS). University of Arizona.

Kosey, E., & Wise, B. (1984). Self-explanatory financial planning models. *Proceedings of AAAI* (pp. 176–181). Austin, TX.

Kotler, P. (1980). *Marketing management: Analysis, planning, and control*. Englewood Cliffs, NJ: Prentice-Hall.

Krantz, D. (1964). Conjoint measurement: The Luce-Tukey axiomization and some extensions. *Journal of Mathematical Psychology, 1*, 248–277.

Krantz, D., Luce, R., Suppes, P., & Tversky, A. (1971). *Foundations of measurement*. New York: Academic Press.

Langlotz, C. (1989). *A decision-theoretic approach to heuristic planning*. Unpublished doctoral dissertation, Section on Medical Informatics, Stanford University, Stanford, CA.

Langlotz, C., Fagan, L., Tu, S., Williams, J., & Sikic, B. (1985). ONYX: An architecture for planning in uncertain environments. *Proceedings of IJCAI* (pp. 447–449). Los Angeles, CA.

Langlotz, C., & Shortliffe, E. (1989). Logical and decision-theoretic methods for planning under uncertainty. *AI Magazine, 10*(1), 39–47.

Langlotz, C., Shortliffe, E. H., & Fagan, L. (1986). Using decision theory to justify heuristics. *Proceedings of AAAI* (pp. 215–219). Philadelphia, PA.

Langlotz, C., Shortliffe, E. H., & Fagan, L. (1988). A methodology for generating computer-based explanations of decision-theoretic advice. *Medical Decision Making, 8*(4), 290–303.

LaValle, I. (1968). On cash equivalents and information evaluation in decisions under uncertainty. *Journal of the American Statistical Association, 63*, 114–129.

LaValle, I. (1978). *Fundamentals of decision analysis*. New York: Holt, Rinehart & Winston.

Lehmann, H. (1988). Knowledge acquisition for probabilistic expert systems. *Proceedings of the Twelfth Annual Symposium on Computer Applications in Medical Care* (pp. 73–77). Washington, DC.

Leinweber, D. (1987). Expert systems in space. *IEEE Expert, 2*(1), 26–36.

Lipson, J. (1981). *Elements of algebra and algebraic computing*. Reading, MA: Addison-Wesley.

LISP/VM User's Guide. (1984). Order #SH20-6477-0, Armonk, NY: IBM Corporation.

Luce, R., & Tukey, J. (1964). Simultaneous conjoint measurement: A new type of fundamental measurement. *J. Math. Psych., 1*, 1–27.

Madni, A., Samet, M., & Purcell, D. (1985). Adaptive models in information management. In S. Andriole (Ed.), *Applications in artificial intelligence*. Petrocelli Publishers.

McDermott, J. (1989, May). *How knowledge acquisition could be easy* (abstract for a talk at Stanford University). Stanford, CA.

McDermott, J., & Forgy, C. (1978). Production system conflict resolution strategies. In F. Hayes-Roth, & D. Waterman (Eds.), *Pattern-directed inference systems*. New York: Academic Press.

McLaughlin, J. (1987). *Utility-directed presentation of simulation tests*. (Memo KSL-87-59, Section on Medical Informatics). Stanford, CA: Stanford University.

Merkhofer, M. (1977). The value of information given decision flexibility. *Management Science, 23*, 716–727.

Michalski, R., Carbonell, J., & Mitchell, T. (Eds.). (1983). *Machine learning: An artificial intelligence approach*. Palo Alto, CA: Tioga Publishing.

Michalski, R., Carbonell, J., & Mitchell, T. (Eds.). (1986). *Machine learning: An artificial intelligence approach* (Vol. II). Los Altos, CA: Morgan Kaufmann.

Milliken, K. (1984). Using expert system technology to automatically assist MVS operation. *Proceedings of GUIDE, 59*.

Moore, P., & Thomas, H. (1976). *The anatomy of decisions*. Penguin Books.

Moore, R., Hawkinson, L., Knickerbocker, C., & Churchman, L. (1984). A real-time expert system for process control. *Proceedings of the First IEEE Conference on Artificial Intelligence Applications* (pp. 132–136). Denver, CO.

Nair, K., & Sicherman, A. (1979). *Environmental assessment methodology: Solar power plant applications, Volume 4: Decision analysis computer program*. (Report ER-1070). Palo Alto, CA: Electric Power Research Institute.

Nelson, W. (1982). REACTOR: An expert system for diagnosis and treatment of nuclear reactor accidents. *Proceedings of AAAI* (pp. 296–301). Pittsburgh, PA.

Nilsson, N. (1980). *Principles of artificial intelligence*. Palo Alto, CA: Tioga Publishing.

Novick, M., Isaacs, G., Hamer, R., Chen, J., Chuang, D., Woodworth, G., Molenaar, I., Lewis, C., & Libby, D. (1980). *Manual for the computer-assisted data analysis monitor*. Iowa City: University of Iowa.

O'Leary, D. (1986). Multiple criteria decision making in accounting expert systems. *Sixth International Workshop on Expert Systems and their Applications* (pp. 1017–1035). Avignon, France.

Pearl, J. (1986). Fusion, propagation, and structuring in belief networks. *Artificial Intelligence, 29*, 241–288.

Pitz, G., & Sachs, N. (1984). Judgment and decision: Theory and application. *Annual Review of Psychology, 35*, 139–163.

Pollack, I. (1964). Action selection and the Yntema-Torgenson worth function. *Proceedings of the First Congress on the Information Systems Sciences*. New York: McGraw Hill.

Poulton, E. (1979). Models of biases in judging sensory magnitude. *Psychology Bulletin, 86*, 777–803.

Pratt, J., Raiffa, H., & Schlaifer, R. (1965). *Introduction to statistical decision theory*. New York: McGraw-Hill.

Raiffa, H. (1968). *Decision analysis*. Reading, MA: Addison-Wesley.

Ray, W. (1981). *Advanced process control*. New York: McGraw-Hill.

Reggia, J., & Perricone, B. (1985). Answer justification in medical decision support systems based on Bayesian classification. *Comp. Bio. Med., 15*(4), 161–167.

Rennels, G., Shortliffe, E. H., & Miller, P. (1985). *Choice and explanation in medical management: A multiattribute model of artificial intelligence approaches*. (Report RSL-85-39, Section on Medical Informatics). Stanford, CA: Stanford University.

Saaty, T. (1980). *The analytic hierarchy process*. New York: McGraw-Hill.

Sarin, R. (1982). Strength of preference and risky choice. *Operations Research, 30*, 982–997.

Sauers, R., & Walsh, R. (1983). On the requirements of future expert systems. *Proceedings of IJCAI* (pp. 110–115). Karlsrue, West Germany.

Savage, L. (1954). *The foundations of statistics*. New York: Wiley.

Scarl, E., Jamieson, J., & Delaune, C. (1985). A fault detection and isolation method applied to liquid oxygen loading for the space shuttle. *Proceedings of IJCAI* (pp. 414–416). Los Angeles, CA.

Schlaifer, R. (1969). *Analysis of decisions under uncertainty*. New York: McGraw-Hill.

Schlaifer, R. (1971). *Computer programs for elementary decision analysis*. Cambridge, MA: Harvard Business School.

Schulman, R., & Hayes-Roth, B. (1987). *ExAct: A module for explaining actions* (Report KSL 87-8, Knowledge Systems Laboratory). Stanford, CA: Stanford University.

Scott, D., & Suppes, P. (1958). Foundational aspects of theories of measurement. *Journal of Symbolic Logic, 23*, 113–128.

Seo, F., Sakawa, M., Takanashi, H., Nakagami, K., & Horiyama, H. (1978). *An interactive computer program for multiattribute utility analysis* (GE18-1980-0). IBM Tokyo Scientific Center.

Shortliffe, E., & Buchanan, B. (1975). A model of inexact reasoning in medicine. *Mathematical Biosciences, 23*, 351–379.

Simon, H. (1987). Two heads are better than one: The collaboration between AI and OR. *Interfaces, 17*(4), 8–15.

Slagle, J., & Hamburger, H. (1985). An expert system for a resource allocation problem. *Communications of the ACM, 28*(9), 994–1004.

Spiegelhalter, D., & Knill-Jones, R. (1984). Statistical and knowledge-based approaches to clinical decision-support systems. *Journal of R. Statistics Society, A:147*, 35–77.

Stephanopoulous, G. (1984). *Chemical process control.* Englewood Cliffs, NJ: Prentice-Hall.

Stevens, A. (1981). *STEAMER: Advanced computer aided instruction in propulsion engineering.* (Technical Report #4702). Cambridge, MA: BBN Inc.

Stevens, S. (1968). Ratio scales of opinion. In D. Whitla (Ed.), *Handbook of measurement and assessment in behavioral sciences.* Reading, MA: Addison-Wesley.

Stillwell, W., & Edwards, W. (1979). *Rank weighting in multiattribute utility decision making: Avoiding the pitfalls of equal weights* (Research Report 79-2, Social Science Research Institute). Los Angeles, CA: University of Southern California.

Strat, T. (1987). The generation of explanations within evidential reasoning systems. *Proceedings of IJCAI* (pp. 1097–1104). Milan, Italy.

Suermondt, H., & Cooper, G. (1988). *Updating probabilities in multiply-connected belief networks.* (Memo KSL-88-27, Section on Medical Informatics). Stanford, CA: Stanford University.

Suermondt, H. J. (1992). *Explanation in Bayesian Belief Networks.* Unpublished doctoral dissertation, Section on Medical Informatics, Stanford University, Stanford, CA.

Suppes, P., & Winet, M. (1955). An axiomatization of utility based on the notion of utility differences. *Management Science, 1*, 259–270.

Swartout, W. (1981). *Producing explanations and justifications of expert consultation programs.* Unpublished doctoral dissertation, Dept. of Computer Science, Massachusetts Institute of Technology, Cambridge.

Sycara, K. (1988). Resolving goal conflicts via negotiation. *Proceedings of AAAI* (pp. 245–250). Saint Paul, MN.

Sykes, E., & White III, C. (1986). Multiobjective intelligent computer-aided design. *Proceedings of the IEEE Systems, Man, and Cybernetics Conference* (pp. 1307–1312). Atlanta, GA.

Tamura, H., & Nakamura, Y. (1978). Decompositions of multiattribute utility functions based on a new concept of convex dependence. *Proceedings of the IEEE Systems, Man, and Cybernetics Conference* (pp. 1362–1367). Tokyo-Kyoto, Japan.

Teach, R., & Shortliffe, E. H. (1981). An analysis of physicians' attitudes. *Comp. Biomedical Research, 14*, 542–558.

Tribus, M. (1969). *Rational descriptions, decisions, and designs.* New York: Pergamon Press.

Tversky, A. (1967). A general theory of polynomial conjoint measurement. *Journal of Math. Psych., 4*, 1–20.

Tversky, A., & Kahneman, D. (1974). Judgment under uncertainty: Heuristics and biases. *Science, 185*, 1124–1131.

Tversky, A., & Kahneman, D. (1981). The framing of decisions and the psychology of choice. *Science, 211*, 453–458.

von Neumann, J., & Morgenstern, O. (1947). *Theory of games and economic behavior.* Princeton, NJ: Princeton University Press.

von Nitzsch, R., & Weber, M. (1988). Utility function assessment on a microcomputer: A reliable, interactive procedure. *Annals of Operations Research, 16*, 149–160.

von Winterfeldt, D. (1980). Structuring decision problems for decision analysis. *Acta Psychologica, 45*, 71–93.

von Winterfeldt, D., & Edwards, W. (1986). *Decision analysis and behavioral research.* New York: Cambridge University Press.

Waterman, D. (1986). *A guide to expert systems.* Reading, MA: Addison-Wesley.

Weber, M. (1985). A method of multiattribute decision making with incomplete information. *Management Science, 31*(11), 1365–1371.

Weber, M. (1987). Decision making with incomplete information. *European Journal of Operations Research, 28*, 44–57.

Weber, M. (1988). Personal communication.

Weiner, J. (1980). BLAH: A system which explains its reasoning. *Artificial Intelligence, 15,* 19–48.

Weld, D. (1984). *Explaining complex engineering devices* (Technical Report #5489). Cambridge, MA: BBN Inc.

Wellman, M. (1985). *Reasoning about preference models.* Unpublished master's thesis, Dept. of Computer Science, Massachusetts Institute of Technology, Cambridge.

Wellman, M. (1987). Dominance and subsumption in constraint-posting planning. *Proceedings of IJCAI* (pp. 884–890). Milan, Italy.

White, C. III, & Sykes, E. (1986). A user preference guided approach to conflict resolution in rule-based expert systems. *IEEE Transactions Syst., Man, Cybern., 16*(2), 276–278.

Wiecha, C., & Henrion, M. (1988). A graphical decision environment for quantitative decision models. In M. Rychener (Ed.), *Expert systems for engineering design.* New York: Academic Press.

Winkler, R. (1972). *Introduction to Bayesian inference and decision.* New York: Holt, Rinehart, & Winston.

Winograd, T. (1972). *Understanding natural language.* New York: Academic Press.

Wright, P., Bourne, D., Colyer, J., Schatz, G., & Isasi, J. (1982, October). A flexible manufacturing cell for swaging. *Mechanical Engineering,* pp. 76–83.

Yntema, D. & Klem, L. (1965). Telling a computer how to evaluate multidimensional situations. *IEEE Transactions on Human Factors in Electronics HFE-2,* 3–13.

Zeleny, M. (1982). *Multiple criteria decision making.* New York: McGraw-Hill.

Author Index

Note: Page numbers in italics refer to bibliography pages.

Subject Index

O

Objective population (opop), definition of, 73
Objectives
  addition of during refinement, 155–160
  Boolean relations on, 83–88
  counterbalanced, 110
  detail of, 131–132, 136
  in empirical observations on choice, 64, 67
  fixing number of, 111
  hierarchy, capture in difference function, 73–75
  inconsequential, 110
  primitive, measurement of, 29
  pruning and presentation of, 107–113
  relevance of, 134, 136
  single, chaining on, 131–132, 134, 136
  sorting and selection of, 83, 96–103
  special, in reformulation of additive multiattribute value function (AMVF), 72–73
  structured in value tree, 29–30, 73–75
  topologies for, 122–123, 168–169
  in VIRTUS knowledge bases, 162
  weights on, 73
Objectives hierarchy. *See* Value tree
Object-oriented value-function computation, 164–165
Opacity. *See* Transparency
Operation explainers, 114–123
  addition, 116–117
  constant, 121
  in diagnosis, 149
  implementation, in VIRTUS, 168–170
  multiplication, 117–120
  subtraction, 120–121
  in topology, 122–123
Operations research, 39
Ordinal-relation concepts, 83–88
  derived, 87–88
  primitive, 84–87
  in selection and sorting of alternatives, 93–96
  in selection and sorting of objectives, 96–103
Output-to-input exposition, 124, 126

P

Parameter assessors, 143–150, 169
Parameter-integrity checkers, 148–149
Parameters
  naturalness of, 181
  relationship among, in multiattribute value function, 25

semantics of, 47, 148–149, 181
Parameter suggestion, 154–155
Parameter values. *See also* Preferences; Sensitivity analysis
  assessment of, 23, 51, 143–148
  bias in assessment of, 3, 23, 186–187
  given by constant explainer, 121
  inference of, 42–43, 144–146
  measurement scale for, 25–28
  modification and repair of, 3, 49, 149–155
  quantitative, included in explanation, 165
  quantitative expressed as qualitative, 66, 70, 116
  tailoring, with VIRTUS, 51
  verification of changes in, 148–149
  in VIRTUS interface, 168
Part worth, 76*n*
Pattern classification of objectives, 96–99, 112, 117
Preference. *See also* Parameter values
  in decision making, 13
  encoded in value function, 32
  priorities as representation of, 18–19
  strength of, 26–28, 78
Preferences
  changing over time, 3, 19–20, 49–50, 142
  using VIRTUS to organize, 50
Primitive weight of objectives, 73
Priorities
  in JESQ, 17–18
  as representations of preferences, 18–19
Priority-conflict-resolution algorithms, 12
Probability, 39–40
Process control actions, evaluation of, 53
Processing models (in JESQ), 18
Pruning strategies, 107–113
  in addition explanation, 117
  combined horizontal and vertical, 112–113
  in difference-function traversal, 117, 130–131
  horizontal, 109–112
  in operations explainers, 130–131
  vertical, 108–109

Q

QBKG, 174–177
Quantitative models, explanation in, 41
Quantitative values, 66, 70, 116, 165
Quantity space, 88

For Product Safety Concerns and Information please contact our EU
representative GPSR@taylorandfrancis.com
Taylor & Francis Verlag GmbH, Kaufingerstraße 24, 80331 München, Germany

www.ingramcontent.com/pod-product-compliance
Lightning Source LLC
Chambersburg PA
CBHW071422050326
40689CB00010B/1938